Let us remember . . . that democracy and with democracy peace, will be extinct if the believers in democratic government will allow their desire for peace to develop into non-resistance towards intolerance, their readiness for self-criticism into a lack of self-reliance, and their recognition of the rights of their opponents into a lack of moral courage to fight those who deny the principles of freedom.

CARL LANDAUER
Harper's Monthly Magazine, 1938

Essays in
Socialism
and
Planning
in Honor of
Carl Landauer

edited by *Gregory Grossman*
University of California
Berkeley

PRENTICE-HALL, INC.
Englewood Cliffs, New Jersey

Essays in

Socialism

and

Planning

in Honor of

Carl Landauer

Essays in Socialism and Planning in Honor of Carl Landauer
edited by Gregory Grossman

© 1970
by Prentice-Hall, Inc.
Englewood Cliffs, New Jersey

13-283689-0

Library of Congress Catalog Card Number:
72-124388

PRINTED IN THE UNITED STATES OF AMERICA

Current Printing (last digit):
10 9 8 7 6 5 4 3 2 1

PRENTICE-HALL INTERNATIONAL, INC., London
    PRENTICE-HALL OF AUSTRALIA, PTY. LTD., Sydney
PRENTICE-HALL OF CANADA, LTD., Toronto
    PRENTICE-HALL OF INDIA PRIVATE LTD., New Delhi
PRENTICE-HALL OF JAPAN, INC., Tokyo

Contents

Essays in
Socialism
and
Planning
in Honor of
Carl Landauer

Alexander Gerschenkron
Harvard University

Reflections on
European Socialism

Professor Landauer's history of Continental Socialism[1] is a magnificent performance. His stupendous erudition is as impressive as his skill in shaping the enormous mass of refractory and heterogeneous material into a well-articulated whole. Few books reveal in a comparable measure the engaging combination of a firm set of personal beliefs with the earnest striving for reasonable interpretation and balanced judgment, even when dealing with antithetic points of view and with historical periods distinguished neither by reason nor balance. Above all, it is a thought-provoking book. It forces the reader who has absorbed the 1500 pages of text and the 250 pages of appended footnotes to re-think many a funda-

1

mental problem of modern historical development. For in Landauer's hands the history of socialism becomes an integral part of European history and is inseparably connected with the painful birth, troublous survival, brief flowering, and tragic fall of the Weimar Republic.

No less than one fourth of the long book is devoted to Germany between the military collapse in 1918 and Hitler's advent to power in 1933. Many causal chains of various lengths had led to the victory of the Nazi movement. It is, however, highly improbable that the final effect would have materialized in the absence of the Great Depression. By the same token, it is plausible to assume that if effective anti-depression measures had been taken and a period of economic recovery initiated, the mortal threat to German democracy would have vanished as quickly as it had arisen. There is little doubt that the inept economic policies that were actually pursued by the Brüning government served to aggravate rather than to improve the economic situation. It is, of course, conceivable that in the long run the deflationary policies might have proved successful. But life or death of the Weimar Republic was then a very short-run problem.

There are a number of mostly indifferent reasons why the suicidal economic policies were adopted and pursued.[2] There are some good reasons why the Social Democratic party lent its support to those highly unpopular policies through the so-called "toleration" of Brüning's rule by presidential emergency decrees. What still constitutes a problem is the failure of socialism in Germany to work out and to propose with proper emphasis a positive policy of combating unemployment—a policy that unlike the hated deflationary measures would have strongly appealed to the Party's membership and voters, and in particular to labor, peasantry, and lower middle class. It seems to me that to a considerable extent, though by no means exclusively, the answer to the problem must be sought in the ideological evolution of the German Socialist movement. Before 1933 its ideological mutation had advanced far enough to make it possible for a leading Socialist and trade unionist to express his willingness to act as physician at the sickbed of capitalism, a statement that, as Landauer rightly remarks, in itself embodied a "theory" of the labor movement (Vol. II, p. 1573). But on the other hand the ideological change had not gone far enough to create a firm belief in men's ability to deal with depressions, except perhaps by facilitating processes that would have taken place spontaneously in an ideal laissez faire economy. In other words, even if the physician had thought about an alternative therapy, he still had grave doubts about its applicability and efficacy. At a crucial juncture in the history of German Social Democracy it appeared that the movement had not liberated itself sufficiently from a set of ideas that was once concomitant with and highly beneficial to its rise, but now put in jeopardy its very existence.

2

The purpose of the preceding remarks should be clear. I am not arguing that a different economic policy advocated by the Social Democratic party from the beginning of the depression would necessarily have changed the course of events. Nor am I saying that the drag of ideology was alone, or even mainly, responsible for the policies actually pursued. Various tactical considerations and the trammels of political feasibilities may have been more important. My only reason for referring to the critical situation in the Germany of the early thirties is that it points up a central problem of the history of European socialism, that is, the relationship between "Ideas and Movements," to quote the apt subtitle of Professor Landauer's book. The following pages are devoted to a few reflections on the nature of this problem.

Ideas are thoughts, and men's actions are determined by their thinking. Without ideas there is no action and no history. Defense of a vested interest or struggle for power for the sake of power must needs derive from ideas. The question whether ideas are "important in history," that is to say, in the intelligible record of men's actions is, therefore, a sham problem. A real problem, by contrast, is that ideas change with the circumstances, that very often there is reluctance to acknowledge the change, both outwardly and inwardly; as a result ideology conceived as a set of proclaimed ideas may no longer be the actual determinant of action. On the other hand, ideologies in this sense die slowly and at times they are apt to rise from their deathbed and put on a show of unsuspected vigor. A significant social movement must have an ideology. It is true that depending on the nature of the movement the ideology in question may be more or less comprehensive, more or less rigid, more or less well articulated. Ideological changes will vary accordingly. Probably no modern mass movements on historical record ever possessed as all-embracing and as clear-cut an ideology as the Marxian Socialist parties on the European continent and among them particularly the Social Democratic parties in Germany and Austria. No other mass movement ever attributed such an importance to the internal consistency and to the intrinsic truth content of its system of beliefs. Under these conditions evolution of that system was indeed a highly complicated process, sometimes gravely inhibiting action and, from a certain point on, creating deep rifts between ideology and policy.

It is not difficult to see why in the second half of the nineteenth century Marxism exercised such a strong appeal to the continental labor movements. For it contained a set of elements that fitted the condition of the working classes of the time in the countries concerned. While the Marxian system was appropriated *in toto*, crucial portions of it, although much discussed in learned fashion, were exquisitely irrelevant. Whether

Marx' labor theory of value was suited to explain the structure of relative prices or whether in connection therewith an unbridgeable gulf existed between the first and third volumes of *Das Kapital*—neither question had any real significance. What mattered was the normative inference from the concept of surplus value to the injustice of the existing economic system. The discontent of people burdened with multifarious grievances was given a justification, deeply anchored in irrefutable science, the latter playing the role of a *Grundnorm* and the syncretic confusion of *Sein und Sollen* creating no difficulty at all. Men conscious of their weakness and inability to seek at once an effective remedy of those grievances were told that the inexorable laws of historical development would lead to the downfall of the system, even though in the process the pressure on their standard of living was bound to increase. But the future was bright. All that had to be done was to recognize that overriding all the conflicts of interest among them there existed a paramount unifying interest. The economic system had created them as a class *an sich*—i.e., as a group of people placed in a similar position with regard to the process of creation (by them) and appropriation (by others) of surplus value. But they were also bound to become a class *für sich*—that is to say, an entity intensely conscious of their common interests. It was not surprising therefore that Otto Bauer, the leading Austrian Marxian, at one point stated that Marxism itself had made it possible to overcome the innumerable conflicts of interest within the working class, enabling it to conduct its class struggle, the impact of a theoretical system thus justifying its own findings.[3]

And the goal of the movement? Its negative aspect was very clear. The capitalist system undermined by its own contradictions would disappear, pushed from the historical scene by a well-applied blow of the organized proletariat. But it would also have developed the productive forces for the creation of the socialist society—the positive goal of the movement again being negatively described as the abolition of private property of capital goods and positively as the establishment of a society that would be stable economically, harmonious socially, and just ethically. But any further anticipation of the character of that society was deliberately rejected as utopian—except that strong anarchistic elements in this ideology ("the dying of the state," "the marcescence of the state") pointed to some sort of cooperative commonwealth and Marx indeed liked to speak of socialism as a system of "associated producers," rather nebulously combined with the idea of central guidance or supervision.

It was always easy to stress the disabilities inherent in this deterministic view, according to which history itself was to take care of solving the social problem, the labor movement confining its direct action to the final blow. Society was apparently seen as a part of nature, and the complete and irrevocable victory of the Socialist movement—the final blow—was itself an integral part of the order of nature. Its occurrence was *naturnotwendig,* as the phrase ran. Was the German Social Democratic party then an association to facilitate the next eclipse of the sun or to assure the arrival of Halley's comet? But strictures of this sort missed the crucial point. For the function of the ideological system lay altogether in the field of social psychology. It does not detract from the scientific elements in the work of Karl Marx to regard the role of Marxism within the Socialist movement as a traditional technique of persuasion quite on a par with divine assurance to the faithful of victory over the infidels. William Liebknecht, a recognized elder statesman of the movement but at the same time its *enfant terrible,* once candidly referred to the instructive experience of Islam whose fatalism imparted superhuman strength to the believer. "The conviction that victory in a fight for a definite goal is ineluctable gives one the forces of a giant."[4] Liebknecht's admission may have been damaging to the tenets of scientific socialism, but the sociological insight it revealed was deep and clear. For the level at which Marxian ideology was most relevant was not that of logical consistency and philosophical defensibility. Precisely because the instrument was an age-old one, although appropriately modernized, its effectiveness must be judged in traditional terms. The Lord did give the city of Jericho into Joshua's hand. Still, much powerful trumpet blowing by the priests and mighty shouting by the people of Israel was necessary before the walls of the city crumbled. For thousands of years men were glad to strive valiantly and to risk their lives in order to fulfill the will of omnipotent deities and to achieve what had been inexorably predestined.

Apart from the general effect on popular attitudes, Marxian ideology had specific implications that were of major importance for the successful evolution of the movement. The belief in the beneficent march of history implied acceptance of technological progress and suppressed any Luddite tendencies from within. The postponement of action implied rejection of any terroristic activity, rife in the pre-Marxian stages of development, which invariably had led to repressive action and had made the movement an easy prey of sanctions by police and courts. For an important formative period "Marxism" meant concentration of all forces on propaganda of ideas and the organization of the movement; and the Party's acceptance of participation in parliamentary elections was primarily viewed as providing a yardstick for the growth of the movement's influence within the population and a tribune for spreading its ideas. This phase of relative passivity, as far as interest in immediate reforms and improvements was concerned, bore clear marks of Toynbee's sequence of withdrawal and return. The movement withdrew into itself, that is to say, into its organization and growth. That it actually was a preparation for a "return" of a different kind from that originally envisaged is another matter.

No proper appreciation of this phase is possible without understanding the position of the industrial worker within the framework of the German or Austrian social structure in the last quarter of the past century. In addition to his economic disability the worker in the industrial towns found himself in almost complete social isolation. To give a few examples: In the city of Vienna, the existence of large and rapidly growing working-class districts meant virtual separation in schools of workers' children from those of the middle class. Workers were precluded from entering certain public parks which were reserved for those higher up on the social ladder. In Linz, the capital of the province of Upper Austria, a police ordinance enjoined workers returning from work from using the sidewalks. The first car on Viennese tramways was regularly used by the better-dressed public, whereas the workers took their seats in the second and third cars, a practice which to some extent survived even the revolutionary upheavals of 1918. It is astonishing how many elements of what nowadays in this country is called segregation existed in the Central Europe of the time, even though the absence of a color line mitigated the sharpness of the discrimination. In Vienna, of course, the existence of the many nationalities of the Monarchy provided additional lines of separation: No one familiar with those conditions can read Gunnar Myrdal's *An American Dilemma* without considering how many things that a Southern white would say about a Negro servant were nearly identical with what a factory owner or middle-class housewife in Vienna would say about a Bohemian worker or a servant girl. This was indeed a situation of profound alienation of the worker from the rest of society. Its basis was a combination of discriminatory legislation (e.g., on labor contracts), administrative measures, judicial practices, and social taboos. Marx once contemptuously upbraided Lassalle for his reference to *Arbeiterstand*, the workers' estate, because estates were peculiar to precapitalist formation; Lassalle, he argued, should have spoken of *Arbeiterklasse*. But one cannot help thinking that Lassalle with his sharp realistic eye saw clearly how naturally medieval attitudes toward the peasantry were assimilated by the middle class in its treatment of industrial workers, to say nothing of the members of the aristocracy and the gentry who still occupied leading positions in the civil service and the judicial system. It was the social position of the worker that Justice Oliver Wendell Holmes must have had in mind when he wrote: "For a quarter of a century I have said that the real foundations of discontent were emotional not economic and that if the socialists would face the facts and put the case on that ground, I should listen to them with respect."[5]

Whether or not the case was put in these terms, it is clear that rigid thinking in terms of two systems separated by the dialectical leap of the revolution was perfectly consonant with these conditions of rigid social stratification. The Socialist movement regarded itself as a revolutionary movement. Revolution was the aim, the only aim. About eighty years ago, a leader of the AFL (which at that time still was in its previous incarnation of Federation of Organized Trades and Labor Unions) had to reply to a senatorial question as to the nature of the ultimate ends of the movement. He said: "We have no ultimate ends. We are going from day to day. We are fighting only for immediate objectives. We are all practical men."[6] That was the voice of the labor movement in a free country unencumbered by the legacy of medieval experience. By contrast: "We have nothing but an ultimate end. We do not fight for immediate objectives. We are proud of our theoretical insight," might have been the retort from the other side of the Atlantic.

And yet it would be wrong to overlook the elements of gradualism that were from the start inherent in Marxian ideology as adopted by the movement. Gradualism was implied in the thesis that the capitalist system prior to its demise must develop all the productive forces of which it was capable. Gradualism was implied in the stress on the necessity to build up a powerful labor movement which at the appropriate time could engineer the transition. Even in that early phase of the movement's history there were, after all, immediate objectives relating to the enormous work of educating the growing masses of industrial labor. And the education was not merely training in the received doctrines. It aimed at creating for the alienated worker a world of his own within which he could move as a valued member among a group of equals, thus paradoxically even increasing artificially his alienation from the rest of society. Implied in the very concept of the future violent revolutionary upheaval was the stress on non-violence during the preceding period. The lapse of the German Anti-Socialist Act in 1890 permitted the revolutionary movement to move within an assured sphere of legality and to abandon illegal activities, such as the smuggling of literature, which had been prevalent during the period of repressions. Finally, the struggle for general franchise in individual states in Germany and on a national level in Austria was an immediate objective. In Austria peaceful marches and street demonstrations, not dissimilar to the civil rights actions of Martin Luther King's days, were abundantly used in the process. Emotional outbursts on the part of the workers would occur from time to time, but the leaders of the movement did all they could to prevent them and patiently tried to make government officials practice restraint and avert the use of repressive force. There was no planning for revolutionary violence. If violence was considered anywhere it was in the *coup d'état* plans of Wilhelm II.[7]

Thus, the deterministic belief in the inevitability of the revolution performed a complex function. This was clearly seen by Bertrand Russell whose very first book, written as early as 1896, was devoted to the German labor movement and showed a sharpness of insight and a prophetic vision of which few contemporaries could boast, and for which the Russell of today may well envy the youngster he once was. He said: "Prac-

tically, the revolutionary tendency is neutralized and held in check by
... the inherent necessity and fatality. This fatalism ... gives the Social
Democracy its religious faith and power; *this inspires patience and controls the natural inclination to forcible revolution.*"[8] This meant that the
determinism of the movement in the sequence of historical reality effectively prepared a nondeterministic and nonrevolutionary phase. But for
the time being ideology and action seemed to be in perfect harmony with
each other, and the rate of growth of the movement was nothing if not
amazing. In the first election after the unification (1871), Socialists received 3 percent of the total vote. In the last election before the outbreak
of World War I (1912), the Party received 4.2 million votes or almost
35 percent of the total. Because of discriminatory allocation of seats to
industrial areas the Party's representation in the *Reichstag* was smaller
(110 seats out of 397), the Catholic *Zentrum* coming closest with its 2
million votes, but even so Social Democracy was the strongest single
political party in parliament and behind the formidable vote stood a
registered party membership approaching the figure of 1 million.[9] The
expectation derived from Marx regarding the irresistible formation of the
proletariat as a class *für sich* seemed to justify itself. This very process
of growth, however, was creating problems that bore directly on the relation between the movement and its ideology. Could a movement that had
come to comprise a large segment of society retain its attitude of splendid
isolation? Did not its rapid growth make it imperative to expand the immediate objectives beyond growth itself?

The debates on this question began surprisingly early. In fact, at the
Erfurt Convention of the Party where a strict Marxian program was
adopted, a plea was made not to ignore the immediate needs of the
workers and to concentrate in particular on four aims: (1) improvements
of legislation; (2) attainment of government's neutrality vis-à-vis labor
contracts; (3) legislative action against monopolies; and finally (4) abolition of tariffs on foodstuffs. But Bebel, the recognized leader of the
Party, easily disposed of this proposal by describing it as *Regierungs-
sozialismus*, and as serving to "obscure the ultimate goal." He admitted
that it was important to advance demands "which no other party could
raise," but he felt that it mattered little how much was actually achieved.
For "only few in this room will not live to see the realization of the
ultimate goal."[10]

Two decades later on the eve of World War I the "ultimate
goal" did not appear any closer. But the attitude toward the immediate
objectives had strikingly changed. In the interval the labor movement had
erected an impressive network of consumers' cooperatives with an at-
tached wholesale society, including a bank of its own and an ambitious
venture into industrial production. A Party Congress in 1892 had declared
that cooperatives could be useful mainly as places of refuge for members

who had lost their jobs because of their activities or when support of cooperatives would facilitate propaganda in favor of the Party. "For the rest," the declaration continued, "party members were to oppose establishment of cooperatives and in particular to fight against the belief that cooperatives were able to exert influence upon capitalist production and to improve the class position of labor."[11] This statement was meant to refer primarily to producers' cooperatives, and the subsequent magnificent evolution of consumers' cooperatives was not foreseen at all. If it had been, Lassalle's iron law of wages and Marx' theory of increasing misery would no doubt have offered sufficient grounds for the condemnation of hopeless attempts to increase the purchasing power of workers' incomes. The attitude toward labor unions had been only a shade less unfriendly, but it did not stop the phenomenal growth of the unions which in 1906 acquired recognition as an equal branch of the labor movement. The official attitude of the Party toward most of the creative innovations that emerged from the union practice gradually changed from initial rejection to tacit tolerance, and finally to grudging acceptance.

Perhaps even more important were the Party's activities in parliament, state legislatures, and municipalities. The original pronouncements were clear and uncompromising: "The Social Democratic party regards the *Reichstag* election as a means of propaganda only and as a test for the spread of its principles, and rejects any compromise with other parties."[12] But the electoral system in operation required agreements among the parties after the first voting round when no absolute majority was achieved. The logic of its position should have prompted the Social Democratic party to count the electoral votes and to pay little attention to the number of seats. But such an attitude was difficult to maintain even on rigid orthodox grounds. Since propaganda from the *Reichstag* tribune was sanctified by the canons of the doctrine and the propaganda potential was believed to vary directly with the size of the Party's representation in parliament, the movement could not remain indifferent to the number of seats it obtained and accordingly electoral alliances with non-Socialist parties came to be regularly concluded. Fleeting as those unions were, they were incompatible with the original attitude of complete introversion. But the development could not possibly halt at this point.

What followed was serious participation in the committee work of the *Reichstag* and a growing concern for the expenditure and revenue side of the budget, even though the Party continued as a matter of principle to cast its votes against every budget; after the early hesitant participation in the *Senioren-Konvent* (The Committee of the Elders) of the *Reichstag* came the election of a Social Democrat to the position of a vice-president of parliament. The consequences of the growing size had to be accepted in the face of much internal debate and criticism.

9

The highly discriminatory electoral system in Prussia kept the Social Democratic representation in the Prussian *Landtag* at a minimum. Even in this case the original policy to boycott the elections was abandoned. But in the South German states the franchise was, or was becoming, much more democratic, and very soon power positions acquired in state legislatures were used with great energy, plunging the Party into deep involvements in current legislative activities and the give-and-take of parliamentary negotiations. Despite protests, admonitions, and threats by the Party, the South German Social Democrats began to cast their votes in favor of the Appropriation Acts, thus committing a major sin against the canons of ideology.

And what happened to those canons in view of the momentous changes in the actions of the movement? The orthodox ideology had indeed been challenged by revisionist criticism. The frontal attack was directed against nearly every fundamental aspect of the ideological system. The theory of increased misery, the elimination of the middle class, the proletarization of the peasantry, the tendency of falling profits—all these were confronted with empirical material and found wanting. These were the main supporting pillars of the belief in the inevitability of the demise of capitalism. The critics challenged the very idea of an "ultimate goal," and Edward Bernstein boldly stated that "the goal was nothing and the movement all." Here was a serious well-thought-out attempt to adjust the ideology of the movement to its practice and by the same token to widen the range of that practice. But the attempt failed. In memorable debates at Party Congresses, perhaps inappropriately but fascinatingly converted into university seminars on Marxism, the revisionist strictures were rejected all along the line. The body of ideological beliefs emerged unchanged. The gulf between ideas and actions was not closed.

One could mention a number of reasons for this result. Germany before 1914 may have been "safely on the road to democracy," as Professor Landauer suggests (Vol. I, p. 373), but there was still a fair distance to go. The government of the country was still responsible to the Emperor. It was not a parliamentary government. The predominant position in the Federal Council (*Bundesrat*) gave Prussia, the state in which Socialist influence remained insignificant, the virtual right of veto over any piece of legislation. Under these conditions Social Democratic participation in the government was neither in the stars nor a very attractive prospect from the point of view of the movement. Hence it was easy for the German party to take, within the Second International, a negative stand on Socialist entry into coalition governments, to say nothing of "Millerandism"—the membership of an individual Socialist in a "bourgeois" government. In addition to the political backwardness of the German constitutional structure—as compared with that of France and England—there was the personal experience—in fact the life story—of the leaders of the movement, and first and foremost of Bebel. Bebel was the living epitome of the history of the movement. He was its cynosure. For more than forty years he had stood at its helm. He had steered the Party through the critical years of the Anti-Socialist Act and had seen the Empire concede defeat and withdraw from the attack upon an opponent who seemed to thrive on repressive measures against him. He had seen the small group with which he had started grow into a movement supported by millions. This enormous success was achieved under the aegis of an ideological beacon that cast a powerful light upon the path traveled by the movement. To accept the view that the very success achieved during the past decades rendered possible, and even called for, a change in ideology was not only a complex mental exercise—it was a menace to unified coherent biographies; rightly or wrongly, but inevitably, it carried with it the strong suggestion that past policies had been erroneous, an admission that was both personally and politically intolerable.

And yet, neither of the two reasons seems sufficient to explain the phenomenon of the unchanged ideology of a changing movement. After the end of World War I the constitutional disabilities vanished. A new generation of leaders had appeared. The Social Democratic parties both in Germany and Austria became strong parliamentary powers engaged in innumerable salutary reforms. They became the carrying pillars, the strongest defenders of the republican system established in both countries. The daily bread of their lives was composed of actions which had been vainly advocated more than two decades earlier by revisionist criticism. The creative policies of the municipality of Vienna and the enormous mass of social legislation were justifiably the pride of the Austrian Movement. They were designed to reform, to make the life of receivers of low-incomes more tolerable and more dignified. They gloried in the resulting improvements of standards of living which were in blatant conflict with the theory of increasing misery. But neither in Germany nor in Austria was there any serious attempt to change the basic set of ideas which still constituted the basic ideology of the movement, the only exception being the programmatic admission of the indubitable fact that large estates were not displacing the peasants' family farm and the programmatic promise that the latter would not be expropriated after the establishment of socialism. But the crucial elements of the ideology—the dichotomy of capitalism and socialism and the inevitability of socialism's advent—remained unaffected by the sea change in actions that was taking place. The ideology as it was formulated in the early years of the movement remained unchanged. The discrepancy between it and current policies was even more striking in Austria than in Germany. For the Austrian Social Democracy, being more "left" than its German counterpart, was much more vocal and articulate in emphasizing its basic beliefs.

Although the Austrian movement had striven valiantly to improve the worker's lot and position within society, it very consciously and deliberately worked to keep the movement and its members in greatest possible isolation from the rest of society. On the job and off the job, the worker remained within the movement. Whether he played football or chess, climbed mountains, raised rabbits, took courses to prepare for high school examinations, sent his children to summer camp, or buried his wife—organizations of the movement surrounded him. The alienation that could have successfully been reduced by the policies of the Party was at the same time artificially maintained and increased by its all-embracing organizational structure. Organizational isolation followed from and was designed to reinforce the purity of ideology.

The split of the labor movement that occurred after World War I no doubt tended to limit ideological adjustments within the Social Democratic party. Continually denounced by the Communists as traitors to the cause of socialism, the Social Democratic party in Germany, where the threat was active and powerful, and in Austria, where it was potential, did not wish to add fuel to the flames of a ruthless and demagogical propaganda. It is extremely unlikely, however, that the dangers of Communist competition can sufficiently explain the tenacity of a creed that no longer fitted reality. Nor can the reason lie in the desire to deceive on the part of leaders whose high moral standards must confound any attempt to cast aspersion on their sincerity. The explanation must be sought elsewhere.

Rosa Mayreder once described the typical history of a social movement as starting from the ideological phase, passing through the organizational phase, and finally arriving at the power phase, or "action phase."[13] The implication was that as movements entered the action phase the importance of ideology—of the basic creed—was diminished and both the exigencies and the possibilities of current situations became the real determinants of action. This did not mean, of course, that "ideas" were no longer of any significance. It did mean that the new ideas differed from the original ideology and that, adjusted as they were to complex and confusing practical problems, they were much less capable of adding up to an internally consistent system. This was a brilliant insight. But what Mayreder's exposition failed to stress were on the one hand the reasons for the continued clinging to a "creed outworn" and on the other hand the fact that the old creed was rarely entirely outworn, so that certain elements of it still remained operational.

Bertrand Russell's keen eye had foreseen much of the road the movement was to travel: "Though it is rash to predict," he wrote, "it seems indubitable that, if the party has a future of power at all, it must purchase power by a practical, if not a theoretical abandonment of some portions of Marx's doctrines. His influence is now [1896] almost omnipotent, but this omnipotence must sooner or later be conquered by practical necessity, if the party is not to remain for ever a struggling minority." But Russell also anticipated the incompleteness of this evolution and the resulting complexities and inconsistencies: "... Those who have seen the strength, compactness, and fervor which this religion gives to those who hold it, will hardly regard its decay as likely to help the progress of the Party. No, not in a formal and critical abandonment of any part of Marxian doctrine lies a tactical solution of their dilemma: rather it is to be hoped that, like other religious bodies ... they will lose something in logical acumen, and adopt in their political activity maxims really inconsistent with their fundamental principles, but necessitated by practical exigencies and reconciled by some more or less fallacious line of reasoning."[14] One can only marvel at Bertrand Russell's ability to discern so clearly *ex ante* what has so often been overlooked *ex post*. The only thing Russell failed to do was to point out the dangers inherent in continued adherence to traditional ideas and in the resulting hybrid system, or mass, of beliefs.[15]

It is perhaps surprising that this conservative tendency should have been at work within movements which, far from being conservative, were committed to change and have in fact brought about momentous changes. They were willing to see everything change except themselves. Marxism was a theory of historical change. In movements that had absorbed some form of Marxian doctrines and had presented themselves as such, there was the general tendency to apply what was considered Marxian analysis to everything around them and before them, but not to their own movement. That was where their dialectics stopped. Most of the time the term "dialectics" is hardly more than an arbitrary metaphysical construct. If it has any operational significance in elucidating historical sequences, it is only in a certain mental predisposition to realize that very often the relation between social phenomena changes so radically that it becomes the very opposite of what it had been. To give an example from an area somewhat remote from Marxian interests: The theory of separation of powers was positively related to democracy as long as the problem was to conquer the legislative area for the parliament. When the evolution proceeded to the point where the establishment of ministerial responsibility to parliament, rather than to the monarch, became the order of the day, the function of the theory was radically changed. By claiming that the executive branch of government must remain reserved to the king, the theory became an obstacle to further democratization. Examples of this kind abound in history, and in this very commonsensical sense the term dialectics, or rather an attitude that is loosely related to dialectics, has proved useful in historical research. Marx and Engels and their successors were untiring in searching for instances of far-reaching change. Such an approach was imbedded in their historical appraisal of capitalism. It would have been most natural for the representatives of Socialist movements to apply such predispositions or expectations to their own movements. If they had, they would have come to the conclusion that an ideology that had once been a major factor in furthering the growth of the movement had fulfilled and exhausted its function so that its relation to the movement had become profoundly transformed. In a period when exerting influence upon practical policies very often depended upon coalitions with non-Socialist parties, the original ideology had grown into an obstacle to reasonable decisions. Admittedly, it was by no means an insuperable one. But in situations where the pros and cons for entering a coalition government were fairly closely balanced, the appeal to what was considered the basic creed could and actually did result in a negative decision. This is illustrated by the history of the Austrian movement between 1920 and 1933.

The problem of coalition governments proved something else much more important. The idea of inevitability was an integral part of the basic ideology. But the concept embraced more than the irresistible advent of socialism. It also connoted the futility of interfering with the elemental forces of economic evolution. This no doubt was good Marxian thinking, but it was not specifically so. Professor Landauer rightly stresses the affinity between liberalism and socialism. From the point of view of laissez faire economics, measures of interference with the free course of economic events were either harmful, or superfluous, or ineffective. As time went on great stress was laid on the last factor in the triad. The economic laws would assert themselves against any attempts at interference. The whole successful practice of Socialist movements through decades was an effective refutation of the doctrine. Was it then obsolete? As the figure showed, it was not with respect to a most crucial area. Marxians and non-Marxians had believed that to modify the course of a business cycle was nearly as hopeless as to modify the course of a planet. In Marxian hands this view had become particularly rigid because it carried with it the belief in an irremediable malady of capitalism. The "system" was subject to periodic crises, a condition which nothing but the abolition of the system could terminate. When the Great Depression struck it was from an ideology whose contact with the actions of the movement had become so tenuous that the Socialists still drew the conviction that the disruptive process must be left to nature, unless one could remove the "unnatural" man-made obstacles to the natural healing process, and that meant lowering wages fixed in collective bargaining agreements and lowering prices that had become sticky because of equally unnatural arrangements. In this sense, it was well in consonance with the basic ideology to support a suicidal policy of deflation, even though such a support was at variance with all the new ideas which had actuated Socialist policies and of which collective bargaining agreements were an

14

essential element. At a fateful juncture a dormant, if not defunct, ideology in alliance with considerations of political expediency that were altogether alien to it, still proved strong enough to paralyze creative initiative and to deflect the movement into the cul-de-sac of deflationary policies.

It is instructive to confront the development of the German labor movement with its counterpart in Russia, especially noting the differences and the similarities. A deep and unbridgeable chasm separates the world of democratic socialism from the Soviet system. But the two trees that have grown so far apart had common roots in the same set of original beliefs. Also, Soviet Russia presents the same case of ideological inertia. Great efforts have been made to stress the "Marxian" character of the official ideology and to evoke the image of an unbroken thread. In reality no more than a superficial acquaintance with the Soviet system and its historical evolution is needed to understand that the determinants of Soviet actions lie on a plane far away from the proclaimed set of beliefs and goals. Whatever may have been true of the origins of the Soviet system, ideology has not been the guiding force in determining the policies of the regime and the resulting processes of change in Russia. The function of ideology was not to guide but to justify. The process of justification has been arbitrary in the extreme. Whatever has been done in response to the demands of given situations and above all in order to maintain the power of dictatorship has been solemnly declared to be in harmony with the basic ideology and has invariably been described as "Marxian." And the resulting absurdities were effectively protected from criticism by the dictatorial control of opinion. But what matters is the paradox of a movement that has produced the greatest upheavals in the history of the country without shedding the conservative urge to preserve, although in name only, a set of beliefs that has become altogether inapplicable to its actions. If the concept of socialism is understood as it should be, in all its breadth as a great humanitarian movement of the nineteenth century, Soviet Russia has long forfeited the claim to be regarded as a Socialist country, and Professor Landauer was quite right in abandoning, or revising, his introductory definition of socialism based primarily on the ownership of the means of production (Vol. I, pp. 5 and 264, and Vol. II, p. 1666). But it is precisely here that the great difference lies between the democratic West and the dictatorial East. Soviet Russia has very good reasons to cling to its original ideology because the implied connection with a humanitarian movement is designed to vindicate the very unhumanitarian policies of the regime and in general the very existence of the dictatorship.

By contrast, it is the interest in the well-being of underprivileged groups of the population that has been and still is the essence of policies of Socialist parties in the democratic countries of Europe. It took the horrors of a Nazi dictatorship and of a new world war to make German and Austrian labor take further steps to liberate themselves from an anachronistic creed. Even now the process is not wholly complete, as witnessed by the reluctance of Austrian socialism in the 1950s to adopt a radical revision of its program. But what the German and Austrian movements have succeeded in preserving was not the pseudoscientific tenets of an ideological system but the ethical norms that stood at the cradle of European socialism when it was born as a movement of social protest against harshness and injustice. The road has been a long one and great things have been accomplished. Immense progress has been achieved in promoting not only the economic but also the juridical and the social emancipation of the laboring man, and the Socialist movements still stand as the guardians of his share in the benefits accruing from general economic progress and the further social transformation that it renders possible. In these circumstances, the German labor movement may perhaps at length appropriate the previously quoted pronouncement of American labor: "We have no ultimate ends. We are going from day to day. We are all practical men."

European socialism has produced a history fascinating in all its aspects: economic, social, political, and intellectual. Professor Landauer's great work is a formidable testimony to the fact. The vicissitudes of ideology within the movement are merely a narrow aspect of its evolution. But they also reveal a broad problem that transcends the boundaries of the Movement. It is a distinguishing feature of social science that its objects never tire of making statements about themselves. This is a blessing and a curse, a fount of enlightenment and a source of confusion. The actors on the social scene may want to deceive and just as likely they may be deceived themselves about their own nature and character. Social movements are movements of men and like individuals they have an urgent desire to see the stories of their lives as consistent unities. Pretended stability in the ways of thinking and believing tends to disguise the processes of change that may appear undesirable from the actors' point of view. But such pretensions should not mislead and confuse the scholar. His task is to penetrate beneath the surface of claims and assertions and to recognize the role of ideology of social movements in its complex functional evolution which includes the imperceptible but steady decline of old beliefs, their sudden resurgence, and their eventual obsolescence.

Footnotes

[1] Carl A. Landauer, *European Socialism, A History of Ideas and Movements*, Vols. I, II (Berkeley 1959).

[2] When I wrote this sentence in the text I did not fully grasp the most important and most sordid reason behind those policies. Now after the appearance

of the shocking memoirs of the man who served as president of the Reichsbank from 1930 to 1933 it is clear that it was not alone prejudice, incompetence, or the debilitating memories of the runaway inflation that let the German government walk the pernicious road of deflation. The crucial motivation lay elsewhere. The Brüning cabinet quite deliberately wanted to use the collapse of the German economy for the purpose of inducing the Entente powers to cancel the reparation debts. Apparently, the plan was to launch reflationary policies *after* the reparation slate had been wiped clean. Cf. Hans Luther, *Vor dem Abgrund, 1930–1933, Reichsbankprasident in Krisenzeiten* (Berlin, n.d.). (Edgar Salin's Introduction is dated July 1964).

[3] Reinhard Weber, Preface to Gustav Eckstein, *Der Marxismus in der Praxis* (Vienna, 1918), p. 5.

[4] *Protokoll der Verhandlungen des Parteitages der Sozialdemokratischen Partei Deutschlands in Hannover 1899* (Berlin 1899), p. 154.

[5] *Holmes—Laski Letters, The Correspondence of Justice Holmes and Harold J. Laski, 1916–1935,* ed. Mark de Wolfe Howe (Cambridge, Massachusetts, 1953), p. 207.

[6] U.S. Senate, Committee on Education and Labor, *Report of the Committee of the Senate upon the Relations between Labor and Capital and Testimony Taken by the Committee,* Vol. I, Testimony (Washington, D.C., 1885), 460.

[7] Cf. Egmont Zechlin, *Staatsstreichplaene Bismarcks und Wilhelms II, 1890–1894* (Stuttgart and Berlin, 1929); Johannes Hohlfeld, *Geschichte des Deutschen Reiches* (Leipsic 1924), pp. 228–31; Fritz Fischer, *Griff nach der Weltmacht* (Duesseldorf 1961), pp. 29–30.

[8] Bertrand Russell, *German Social Democracy, Six Lectures* (London 1896), p. 6. Italics supplied.

[9] 982,850 in 1913. Cf. *Protokoll über die Verhandlungen des Parteitages der Sozialdemokratischen Partei Deutschlands in Jena 1913* (Berlin 1913), p. 13. For the data on voting strength cf. Franz Mehring, *Geschichte der deutschen Sozialdemokratie* Vol. IV (Stuttgart 1919), 16, and *Statistisches Jahrbuch fuer das Deutsche Reich* Vol. 33 (Berlin 1912), 327.

[10] *Protokoll über die Verhandlungen des Parteitages der Sozialdemokratischen Partei Deutschlands in Erfurt 1893* (Berlin 1893), pp. 163, 172–74, 179ff.

[11] *Protokoll über die Verhandlungen der Sozialdemokratischen Partei Deutschlands in Berlin 1892* (Berlin 1892), p. 220.

[12] *Handbuch der Sozialdemokratischen Parteitage, 1863–1906,* ed. Wilhelm Schroeder (Munich s.a.) p. 388.

[13] Rosa Mayreder, *Typischer Verlauf sozialer Bewegungen* (Vienna 1927).

[14] Bertrand Russell, *op. cit.,* pp. 143, 161.

[15] Not that the existence of hybrid beliefs should in itself provoke astonishment. As John Morley once said: "It is only too notorious a fact in the history of belief, that not merely individuals but whole societies are capable of holding at one and the same time contradictory opinions and mutually destructive principles." John Morley, *On Compromise* (London 1888), p. 68.

Bernard Cazes
Commissariat Général du Plan
Paris

Landauer's

Theory of National Economic Planning

Revisited

The second edition of the *Theory of National Economic Planning* by Carl Landauer takes us to 1947, in other words, to the prehistory of economic planning in the western industrial countries. The Dutch Central Planning Office dates from 1945, but it has been dealing only with annual plans, and in France the *Commissariat Général du Plan* was not established until early 1946. One may therefore say that this book was written without what for the theorist is a reassuring safety net—the observing of events or developments that have already occurred or are in the process of occurring. (Incidentally, these are the same conditions under which French planners had to begin their work.) A retrospective examination twenty years later therefore confers on anyone who undertakes it the easy advantage of a certain hero in a prewar French film comedy who found himself transported to the court of Francis I with the portable Larousse dictionary in his luggage.

I believe, however, that the venture is less futile than one might suppose. First, because the *Theory* in several of its parts survives confrontation with ensuing reality very well; second, because it is instructive to ask why in certain respects this reality took an unforeseen course. In order to do that, I shall regroup the book's chapters into four major categories: the nature and role of planning, planning and democracy, methods of preparing a plan, and problems of execution.

The Nature and Role of Planning

The problem of the meaning of planning is treated in Chapters I and IV of the *Theory*. As his point of departure Landauer describes the price system's inadequacy as an instrument for coordinating economic activities due to the failure of this system to reflect anything other than the present relation between supply and demand or to furnish any indication of future relations that may result from present economic decisions. In other words, the market is "insufficiently forward-looking"[1] and must be complemented by the action of an "anticipatory" agency whose tasks would be: (1) to examine the plans of enterprises and to determine what inputs these will absorb and what incomes they will distribute; (2) to ascertain how consumers will react to changes in supply and demand; (3) to modify projects when indicated, so that they may become mutually compatible and preferable to all conceivable alternatives for a given hierarchy of incomes. To Landauer, the result may properly qualify as a national economic plan, and he further explains his definition of planning as follows:

> Guidance of economic activities by a communal organ through a scheme which describes, in quantitative as well as qualitative terms, the productive process that ought to be undertaken during a designated future period. To achieve the main purpose of planning, these processes must be so chosen and designed that they secure the full use of available resources and avoid contradictory requirements, making a stable rate of progress possible (p. 13).

This definition describes the *function* of planning but not its *purpose*: its function is to coordinate economic activities better than the market mechanism could, in order to achieve consistency of decisions and conformity to an optimum. The goal, according to Landauer, is the maximization of consumer satisfaction, taking account of such other objectives as education, where free consumer choice might lead to undesirable outcomes. But he does not exclude the possibility that production planning might serve objectives other than consumption—military power, culture, preservation of natural beauty, etc.—or that the choice of coordination through planning might serve no motive other than to enhance efficiency in the productive process. One may prefer planning because it excludes competition and its hazards or because it offers a frame of reference for measuring gains and losses from the choice of less efficient forms of economic organization, for example, autarky or the preservation of small business.

In other words, planning represents a qualitative change, important insofar as it substitutes deliberate for automatic coordination and offers society the opportunity of calculating total costs and benefits of the course it wants to choose. Thus planning is not identical with government control of the economy,[2] and it is interesting to note that at about the same time Pierre Uri, then working at the General Planning Commission, made the same fundamental distinction:

> Planning is unconcerned with the irritating conflict between *dirigisme* and liberalism. For it is still necessary to decide whether or not *dirigisme* should be defined as the institution of physical controls on production, exchanges, and prices, or as an over-all design imposed on the economy. Experience shows that it is possible to practice a kind of *dirigisme* in the first sense without any coordination or overall philosophy, that is to say a *dirigisme* without plan.

For Landauer, the planning process exhibits two characteristics: it is the future image of an economy in the process of growth, which contains as an integral feature the consequences of that growth on inter-sector relations (and therefore on the level of production) and on the structure of final demand; it is, furthermore, a means of testing government policies against the criterion of economic growth, since it permits an evaluation of the incidence (favorable or unfavorable) of these policies on growth. It is therefore a technique that, although primarily related to the problem of growth, lends itself to the pursuit of other objectives. The *Theory* thus emphasized the two major arguments which will never cease to be invoked by supporters of planning: (1) planning ensures a greater and more orderly expansion of production, and (2) it offers a nation the opportunity to examine the goals and means of its development instead of submitting to the development fatalistically.

Are these arguments well founded? Does the experience of Western European planning justify the expectations of those who hoped for more rapid and deliberate development? The first question calls for a yes with a qualification, because the honor roll of economic growth does not include only countries practicing economic planning. Nevertheless, there are reasons to believe that in France the expansion realized during the decade of the fifties was attained with a slightly smaller investment than was required in other countries to reach similar rates of growth.[3]

As to the possibility of effecting deliberate choices, there is no doubt that the discussion of the major options of the Fifth Plan late in 1964 permitted for the first time the initiation in parliament of an open debate on the goals of development and, to a lesser extent, on its means. But it must be noted that the latitude thus offered can include only alternatives capable of being expressed numerically and not the more qualitative aspects (the quality of the environment for instance), and even among quantifiable objectives only those whose costs and benefits can be measured in monetary terms and whose profitability can be calculated.

Society, Paul Valéry said, has a tendency to pay only for what it sees, and if the planning process helps perceptibly to compensate for this impaired vision it nevertheless relies on economic analysis which, in turn, sees only what is paid for.[4]

Planning and Democracy

By 1967 the compatibility of planning and democracy had by no means become an obsolete question since, as cogently noted by Professor Neil W. Chamberlain:

> The Western endeavor to preserve as large a measure of freedom of private action as possible and still achieve public objectives, involves a number of basic philosophical dilemmas which can only be resolved by political compromise rather than some guiding principle.[5]

But obviously twenty years ago this compatibility was much more controversial, perhaps because the single example of planning then known, that of the USSR, could suggest pessimistic conclusions.

Landauer first attacks this problem by considering the means of economic pressure that the state can derive from the planning process. He has little trouble showing that the power to hire and fire employees at will has in the past lent the employer an instrument of power that we would be hypocritical to pass by in silence. Furthermore, public authority now has various means of taking action (police, power to levy taxes) whose use is regulated and does not, with few exceptions, lead to abuse. Finally, the ability to ensure full employment pursuant to a plan provides an economic security that cannot help but reinforce democratic institutions.

Landauer then takes up the problem from a different perspective: will planners not want to take advantage of their positions to impose their preferences as to objectives and methods of production? For practical purposes it is necessary to distinguish between these two aspects, for the first relates to the size and composition of demand, whereas the second concerns production functions.

With respect to the first point, Landauer believes it necessary to subject planners to a general rule which he formulates as follows:

> The consumers must be given what they wish to have within the limits of available resources, unless their collective will, expressed by the representative institutions of a democracy, approves deviations in favor of educational aims, social needs, or of a greater sacrifice of present to future needs (p. 233).

In addition, these resources "should be used as efficiently as possible" (p. 235). The reason for this rule, no doubt, is the wish to exorcise the bad memory of Soviet planning and to counter the "anticonsumption" attitude of certain non-Marxist planning theorists, such as Barbara Wootton. But at the same time, the adoption of this principle permits Landauer to answer Hayek's objection that planning will mark the end of the rule of law because government would no longer obey regulations defined in advance.[6] Experience shows that although western planning in no way impairs consumer preferences with respect to allocation of their expenditures, it nevertheless seeks, for reasons of consistency (the need to ensure equilibrium between resources and expenditures in goods and services), to influence the volume of consumption spending and also to combat what Galbraith has called the "social imbalance" between individual and public consumption. In this sense, public consumption shows a weaker "time preference" than that of individual consumers, as Landauer rightly notes in the *Theory* and in his recent work, *Contemporary Economic Systems*. Yet, in my opinion, it is important to observe that this only reflects the difference in view between the "leadership" and the people's representatives; and that, moreover, singularly effective devices exist in western societies to guard against any attempt to curb the impetus of private consumption in favor of forms of welfare different from those which satisfy the "industrial system."[7]

The second point relates more to economic theory (and to economic policy) than to the connection between planning and democracy because it introduces the relation between micro and macroeconomic points of view. The question it raises is basically how best to approach the optimum—by decentralized economic decisions that are closer to the actual conditions of supply and demand or by centralized economic decision making that can take better account of externalities? It would be imprudent to respond in a definitive way; rather, it seems important to establish the closest possible connection between various levels of decision making, so that different points of view and different experiences may at least become known to one another, influence one another, and, thanks to this exchange of information, avoid grave errors. That, in my opinion, is one of the essential justifications of economic planning.

In any case, one can credit Carl Landauer for recognizing that planning confers greater "calculability" on government actions, since the measures it takes may be tested against the goals of the plan. I shall cite as a recent illustration of this point the "warning signals" of the Fifth Plan, thanks to which, it is said, "changes in strategy, such as the interim plan in the spring of 1960 or the stabilization plan in the fall of 1963, can no longer be regarded as *ad hoc* improvisations—nay, the disavowal of policy—but form part of a permanent pattern."[8]

But might not democracy be endangered by the counteroffensive of those who at any cost oppose planning? One may note at the outset that many measures deplored by partisans of laissez faire have been and are being taken even in the absence of any planning. Furthermore, in a pluralistic democratic system it is always possible to turn back, although these vacillations risk being incompatible with the continuity of purpose and of action necessary to the success of a plan. It is essential to distinguish between *structural* instability caused by the succession of different political parties in power and the *conjunctural* instability derived from the right of parliament to reverse itself.

Structural instability is inevitable because it is the normal consequence of a pluralistic form of government in which parties compete for the exercise of power, although it will be more or less pronounced depending on the stability of the government itself. In France, the supporters of the parliamentary form of government have sought to harmonize the timetable of planning with that of political life according to the formula "one legislature, one administration, one plan." Nevertheless, a technical difficulty of scheduling occurs owing to the duration of the drafting phase of a plan. It takes almost three years to prepare a five-year plan, and during this period parliament is asked to vote on two occasions: first, on the major options of the plan, and second, on the definitive document. This double intervention by parliament, inaugurated in the course of the preparation of the Fifth Plan (1966–1970), was considered necessary to permit legislators to debate a text that was both provisional and reduced to its major outlines. But for the same reason it becomes impossible to synchronize the end of one legislature (and the general elections), the expiration of the plan (which permits judging the administration of the majority in power), and the selection of the principal options of the plan in preparation, since at least one year elapses between the vote on the options and that on the definitive plan. However, one can coordinate the transition from one plan to another with the date of the general elections, but then one must abandon the substantively rich preliminary debate on the options.

The instability that I have called *conjunctural* and that relates not to the succession in power of political coalitions with differing goals but to the possible disagreement between what the plan proposes and what parliament may dispose may occur on two occasions, either at the moment of the vote on the plan or in the course of its execution. The solution proposed by the *Theory* is a sort of suspensive veto, requiring legislators to reflect twice before jeopardizing the equilibrium of the plan. In France an analogous mechanism actually exists, that of the blocked vote provided by article 44, 3° of the Constitution, under which the government, having submitted a legislative proposal to the National Assembly, may ask it to express itself "by a single vote" on all or part of the text in question and to retain only amendments proposed or accepted by the government.[9] We might add that although there are procedures permitting the executive to preserve the consistency of its plan notwithstanding changes proposed by the legislature, there is no corresponding reverse regulatory mechanism endowed with the same character of *ultima ratio* toward the economic policy of government. The legislature could not intervene unless, in accordance with Andrew Shonfield's suggestion,[10] parliament "equips itself with a corpus of specialist ability" by means of which it could closely follow the execution of the plan and evaluate the extent to which the government's current economic policy does or does not conform to it.

The chapter in the *Theory* devoted to "Economic Planning and Democracy" constitutes a sort of conclusion in which Landauer asked himself what the chances were for economic planning in the United States and in Western Europe. For the United States he refrained from making any categoric prediction for, basically, in his book he did not try to foresee what was likely to happen but instead tried to persuade the reader that there was no antinomy whatever between planning and democracy. For Western Europe, on the other hand, he tried to estimate the probability that planning would be adopted.

On this subject he expressed a concern that the future has only too amply justified:

> The European nations, however, seem to be in danger of committing one very serious mistake. From England as well as from the continent we hear much of socialization, but hardly anything of serious attempts at full planning. The term planning is used very frequently, but without the idea that

24

the economy should be guided by a single unified plan. Rather planning is thought of as a sort of supplement of socialization. ... In Britain as elsewhere the emphasis is on public ownership and not on national planning (pp. 255–56).

The conduct of the first two postwar Labor governments well illustrates this double illusion according to which it is necessary, on the one hand, that nationalization must be the first step, so that thereafter one may contemplate planning; and, on the other, that this planning is ultimately not quite so indispensable once there has been nationalization. The idea that one should separate these two notions and reverse their order of importance has made slow headway. Paradoxically, it was under a Tory government and under pressure from certain industrial quarters that the National Economic Development Council was created in 1961. The true role of planning has been perceived very slowly; for a long time there has been insistence on seeing it (and hailing or deploring it according to prevailing mood) as a substitute for allocation through the market, when in fact it is a complement to it. In this view the problem is no longer to replace the one by the other but to make them coexist—which also forces us to rediscover a very old question in modern guise, that of reconciling collective benefit with individual interest.

Preparing the Plan

The distinction between preparing and carrying out a plan is slightly arbitrary insofar as the manner in which a plan is prepared affects its chances of success. Thus it seems that in France the participation of employer organizations and of a certain number of business executives in the preparation of the plan was an important element in influencing the business community. At the same time, contacts between planners and government leaders in the course of plan preparation are very important because they help policy makers become aware of those problems of economic policy which will arise when the plan is put into operation.

Nevertheless, Landauer is right in emphasizing that planning must be accomplished in two steps: "First, a plan must be compiled; second, it must be executed" (p. 14), because in the first stage the plan should be as complete as possible and take account of all economic processes, whereas in the second stage the incentives or constraints can be limited to specific areas and the remainder can proceed without public intervention.

The partial character of specific interventions in behalf of the plan is not unrelated to another observation of Landauer's which concerns the content of the plan. We have seen that, for Landauer, the purpose of a plan in a pluralistic democracy must always be the maximization of consumer satisfaction, allowance made for deviations from this rule which might be approved by the political rulers of a country. Landauer returns to this principle in Chapter II (devoted to the preparation of the plan) to observe that consumers' choices are independent of political choices because the allocation of the resources destined for consumption is determined by the decisions of consumers to buy or not to buy this or that good or service. But there are areas where the allocation of resources can be accomplished only by political decision. Such is the case where the community as a whole decides that consumers' preferences would lead to non-optimal results. Thus, for education and public housing a country usually spends more than would be justified by householders' preferences (or, in the case of narcotics, less than drug addicts might wish). The same is true in the matter of "time preference"—our concern for the future is more marked when we act as citizens than when we act as consumers. In all these areas, conflicts cannot automatically be resolved by "competitive bidding" because demands may be incompatible. A political decision is therefore required.[11]

Thus in some instances the state will have goals of its own that it will incorporate in a plan, and at other times the plan will register merely consumers' preferences. To this basic hypothesis Landauer adds others, no less essential, including the preservation of the monetary system of the market and of private enterprise as economic institutions, not because he professes an a priori attachment to them but because he does not believe that to be effective planning requires a complete overthrow of the institutional framework.

In reading the remainder of the chapter that deals with the manner in which a plan should be formulated, one is immediately impressed by the exclusively technical character. If one may distinguish two aspects in the problems of formulation—the exchange of various points of view (la concertation) and the calculations—the first aspect is totally absent not only from the chapter but from the entire book. It seems as though the planners were working by themselves, without any direct contact with the realm of production. Perhaps this may be interpreted as a reaction against the tendency of many theorists at that time to entrust planning entirely to the producers, at the risk of creating a "corporative" economy and of stripping the public authorities of part of the political power which universal suffrage had bestowed on them (see especially p. 108). If so, it is a very reasonable reaction, which has not lost its point because the nostalgia for the "democracy of the producers" has not lost its hold and continues to punctuate discussions about democratic planning. It is nevertheless worth noting that if one pushes this reaction too far, one risks robbing a plan of most useful technical and psychological cooperation.[12]

As to technique, Landauer stresses a problem which is now beginning to be appreciated but of which one did not really become aware in France until the formulation of the Fifth Plan; namely, the need to deal at the same time with planning in physical quantities and planning in value terms. It showed real daring for Landauer to write in 1947:

> If we want to decide which procedures are worth undertaking or are preferable to others, we cannot rely exclusively on a calculation in terms of physical quantities; we must supplement it by calculations in terms of economic value units (p. 37).

At that time a rather schizophrenic approach prevailed, according to which the capitalist economy was dedicated (for better or worse) to monetary calculation, whereas the planned economy (again for better or worse) would calculate only in physical quantities. Nobody could imagine the possibility that this gap might some day narrow. Yet, this is just what has happened. The French Fifth Plan includes an attempt to program in terms of value, that is to say, to project relative prices and real incomes consistent with physical objectives, whereas the eastern countries are trying to base their planning on a more rational price system and on a more decentralized system of decision making.

Doctrinaire prejudices are not alone responsible for the time it took programming in value terms to come into use. It must be recognized that the purely technical difficulties are also great. It was necessary to have a comprehensive system of accounts embracing all transactions in goods and services and all flows of incomes and savings (which in France is now called a "comprehensive economic table" [*tableau économique d'ensemble*]), and be able to project this table into the medium term— which presupposes a knowledge of the economic interrelations among its different parts. But "the judgments made about the relation between an easing of the labor market, on one hand, and the development of prices and wages as well as the increase in productivity and participation rates, on the other hand, were at the core of the discussions concerning the main features of the Fifth Plan, while economic theory and empirical knowledge could not contribute much to clarify the issues debated." At the same time it is indispensable to have a better knowledge "of the reactions of economic agents to financial stimuli and of the phenomena affecting changes in relative prices."[13]

Having mainly domestic demand in mind, Chapter II predicts in passing, quite correctly, that planning can greatly benefit from forecasts of household consumption by econometric methods. The problem of foreign trade is treated in another part of the book (Chapter V, "National Planning and International Relations"), but Landauer sees it chiefly from the angle of the compatibility of planning and freedom of trade. One senses that he seeks to demonstrate that planning does not inevitably

27

call for protectionism. His arguments are altogether pertinent, especially when he emphasizes a point that could have been made by Alfred Sauvy, that planning for growth makes it evident that true scarcity correctly refers to the available resources and not to the opportunities for their use. Nevertheless, until 1959 French planning operated in a very protected environment, and for a long time foreign trade was treated essentially as a relatively secondary quantity: "foreign trade [had] the function of providing for the economy's basic import needs, and exports [were] of importance to the extent that these pay for the necessary imports."[14]

Reduction of trade barriers introduces a great uncertainty into forecasts of foreign trade and therefore also of the levels of activity of export- or import-competing sectors. Hence, the execution of the Fourth Plan shows substantial discrepancies between forecasts and realizations by industrial sectors.[15] It should be recognized that Landauer's optimism as to the possibility of predicting the medium-term development of exports and imports by product ("there is little reason to fear that a planning country will encounter major difficulties because of unexpected changes in its opportunities to buy or to sell abroad within the few years of a plan period" [p. 175]) has not been confirmed by the facts and that variations in foreign trade represent a very important source of uncertainty regarding the success of the plan. To be sure, the *Theory* contains two tables on the structure of German exports by country and by commodity for 1913 and 1929, which indicate great stability between those years (pp. 174–75). But for a shorter period—1959–1965—the table for France demonstrates a very clear geographic reallocation of exports:

	PERCENT OF TOTAL EXPORTS	
	1959	1965
E.E.C.	29.1	40.6
E.F.T.A.	12.7	15.6
Eastern countries (except China)	2.9	3.4
Other European countries	2.9	5.6
U.S. and Canada	9.1	6.7
Other developed countries*	1.7	2.3
Overseas countries of the franc zone	30.8	15.6
Developing countries outside the franc zone	10.8	10.2

* Japan, Australia, New Zealand, South Africa, Israel.

Source: *Rapport sur les Comptes de la Nation pour 1965*

Exports by *commodity* are listed in the French national accounts not as percentages of the total but as percentage increases (by volume) between 1959 and 1965. Here again one finds great disparities. The total increase is 62.5%, and by commodities as follows:

— 29% for solid and gaseous mineral fuels
+ 24% for iron ore and ferrous products
+ 42% for textiles, garments, and leather
+ 66% for products of machinery and electrical industries
+121% for chemical and rubber products
+181% for agricultural products and timber

The underestimation of the dynamism of international trade and of the unpredictability of its development is not surprising. No one I know, except obviously the extreme supporters of free trade (who unwittingly become clairvoyant as their wishes are realized), was in a position to foresee how much the prosperity of the industrialized capitalist economies would depend on the intensification and diversification of international trade, and the ensuing consequences of any attempt at non-autarkic planning.

But it is precisely this difficulty of reconciling autonomous economic development with dependence on foreign trade that has led to questions regarding the usefulness and possibility of planning international trade. Landauer thought that when the major countries began to plan their economies they would create "some sort of international agency for the drafting of schemes for development" (p. 179). This international agency "would endeavour to find out where every commodity could be produced with the least social cost and where investment capital would be most promising" (p. 180). However, he did not consider this institution to be a precondition to national planning. The weakness of an unplanned economy arises because no economic agent knows the intentions of any other and thus cannot anticipate the conditions on which the success of his own activities depends. The existence of a sufficiently large number of planned economies would thus insure exactly this communication of intentions. Moreover, Landauer believed that the connection also ran the other way—an international plan is hardly conceivable without a sufficient number of national plans to support it. As he envisioned it, the international planning agency would have had a very ambitious task as it would have been directing production on a worldwide scale.

At the present time the problem appears in somewhat different terms: since the development of international trade may induce trading countries to curb their growth to guard against inflation, which would jeopardize their ability to compete, would it not be advantageous to introduce a certain amount of coordination into world trade even if the number of countries with planned economies is still limited?[16]

From this standpoint the question is not whether international planning should precede or follow the initiation of national plans. Rather, it is a matter of trying to compare foreign trade forecasts by country to bring out their consistencies or inconsistencies. Then, if necessary, one would look for ways to coordinate by means of international negotiations with respect to the redistribution of production, particularly in regard to structurally stagnant sectors where competition is unable to bring about a lasting long-term adjustment of production and markets.[17]

Technical progress along with foreign trade is another important source of uncertainty for planning purposes because it modifies the matrix of technical coefficients of the input-output table. P. Maillet's[18] calculations show that technological change (including substitution between primary materials and between energy products) has had very different impact on different sectors:

> It would have greatly slowed that growth of coal mining and, to a smaller degree, of agriculture, transportation, and textiles. Conversely, it would have favored the growth of electric power, oil, chemicals, and of the machinery industries. Finally, it would have had relatively little effect on the growth of construction materials, wood and paper, and services.

Yet the *Theory* is concerned with technical progress, not from the point of view of uncertainty for the Plan's projections but from the standpoint of the possibilities for long-term expansion and the risk of an excess of savings over investment opportunities. Landauer's conclusion was that there is no clear tendency toward a diminution of the capital-output ratio in industry and that in any case the economic needs of the underdeveloped countries are so enormous there is little danger of a shortage of outlets for savings.

Has economic thinking advanced much since that time? The studies of Simon Kuznets confirm that there is no secular tendency toward an *increase* in the capital coefficient. "The American development seems to show a period of increase followed by one of strong decline,"[19] perhaps under the influence of capital-saving innovations and of the relative progress of tertiary activities. That does not quite confirm the fears of an excess of savings that Landauer attempted to dispel in his book. International tension, a sense of responsibility or enlightened self-interest with respect to the rest of the world, proliferation of inventions and discoveries, inadequate levels of living—so many opportunities and stimuli for investment, and if there is a danger it will rather be found, as Landauer foresaw, on the side of an insufficiency of savings.

1. Let us divide this immense problem into two subproblems: how to follow the implementation of the plan, and how to influence it so that it will be consistent with the predetermined objectives. This is the order which the *Theory* follows, since Chapter III ("The Execution of the Plan") opens with consideration of the need for "control figures," depicting at regular intervals how the plan is doing and permitting the planners to alert the government when there is need for corrective measures. Here Landauer indicated one of the crucial problems of planning, and even in France this problem has not received a wholly satisfactory solution. Indeed, the question is a complex one because, on the one hand, observation must be continuous as well as at the end of each significant period (calendar year, fiscal year, and five–year period); and, on the other hand, the phenomena to be observed are of two types, namely—to use Gerhard Colm's[20] concepts—*performance goals* pertaining to the general progress of the economy and *achievement goals* relating to specific objectives. The interconnection between these two requirements can be represented as follows:

	PERFORMANCE GOALS	ACHIEVEMENT GOALS
Current Indicators	Warning Signals	
Results during a period (1 year, 5 years)		Physical or financial results

In this very schematic table the two blank boxes correspond to what might be called the absence of a problem. It is of no advantage to report continuously on the development of achievement goals (primary schools, hospitals, etc.). As to performance goals, it is common to report periodically movements in the general price level, employment, and GNP during the year (e.g., in the reports of the CEA in the United States or in the annual national accounts in France). But it is in the two other boxes that the greatest difficulties appear. In the first box, it is necessary to reconcile the indicators of economic activity with the annual progress of the plan, and in the second box, to reconcile the accounts that trace the course of public expenditures with the planned objectives established for the final plan year (and not year by year) which are based on concepts often different from those employed in government accounting.

On the first point, I have already mentioned the warning signals (*clignotants*)[21] devised to reveal inflationary or recessionary tendencies arising during the implementation of the Fifth Plan. They bear on the development of the general price level, the rate at which exports cover imports, investment in plant and equipment, growth of total and industrial production, and employment. These are not early business cycle indicators but a means of taking official note of any deviation between actual economic development and the *ex ante* path specified by the plan and of indicating the need for intervention to re-establish the equilibrium. (It is probable—and desirable—that this intervention would operate before the warning signals began "blinking.")

The second point concerns primarily the expenditures for public investment.[22] In this respect the Plan fixes, by major category of investment, the total value of expenditures to be undertaken during its five years and the corresponding total appropriations to be included in the state budget. As a general rule, the Plan does not specify either the technical characteristics or the estimated cost of each investment item. At the execution stage each ministry works out, in greater or lesser detail, its multi-year investment programs, though their realization depends on the inclusion of corresponding funds in the state budget. But as the 1966 annual report of the Cour des Comptes shows, these multi-annual programs and the direction defined by the Plan do not always correspond to each other. Furthermore, the appropriated funds are not always used in accordance with the multi-annual programs, or are used only with delay. The improvements needed are certainly more of a technical than of a political order, but they are no less important insofar as they bear on the effectiveness of public finance effort in regard to investment and the public's faith in the objectives of the Plan.

2. Andrew Shonfield in his forementioned book, *Modern Capitalism* (Chapter X), outlines a very illuminating typology of the styles of planning in Western Europe, which describes the manner of execution of a plan as envisaged by the *Theory*. Shonfield examines:

(1) "The intellectual approach" or "indicative planning in its purest form." If the plan succeeds, it is because of the quality of intellectual analysis performed by the planners who manage to convince their public and private counterparts of the correctness of the views presented to them. The plan, like the market, is a emitter of signals, but it is a better guide.

(2) An approach that "relies on reinforced governmental powers."

(3) A type of planning that "places its reliance instead on the corporatist formula for managing the economy. The major interest groups are brought together and encouraged to conclude a series of bargains about their future behavior, which will have the effect of moving eco-

nomic events along the desired path. The plan indicates the general direction in which the interest groups including the state ... have agreed that they want to go."

Shonfield concludes that French planning combines chiefly the first and second approaches. The position adopted in the *Theory* is quite analogous. We have already indicated how reticent Landauer is with regard to all collaboration between employer and trade union organizations. By contrast, he insists again and again that the plan exercises its influence because it discloses in a concrete and reasonable form the possibilities for expansion inherent in each sector of the economy. Nevertheless, it is clear that in Landauer's scheme the means of action at the disposal of the public authorities play a decisive role, not in the form of recourse to compulsion (since that for him is only a last resort) but by seeking to obtain a voluntary acceptance of the plan. "The way to achieve such voluntary acceptance is to make it visibly profitable to the individual entrepreneur" (p. 78). For this purpose he suggests a system of state compensation for any losses incurred by an enterprise as a result of complying with the Plan's instructions.

Landauer also refuses to endorse compulsion in wage negotiations (he prefers the creation of an arbitration procedure which would prevent any wage agreement that would lead to excessive or insufficient increases in remuneration), in choice of occupation, in personal consumption, or in saving. Western European planning experience has obviously not unfolded in rigorous conformity with the expectations of the *Theory* in that each enterprise may at its risk choose a growth policy different from that proposed by the plan. Yet I see only two points where the future outlined in the *Theory* was too optimistic: the predictability of consumption trends, and income policy.

Landauer thought he could safely write (p. 104):

Changes in consumers' tastes are no important source of economic insecurity or instability, and the planning board can calculate them in advance with sufficient accuracy.

This is true for aggregate consumption but not for consumption by category of goods or by function. For example, for the Fourth Plan, the Report on the National Accounts for 1965 noted a significant discrepancy for "home furnishings" and "vehicle purchases." Similarly, the increase in new housing construction between 1959 and 1965 amounted to 72 percent compared with a projected rate of only 28 percent (the review of performance demonstrates, however, that the discrepancy could be attributed only to economic accidents, but even if this explanation is valid it shows that prediction for the medium term is a hazardous task).

However, Landauer thought that planning would rationalize class struggle by letting the division of the national income depend on economic or social considerations and not on the relative strength of the combatants. Although this point of view remained valid in 1967, the difficulty of defining technically nonrefutable criteria and the distrust on the part of social groups of procedures that would involve state intervention and/or centralization of negotiations have until now impeded the establishment of an agreed income policy.

The *Theory* did not purport to be an explicit prediction of the shape of planning in the noncollectivist countries during the ensuing ten or twenty years, but I do not think I would misrepresent Landauer's intentions by hazarding an overall judgment on the predictive value of his book. After all, a theory that correctly explains the facts cannot be without interest from the point of view of prediction. So considered, the *Theory* seems to me to have presented very clearly and very accurately the conditions for the functioning of an effective plan in a so-called capitalist economy and the pitfalls it must avoid in order to succeed— respect for economic freedom, recourse to incentives rather than to compulsion, assignment of a significant role to the state, importance of problems of consistency, and need to program in value terms.

Planning, where it exists, has not invalidated the *Theory* and that, for a book on economic planning, is no small success. But the *Theory* suggested an economic universe appreciably different from that which has finally emerged: a universe quite largely predictable, where the major problem was more to demonstrate to business that expansion with equilibrium was practicable than to discover possible and desirable ways of economic development. Liberalization of trade, dynamism of private consumption, acceleration of scientific and technical progress, and population growth have led—and continue to lead—the Western industrialized economies in directions as yet only barely discernible. "Man has henceforth the *material* means, inconceivable only yesterday, to forge his destiny. This capacity is no less for ill than good."[23] Planning, formal or (as in the United States) informal, has succeeded in warding off the specter of a new Great Depression. Will it be able to introduce order and sense into the unleashing of productive forces grown too powerful to permit their channeling by market mechanism alone?

Footnotes

[1] P. Massé, *Le Plan ou L'Anti-hasard* (Gallimard, 1965), p. 113: "The great deficiency of natural mechanisms is their failure to be sufficiently forward-looking."

[2] *Ibid.*, p. 13. "All planning is government control, but not all government control is planning."

34

[3] On this point see U.N. Economic Commission for Europe, *Some Factors of Economic Growth in Europe During the Fifties*, Geneva, 1964, and O.E.C.D., Document C.P.E.—W.P. 2(62), Appendix, mimeographed, 1962.

[4] It is nevertheless possible to improve economic calculation in the sense of better cost and benefits accounting; see for instance Orris C. Herfindhal and Alvin V. Kneese, *Quality of the Environment* (Baltimore: Johns Hopkins Press [for Resources for the Future], 1965).

[5] "Western Economic Planning and the Convergence Thesis," mimeographed, p. 6.

[6] While smiting the strawman of tyranny-through-planning, Hayek has unwittingly raised a very real problem, that of the transition from "monocracy" to "telocracy," to use the very evocative terminology of Bertrand de Jouvenel (cf. his essay, "On the Evolution of Forms of Government," in *Futuribles*, Vol. 1 (Droz, Geneva, 1963), 92–94. It is apparent that planning is a symptom of that transformation but not its effective cause.

[7] This is the expression used by John K. Galbraith in his book, *The New Industrial State* (Boston: Houghton-Mifflin, 1967) to designate those industrial and commercial corporations which are largely free of market constraints and hazards as a result of their own planning.

[8] "Rapport sur les Options du Ve Plan," *Journaux Officiels* (Paris), 1964, p. 51.

[9] See Pierre Avril, *Le Régime politique de la Ve République* (L.G.D.J., 1966, 2° éd.) and his article on the blocked vote which appeared in *Revue de Droit Public*, 1965, N°3, pp. 444–52.

[10] *Modern Capitalism* (London: Oxford University Press, 1965), Ch. X, p. 236.

[11] Carl Landauer thus implicitly formulates a definition of a political decision entirely comparable with that which Bertrand de Jouvenel was later to propose independently in *The Pure Theory of Politics* (Cambridge University Press, 1963, Pt. IV, Ch. 2): "Where conflicting instigations to do would result in placing members of the set in attitudes destructive of the set as a working system ... then there must be elimination of conflicting instigations, one of which, and one alone, is elevated to a position of a 'command,' which alone can be uttered and which precludes the utterance of any conflicting instigation" (p. 113).

[12] Landauer has moreover corrected this too extreme view in his *Contemporary Economic Systems* (Philadelphia: J. B. Lippincott Co., 1964). See particularly pp. 281ff.

[13] "Méthodes de programmation dans le Ve Plan," *Etudes et Conjoncture* (December 1966), pp. 103–4.

[14] Bela Balassa, "Whither French Planning?", *Quarterly Journal of Economics*, November 1965, p. 542.

[15] *Rapport d'exécution* du Plan en 1965 et 1966 (Paris, Imprimerie Nationale, 1966), Vol. II, see particularly tables Nos. 40 (Industries chimiques) and 43 (Industries mécaniques et electriques).

[16] See for examples the propositions formulated by a French economist, Professor Lassudrie-Duchêne, of the Faculté des Sciences Economiques de Bordeaux, in *Le Monde*, February 8 and 9, 1967.

[17] See the report of Henri Aujac on *L'Adaptation des secteurs industriels*, O.E.C.D., May 1965.

[18] P. Maillet, "Disparités sectorielles dans la croissance économique: influence de la demande finale et de l'evolution technologique en France entre 1950 et 1963," *Revue d'Economie Politique*, special issue 1965 on "Recherche et innovation dans l'industrie."

[19] P. Massé, "La Prospective économique," cours de doctorat 1965–66, Faculté de Droit et des Sciences Economiques de Paris (mimeographié), pp. 75ff.

[20] "National Goals and the American Economy," *Financial Analysts Journal*, Nov.–Dec. 1964.

[21] On their functioning, see the explanations given in the appendix to the report cited in footnote 15.

[22] For the sake of completeness, one should also mention what the Fifth Plan has called the "structural objectives," i.e. the creation of major industrial groups, but it is impossible *ex ante* to formulate such objectives in numerical form.

[23] Raymond Aron, *Trois essais sur l'âge industriel* (Paris, 1966), p. 239.

Abba P. Lerner
University of California
Berkeley

Some Thoughts on
Landauer's *Theory of National Economic Planning*

It is really unfair to write a review of a book on current issues in economics from the vantage point of almost a quarter of a century of hindsight. It is almost impossible to resist the temptation to take potshots at evidences of the backwardness of the past when struggling with new ideas that are now old hat. But what is surprising in a rereading of Carl Landauer's tract for the aftermath of World War II is the degree to which its basic lessons seem even more appropriate and more urgent now than they were then.

The two most important reasons for this are Landauer's unwavering concentration on the freedom and prosperity of the individual human being and his generous flexibility in the interpretation of *planning*. He never allows either the abstraction *society* or the instrument *planning* to usurp the position of the true human objective, and his *planning* is able to embrace all measures that contribute to the establishment and the maintenance of the good society.

It is probable that Landauer would protest the second reason, and it is almost certain that he would have done so while he was writing the book. But his humanism and his wisdom saved him from the twin sins, in dealing with *market* and with *plan*, of elevating either of them from means to end and casting the other out as an inherently wicked instrument of the devil. This involved stretching *plan* to include free competitive markets or inequalities of reward whenever they would serve human freedom and prosperity and rejecting doctrinaire socialization or nationalization whenever they would threaten these ends. His deep concern with the imperfections and inadequacies of the actual markets never submerged his economics. Even his insistence on *full planning* and his warnings against *partial planning* can be interpreted as merely requiring that economic policy be *comprehensive* as well as intelligent and humane. He disclaimed any hot line from "history" that granted inevitability, even to his *flexible planning*, as the wave of the future. Instead he sought the minimum of change required to achieve the ends.

This underlying humanism so permeates the book that even when the reviewer succumbs to the temptation of hunting up some dated wrinkles or blotches he finds that they are frequently also marks of maturity and wisdom. There are, for instance, many indications of addiction to the invocation of Say's law against the full acceptance of the Keynesian revolution, but Landauer's classicism, in the pejorative sense of the term, is almost completely neutralized by his innocent qualification (modestly enclosed in parentheses) when referring to "that part of Say's reasoning which nobody who believes in the possibility of theoretical explanation of economic phenomena can reject: namely, that . . . the money earned in one type of employment (*if it is not hoarded*) will be spent on the products of other branches of production and thus sustain the employment of a corresponding number of workers there" (p. 70, n. 53, my italics; all page references are to the 1947 edition). It was probably not quite clear when this was written that *hoarded* is synonymous with *not spent*, for Landauer would surely not have taken the trouble to tell us that "money . . . (unless it is not spent) will be spent."

The parenthetical qualification almost succeeds in turning into a harmless truism the pernicious denial of the possibility of a *decrease* in aggregate money demand (to say nothing of Say's denial of the possibility of a more general *insufficiency* of money demand). But what is really important is his vision that functional finance is not enough—that "for good or for bad reasons Congress and the administration will hardly carry deficit financing to the point at which it would create full prosperity" (p. 148) and that "even before the injection of money has produced a state of full employment, sellers ... will demand and obtain higher prices" (p. 211) so that some kind of wage and price setting by compulsory arbitration is necessary for maintaining full employment—and this is part of the *plan*.

Essentially the book was an attempt to marry classical economic theory with the social democratic notion that what was wrong with capitalist society was the absence of a *plan*. The classicism, it is true, was already somewhat disillusioned with its affair with "laissez faire," and the romanticism about planning was rather spoiled by the clear recognition that planning must be a means and not an end. But enough of these hangovers remained to render the book a most interesting study of how largely they came to be dissolved by the application of common sense in clearing the path for the rational application of economic understanding to liberal social policy.

A lingering remnant of classical economics appears in an unruly team of preconceptions, which on the one hand envisages a natural tendency to full employment and thus would thrust the Keynesian heretics into limbo with the "underconsumption theorists" who have failed to understand "Say's reasoning," and on the other hand supposes that business cycles are a necessary and even a functional element in economic growth in an unplanned economy. This uncomfortable team seems to require a *plan* for its elimination and to be in part responsible for a downgrading of Keynesian economics or of functional finance as a means of achieving continuous adequacy of effective demand for permanent prosperity, unless these are part of a national economic plan. Keynesians and "functional financiers" tend, of course, to see the level of effective demand as of primary concern and the accompanying planning as of secondary importance. This most good-humored debate fizzles semantically into a footnote as to which of these approaches is of the essence and which should be "relegated to a kind of footnote" (p. 120, n. 23).

On the other side we can see a nostalgia for *physical planning*. Physical planning "is basic to value planning," yet "the planning board must not draw up two separate plans, but two interdependent columns of the same plan" (p. 64). The coordination of the two plans, however, remains a mystery and even "one of the best informed writers on the economics of the Soviet system" is unable to throw any light on the secret of how they have coordinated their "material balance sheets" with their "synthetic balance sheets" (p. 67, n. 52). But once more common sense and human feeling come to the rescue, and the detailed discussion of how the plan should be made and how it should be executed in a society of free men in which consumers' sovereignty is an aim that must not be transgressed for the conveniences of the planner resolves the economy into a very large number of decentralized *firms* guided by equilibrium prices. The apparent need for the planners rests on a belief that "it is infinitely more economical" (p. 62) for the equilibrium prices, at which all supplies equate all demands, to be worked out "on paper" at the planning center.

In the quarter century since the book was written the secret of how the "planned" socialist countries solved their "synthetic balance" has been resolved by the revelation that they didn't know how. They are now gingerly adopting bits of the free market mechanism to help them improve their efficiency and make their economies somewhat more subservient to consumers' sovereignty, showing that they had more to learn from Landauer than he from them.

In the discussion of value calculations, Landauer confronted the Mises-Hayek school that asserted the impossibility of market prices being developed in a socialist economy. In the course of presenting the well-known answer to this (associated with the name of Oscar Lange), Landauer glides into another debate on the measurability of utility where he errs in supporting the quite unnecessary (and invalid) proposition that the possibility of establishing marginal rates of substitution between commodities and relative prices of commodities proves the measurability of utility. Although wrong, this does not affect anything of importance in the real issues dealt with by Landauer.

The strength of the book, in short, is to be found not in its refinements of economic theory but in its social philosophy and devotion to democracy. It impinges on economic theory when it states that rationing was evidence of a failure of foresight (p. 103), but it appears in full strength in the correction of careless Socialists like Harold Laski who made it easy for Hayek to assert that they were prepared to sacrifice freedom for the sake of planning; or of overnarrow definitions of democracy, like that of Herman Finer, who would identify it with majority rule; or of impatient Socialists like Barbara Wootton who seemed ready to sacrifice at least some part of consumers' sovereignty because of alleged incompatibility with planning (p. 27) and who played with the notion of removing basic decisions for the institution of planning from democratic control because planning would not work if it was "revocable" (p. 246). In particular I would like to recommend for current rereading the chapter, "Economic Planning and Democracy," for a distinguished and penetrating analysis of the *formal* and the *substantive* in the Rule of Law, where the line is finely drawn between the dangers of holding to it too rigidly and the dangers of departing from it too lightly.

Today, much more than in the 1940s, the improvement, and perhaps even the preservation, of democratic society depends on the understanding of the observance of this line. We are being threatened by destructive conflict between those who would defend evil because it is part of the existing legal order and those who would destroy the whole existing order because of injustices that it contains. Impatience lends appeal to the Marxian saying that philosophers have long been explaining society —helping us to understand it—and the time has come instead to change it. Landauer reminds us that without understanding we cannot know that the change will be for the better.

Rudolf Bićanić
*University of Zagreb**

Three Models
of Planning
in Yugoslavia

J.

Twenty years of experience have brought forward changes in planning to its actors, its ends, its means, and to the environment in which these changes are being carried out. It would be completely out of place to consider that these changes were made only for ideological reasons or for theoretical predilections for one type of economic planning rather than another. On the contrary, most of the changes in Yugoslavia have been

* This essay was submitted by Professor Bićanić shortly before he died in 1968.

the result of the pressure of facts against preconceived ideas and have meant a search to reconcile theory with changing conditions of development and political expediency with theoretical concepts. We have to bear in mind that the different areas of this country are very varied in their endowment of natural resources, that its regions have an individual historical inheritance and geographical position, that it is a country of multinational composition, and that the levels of social and economic development of different areas are very distinctive. This has demonstrated much quicker and more clearly the weaknesses and the forces in the planning mechanism of the Soviet pattern, which might have been concealed for some time longer in a less complex country.

In this paper, we shall consider planning experience in Yugoslavia, which can be summed up in the form of three models. We shall name these models of planning according to their main characteristics: the centralized, the decentralized, and the polycentric.[1]

The *centralized* model of planning, a curious crossbreed of Marxist-Keynesian economics, is still considered in theory by some economists, mainly abroad, the most rational planning pattern, even by those who do not agree with its political presuppositions. Centralization is thought to be almost equal to rationalization and generalization of the social interest.

We find that this picture of centralized planning is overrationalized. One has to realize that limitations of this rationality have become manifest in all planning systems in operation, even in the most centralized ones.

There are at least four characteristics of such limitations:

1. Planning does not deal with a homogeneous environment because the levels of development and the degree of socialization of different areas and sectors of the economy are so varied that there is no possibility of bringing them all under the same pattern of a homogeneous plan. Equilibrating such resources and requirements cannot be done by one single method of planning, even under a macroeconomic disguise. There must be—and there always has been—a difference between planning agriculture and planning manufacturing industry, between planning international trade and planning domestic trade, between planning banks and planning physical production, and so forth. This *de facto* heterogeneity is concealed in the uniformity of central planning.

2. Another limitation is that the plans are presented in their final form as a unified and consistent rational ("scientific") decision of the top planning decision makers. The whole procedure of how to reach these central decisions, what norms to apply and where the initiative comes from, and how free the channels of initiative are is not taken into consideration. Empirical voluntarism of the top political decision makers, the irresponsibility of their economic gray eminences, the blocked initiatives of those

below, the arbitrariness of the models used, and the omission of important economic activities from plans—all this is concealed in the authoritarian procedure of centralized planning. The main objection to this type of centralized planning is that these ways are not institutionalized but are left to political arbitrariness and bureaucratic whims of the central planning authorities, which results in maximum tension between planners and those for whom the plans are made.

3. Planning in its centralized form is not a system in which rational planning methods can be satisfactorily applied. Just because it is centralized the central authorities object to or prevent any kind of rational formalized models from being used and prefer to keep within the framework of macroeconomic empirical decisions of political actors. In a system where there is monopoly of power in one center that is not checked or counterchecked, such a system is not only possible but seems to be natural.

4. Another exception to centralized planning is that such macroeconomic planning is not an all-embracing system, as it is often supposed to be, but is limited to some sort of internal closed equilibrium of variables and objectives chosen to suit the central planner, which leaves out all other activities that are not approved or recognized by him in his plan. It is a perfect opportunity to conceal the actual biases of the central planner.

The *decentralized* model has its own rationality, which is also limited. But the inequality of functions of the dominant *center* and the (*ex definitione*) dependent *periphery* creates tensions that are an obstacle to rationality in planning. For this reason a system that takes into account all the centers of activity in an appropriate way is more efficient and more successful than either a centralized system or a decentralized one.

The *polycentric* model is less homogeneous than the centralized system seems to be; its heterogeneity is recognized and institutionalized; therefore, it is in advance taken into account in an organized way. The polycentric system is less arbitrary because of the possibility of checking one dominant center by others.[2]

II.

We shall now describe the three models of planning in Yugoslavia by discussing certain basic elements of planning and how they are organized. This should give a better understanding than taking the three types in chronological order. We shall consider the role of the actors, the objectives, the means of planning, and the environment in which the planning action takes place.

1. The actors

As stated in the Yugoslav Constitution of 1946, the main actor in the period of centralistic planning was the state, which directed the development of the economy through the overall state plan.[3] The centralized state sector of the economy was meant to be the main field of planning action. In the second period, that of decentralized planning, instead of a *state* plan the constitutional law of 1953 mentions a *social* plan. Instead of one overall plan setting the frame for all actions in economic life there were autonomous plans based on self-management of enterprises, and the sequence was self-government plans of cities and districts, of republics, and finally of the federation. This social plan had to secure the planned development of the economy as a whole, which in practice meant mainly centrally planned investments.[4]

In 1963 the new constitution established new principles of planning —their purpose was to attain self-management of enterprises, realize individual and common interests of the working people, and stimulate their initiative. Planning in working organizations was put on an equal footing with that of social-political communities (communes, districts, republics, and federation), indeed, priority was given to planning in enterprises.[5]

In the *centralized* system of administrative planning, all actors were organized in the pattern of a social pyramid in which decisions were made at the top and then proceeded down to the bottom. The Five-Year Plan was created by the federal Parliament which was at that time a rubber-stamp institution of the federal government which in turn was controlled by the Political Bureau of the Communist party. A similar organizational relationship existed on the lower levels of planning. The basic characteristic of this system was that actors at the higher level set the limits to the planning decisions of the lower levels in the social pyramid. Thus those on the lower levels could move only within the framework of the ceiling set by those higher in the administrative hierarchy.

In the *decentralized* system of planning such decisions no longer completely followed the line of communication from the top to the bottom of a pyramid. With regard to actors the main difference was a link built into the system making communication possible on the lowest horizontal level of the social pyramid, that is, the socialist enterprise. This link was secured through the market mechanism. The second characteristic of the decentralized model was that no ceiling of targets was set by the top federal plan. Of course, talks and discussion went on between the republic and federal planning authorities and between local authorities and republic planning institutions, but no ceiling existed. If a republic was able to find ways of overreaching the target set by the federal plan and set its own targets[6] it was free to do so; the same was true of local authorities. This change in the planning decision making and a certain liberalization of the position of the lower centers in relation to the higher ones was not only a matter of principle but also of political convenience —since the central plan could not fulfill all the demands and expectations of those lower in the social scale, it was necessary to let those planning units that wanted to make additional efforts by their own means have additional planning targets. It still suffered from the prejudice that over-fulfilling the plan was a good thing and not a sign of bad planning.

The third model of planning has taken a *polycentric* pattern in which the contacts can be made on a horizontal line, and the top center has been split into many centers of decision making, all on an equal footing.

One should not think that polycentric planning is a system with no central plan at all. Indeed, there are several central plans that have different actors, targets, size, and means in various fields. What matters is that none of these central plans has an overruling power and undisputable priority objectives set against any rational examination.

The first model of planning takes as its pattern a social pyramid and the second a pyramid with horizontal rungs of communication at the lowest level. The centralist system operates only by communication up and down the pyramid. All connections among economic units take place through higher levels in the hierarchy. In the decentralized system the market mechanism operates on horizontal left and right enterprise-to-enterprise lines. The pattern of polycentric planning is a matrix, and this matrix shows an interconnection between all decision-making planning agencies. In this case every planning unit can make plans on its own, what matters is that these decisions are all registered within the framework of a matrix and made consistent with such a matrix by check and countercheck. The effectiveness of planning depends on the connectedness and the degree of social integration,[7] the transparency of the economy, and the speed of information between the actions of the planners and those for whom the plans were made.

2. *Planning instruments*

The character of planning instruments has changed in the three different models. In the *first* model these instruments were mostly administrative: rules, orders, government regulation, administrative acts and directives imposing the planning targets and ordering what must or must not be done, and the great number (fourteen) kinds of disciplines were to be respected. The modest counterpart to these norms was moral stimulation: awards of orders, flags, titles. In the *second* model the planning instruments were economic: wages linked to accumulation of funds, profit sharing, income sharing, interest rates, multiple exchange rates, and so forth. Workers' councils, pursuing the economic interests of the working collective of the enterprise, decided about their autonomous plan and in doing so they at the same time implemented the planning targets and thus fulfilled the objectives of the social plan. Thus, instead of administrative instruments economic instruments were introduced, and concurrently the initiative of the workers was freed from the iron shirt of state administration.

It was expected that economic interest would be a stimulation to workers to fulfill social objectives. What happened, however, was just the opposite. Indirect planning turned into direct planning as a result of bureaucratic interference. Most of the enterprises had pressure put on them by the local planning authorities, pressed by those above, to accept planning targets that made them pay into the government budget a certain global sum.[8] In this way the government's share instead of being a dependent variable became a *constant* around which all other elements of socialist income turned. This was a *de facto* redistribution of anticipated (i.e., as yet unearned) income.

In the *third* model the income to be distributed not only had to be produced but the product also had to be actually sold (realized), so that only what was earned could be distributed by the enterprise. Workers' management had developed from an instrument of stimulation for the fulfillment of social plans into a system of business management and from this into a system of social organization—the whole concept of socialism had become based on it.[9] Following this principle, de-statization of the economic system was indispensable. The consequence has been that new methods of planning are being introduced to correspond to this new system.

In a spatial sense the *first* model meant that the federal plan as an overall state plan was the overriding one, placing the ceiling on the targets of the republics' plans which in their turn provided the ceiling for the local plans. This was the territorial line of planning. Another line was provided by departmental planning along the three-level line of administrative subordination: *ministry, directorate,* and *enterprise.* There was a distinction between ministries of federal importance, which planned only within the framework of the federal plan, and ministries of mixed federal and republic jurisdiction, which planned within the general framework of the federal plan but were subject to the administrative control of the republics' ministries. Local authorities had only a small area of jurisdiction, mostly in handicrafts and very small industries, in which they could plan with no limits set by the higher planning authorities.

In the *decentralized* system differentiation of enterprises between federal, republic, and local was abolished and all enterprises were connected to the planning system at the level of the local authorities, through the intermediary of the local plans. Unity of space in planning was achieved, as opposed to administrative heterogeneity of the planning space in central planning, so that there could not be in operation throughout the same area several plans of different administrative levels without proper connection between them.

Since *decentralized* plans were territorially bound, there soon developed a tendency toward a closed system based on boundaries of administrative units of the country. Every republic and every commune had under control its own enterprises operating within its administrative frontiers. The federation followed an autarkic policy toward foreign countries, and the lower units tried to copy this within their own jurisdiction, basing themselves on a concept of a closed planning system. Moreover, as the enterprises were the source of fiscal income of the local and republic authorities and also of the federation, a great struggle developed as to who was to have the income from taxing the enterprises. One could say that administrative boundaries prevailed over economic considerations if it were not that even these economic considerations were politically biased and what was in favor of the center was considered optimal.

To counteract this a system of *polycentricity* is at present being developed, under the impact of the economic reform. In this polycentric system autonomous planning by enterprises plays the main role, and the authority of the territorial administrative units is reduced in planning so that it is possible for enterprises to develop commercial and contractual (long term) links with other enterprises across administrative borders and take part in their activity to a much greater extent than before. They are led not by the command of administrative planning but by their economic interest.

This naturally leads to a difference in the role of initiative of the actors in planning. The authoritarian system of centralized planning operated under guidance by directives of the central, that is, federal authorities. There was punishment if the plan was not fulfilled and reward if it was. This system sapped the energies of the working people and the managers immediately, and it turned them into passive performers of the will of those superior in the administrative pyramid. On the other hand, the consequence of the same system was that they were free of all responsibility but one—to do what they were told by the plan. The top planning authorities had to provide them with the necessary resources and instructions and means to implement the plan in current and investment activities.

When it was realized how much damage this system of bureaucratic administration was doing to the economy, workers' management was introduced in the factories and socialist enterprises. But in the system of *decentralization* the power of the workers' council was limited to the planning of current activities. It was considered the role of the federal social plans to direct the policy of investment for economic growth. However, it is not possible to separate current from growth activities.

Every successful management tends to make its enterprises grow, and this was subject to obstacles set by central planning.

The enterprises obtained autonomy of planning in the current operational field but not freedom of decision making in the organizational field and even less in the field of regulation, where they were strictly bound by administrative rules. This is being changed in the third model. The economic reform envisages planning of enterprises extended to autoregulation of their activities. This again has led to a two-track policy because, although autoregulation means that the enterprises are free to decide what to do, they are no longer under the shield of the government budget, funds, and administrative subsidies and therefore have to stand on their own feet and be responsible for their own decisions.

A significant change has taken place in the *time* dimension of planning. In the first period of administrative centralized planning there was one all state Five-Year Plan with ramifications on both territorial and departmental lines. This perspective plan was split into five annual plans and these into trimestrial plans, which were the smallest time units for overall national planning. In fact, this first Five-Year Plan (1947–51) had to be prolonged for one year. The plans of the enterprises were made not only on annual and trimestrial bases but also in monthly and ten-year periods. These short planning periods led to a *de facto* division of labor between those in the enterprise who continuously planned and had no experience in the implementation of plans and those who carried out the plans in a merely routine way.

In the period of *decentralized* planning, during the first five years (1952–56) only annual plans were made because the economy was in a transition period searching for new patterns of organization. Trimestrial plans were abandoned altogether as being of too short a period for planning an economy on a national scale.

The period of the next five years (1957–61) was included in the second five-year perspective plan whose objectives were achieved in four years (ending in 1960). The economic reform introduced a five-year perspective plan (1966–70) and abandoned operational annual plans as being too short a period for planning. (Suggestions were made to introduce a two-year planning period.) In the struggle for stabilization of the economy annual planning was considered an obstacle to stabilization, which is true for the type of planning that had previously existed. On the other hand, it was stated that planning in an economic system like the one introduced by the reform required further study.

3. *Planning objectives*

In the *centralized* system of planning the targets were stated in absolute figures. We would call this a system of *global* planning, in

49

which the targets are set in physical units or in value terms. This system can also be called a system of *direct* planning. In the decentralized system, direct planning was considered inadequate because it set the targets and did not stimulate workers to produce more goods with greater efficiency and economy. Therefore, the system was changed to a system of *parametric* planning. Parameters of action called economic instruments were set, and it was left to those planning the enterprises to find their own optimum within the constraints of these various instruments. If the planner was a good one, the optimum that the enterprises found should be close to his planning target. A competitive struggle developed between the enterprises and the social plans as to how to find the optimum. There was a continuous hide and seek in this game where the gain was not always on the side of the social planners, who tended to suffer from their professional disease: authoritarian overoptimism. Moreover, in the *decentralized* system the parameters of action were each set separately and almost independently. There was no formalized model of planning that would secure consistency in the fulfillment of the targets. Therefore, it was difficult to find a common yardstick to judge the effectiveness of the fulfillment of the plans. A system had to be evolved that would take into consideration the activity of the enterprise as a whole. This system is now seen as one in which the parameters of planning are arranged into one consistent matrix, and it may therefore be called a *matrical* system of planning. Efforts to establish such a system are meeting with all sorts of resistance attacking its consistency, starting with the political actors in the central government and its bureacracy and ending with the dictatorial managers in some enterprises. But there is no way out. Sooner or later such a system will evolve and work efficiently. On one side it provides ample opportunity to develop the initiative of the workers in the enterprise and on the other side their activity is interconnected by a flexible method of planning by matrix with other mechanisms.

The *centralized* system was based upon planned *prices* as instruments of distribution. These prices were planned in all constituent parts that were fixed and not linked to the real costs for reasons we shall develop later. All interenterprise relations were planned by fixed targets, and each enterprise was told what price to charge other enterprises and what to buy from them. Any possibility of choice of products or questioning of quality or assortment of goods was ruled out by the system. If it were not for the "comrades' agreements," this thoroughly "rationalized" system could not have operated. There was a marked difference between the real requirements of the enterprises, necessary for the implementation of imposed planned targets, and the centrally planned resources which the planned prices expressing averages of the averages could not bridge.

To avoid this, it was necessary to abolish the centralized planning system and to put a more decentralized and responsive one into operation. This system replaced rigid planned prices by market prices. Although the market was a very imperfect one, with many elements of the price structure being defined by administrative methods, it was a much more flexible and successful system than the centrally planned one. It came closer to real costs and expenditures. But the manipulation of prices by administrative methods was a great temptation for "creating profitableness by political means," and therefore many enterprises were created based on mere political decisions, and their prices were made adjustable to this imperfect market by subsidies, tax reductions and exemptions, and other methods of income redistribution by political power. This gradually made the whole system so full of exceptions that it required a general overhaul. On the one hand, prices that were set administratively soon became monopolistic, although there was no capitalist bearer of the monopoly. On the other hand, such prices were much higher than real costs and still higher than prices of comparable products in other countries. Some prices were deliberately kept low, such as agricultural prices (wheat, meat). Others were kept below the domestic profitability line by subsidies, but still much above world market prices (pig iron, coal). However, prices of manufactured consumer goods were kept high and prices of capital goods rose rapidly. These were the results of forcible though planned maximization of growth and accelerated industrialization.

The third point was that this system enabled the federal authorities to allocate for their plans the foremost priority and to distribute the national income in their own way, not forgetting to take the lion's share for their specific interest, the central bureaucracy. The system soon created tension between federal bureaucracy and business management which were eventually separated from each other by the introduction of the new economic system. The former wanted general provisions in the social plan, which would enable them to act arbitrarily according to their own preferences, but the latter had little use for such general rules of the plan—after paying taxes, making contributions, and receiving subsidies, the enterprises worked on their own in current transactions, hoping to solve most of their problems by requesting credits for new investment. This system finally became so inoperative that a crisis developed, first during 1961 and 1962, which was patched up and the main issues postponed, but in 1965 it was no longer possible to delay and economic reform was introduced. This had as its main targets the stabilization of the economy and the creation of a more realistic economic system by structural changes. After various attempts to introduce an internal distributive system similar to an income-price system, it was decided that the best objective measurement of the efficiency of enterprises would be prices on the world market, which meant that enterprises should plan on the world market price level, taking into account only normal tariff protection. Of course, this has created some difficulties in planning, but it does mean that a yardstick has been found to measure the effectiveness of enterprises.

The *distribution* of a gross national product is very significant in these models of planning. In the *first* model, this distribution was made according to the decision of the supreme political body deciding on the central plan. Distribution of every product started by distributing a global quantity produced in the country (plus a 6 percent *planned gain*) by a system of weighted averages from the top down to the lowest level of the economic unit, on the three-level scheme: ministry, directorate, and enterprise. This meant that nineteen thousand groups of centrally planned commodities were distributed among 165 ministries, several hundred directorates and their eight thousand enterprises. The planning requirements of the six republics with 360 districts and 7,104 local people's committees ranked lower in priority. As these levels were varied, many of these averages gradually became less and less connected with reality the further away they were from the center, and in the end they had nothing in common with the true requirements of the population.

The system of centrally planned income distribution thus had to be abandoned, and another system of distribution by planning was introduced. In the first system there was a 6 percent general rate of interest introduced on fixed assets and later on total working capital, which the enterprises had to pay annually into the general investment fund as their contribution for the use of the capital that had been put at their disposal by society. This rate was introduced by law and not changed by the annual social plans.[10]

Another instrument of income distribution was the share taken from the enterprises by the federal government in the form of a 50 percent participation in the profit of the enterprise. The turnover tax still remained the main instrument of accumulation and went to the federal government budget. In fact, the rates of the turnover tax were changed so many times that finally there was no system left in the great number of very varied rates of taxation. The turnover tax that was originally meant to be the chief instrument of equilibrating effective demand with inadequate supply lost this function almost completely and retained its fiscal character.[11]

Thus the workers' councils after so many proclamations of self-management were left with approximately 26 per cent of the income of the enterprise as the workers' personal income (instead of wages). The enterprise funds received not more than 14 percent of the income. The rest (60 percent) was appropriated and administered by the social plans of the federation, republics, districts and communes.

In the third model it was decided that the income of an enterprise belongs to the workers of that enterprise and that redistribution by the government is an imposition by a third factor. The principle adopted was that income should be disposed of where it is earned, and this is in the enterprise as the labor theory of value would require. It was considered reasonable that the government should take away from the enterprise about 30 percent of the gross income and that the rest should be spent according to the decision of the workers' management for the personal income of the workers and for the funds for investment in the enterprise. As a consequence, ultimately 70 percent of enterprise income will be exempt from redistribution by the annual social plan and will be left to be distributed by the autonomous plan of the enterprise. The justification for this is the necessity to carry out modernization and to replace obsolete capital and equipment, and this can best be done by the enterprises themselves. No central authority and its experts can have the detailed technical knowledge of modern innovations and information concerning an actual situation and what is needed in the way of modernization in eighty-five hundred factories as the business enterprises themselves have.

4. The environment

In the *centralized* authoritarian model the overall state plan was operating in a universe of its own creation, and the only question was to fulfill the plan with no regard to what would happen outside. The number of planning targets was very great but still not enough to contain all the actors, objectives, and forces of economic activities in the country. The plan was based on a closed planning mechanism that did not care about such other activities; it "socially recognized" only that part of economic activity that was included in its targets.

The *second* model introduced great innovations. Activities other than planned activities were also to be taken into account by the economic policy, and the monopoly of the plan was to a great extent weakened.

In the *third* model it was officially recognized that there are many activities of social importance other than those included in the plan, and it is in the interest of socialism that these initiatives be given attention even outside the planning mechanism.

This had already been stated in the program of the League of Communists in 1958: "The experience of Yugoslavia, and of a number of other countries, indicates that a social economic plan, no matter how perfect it may be, cannot exhaust the limitless possibilities, forms, and initiative afforded by the spontaneous development of economic forces. That is why the economic system and plan must not deprive the working man, enterprise and other social economic units, of that essential degree of independence without which no conscious initiative is possible and Man ceases to be a creative being."[12]

And the program of 1964 was still more explicit in emphasizing the change of the role of planning in giving guide lines for general conditions of development. "In a situation where direct producers themselves decide about investment and capital development, the function, system and method of planning are becoming an instrument in the hands of producers and of the community, for providing guide lines for economic development. The Federation, the republics and other socio-political communities should be primarily responsible for the creation of general conditions for harmonious economic development, but in doing so they should refrain from directly disposing of financial resources, this being the essential precondition for the implementation of the principles of income distribution according to labor input."[13]

Therefore socialist economic policy has to consider that besides the internal equilibrium, set by the requirements of the consistency of the formal plan, the external equilibria between planned targets and nonplanned activities should also be taken into account. Such an attitude leads to changes in the methods of planning in the direction of an open and polycentric planning mechanism. The plan has come to be considered only a guide and an indicator of social objectives and not an order or an obligation. Although it looked as if the first planning model included many more economic activities because the formal targets were much greater in number, the third model can in fact plan many more activities; only methods have had to be changed.

In the first model only the volume of foreign trade at planned prices was devised for both exports and imports. Between the internal planned economy and the external market there was no direct contact. Contact went through the buffer of the equalization fund in which all gains and all losses—but mainly losses—between the domestic planned prices and the prices achieved on the foreign markets were centralized. In the second model, planning of foreign trade was based on commercial operations of various enterprises which expected to be able to carry out their transactions under the principle of covering their costs by their proceeds. Thus, the risk was decentralized as there was no longer an equalization fund centralizing the risks, and enterprises could enter into commercial transactions and other relations with foreign enterprises. Their income or profits were part of their own benefit. Informal pressure was put on them by government agencies in order to achieve a certain amount of export; this pressure varied from commodity to commodity and from country to country (multiple rate of exchange) in fulfillment of foreign trade targets. These targets were not set by the annual social plan; they were more or less operational targets of the government foreign trade agencies or of the national bank to achieve foreign currency funds and to keep the flow of payments abroad going.

The first planning model was based on the supposition that national autarky can be put into operation at once, and the closed centralistic plan was considered its political expression and main instrument. From the planning point of view this meant that import targets (mainly capital goods) needed for fulfillment of the plans were set up as planning requirements that exports had to cover at all costs.

The second planning model extended the objective of achieving national autarky over a longer time period which had to be accomplished through balanced growth. Commercial transactions with foreign countries were considered temporary concessions to national autarky. Nevertheless their magnitude and duration demanded that the cost be balanced by proceeds on the micro level. Multiple rates of exchange replaced the role the price equalization fund played as the main planning instrument in foreign trade.

The third planning model was formed on structural build-in into the world division of labor, with customs duties as the main instrument of trade policy and a uniform rate of exchange. The whole conception of autarky has been abandoned, which implies further liberalization of foreign trade and gradual liberalization of foreign currency control until convertibility is expected to be reached. Planning has undergone quite a substantial change. As in other fields, enterprise planning plays the leading role and social plans are reduced to more or less a forecast of operations. There are two important exceptions: all purchases from centrally planned social economies are made through one single enterprise playing the role of commissioner-distributor for each commodity of each country, and the bulk purchase of food and certain raw materials is made by the state directorates for food and reserves.

On the other hand, social plans have to examine the fields of activity in which Yugoslavia and its republics have comparative advantages. Foreign trade planning will undoubtedly undergo further changes.

Footnotes

[1] A more general analysis of the development of the Yugoslav economy can be found in Rudolf Bicanic, "Economics of Socialism in a Developed Country," *Foreign Affairs*, July, 1966.

[2] For polycentric planning see Rudolf Bicanic, *Problems of Planning, East and West*, Part II (Institute of Social Studies [Mouton], the Hague, 1966).

[3] "In order to protect the vital interests of the people, to further the people's prosperity and the right use of all economic potentialities and forces, the state

directs the economic life and development of the country in accordance with a general economic plan, relying on the state and cooperative economic sectors, while achieving a general control over the private economic sector." *Constitution of the Federative People's Republic of Yugoslavia,* 1946, Art. 15.

[4] "The self-management of producers in economic life consists of: the right of business organizations to set their economic plans independently" (Art. 6). "Self-government by the working people in communes, cities and districts especially consists of ... the right of the people's committee autonomously to decide about the budget and social plan" (Art. 7). "The social plan of the Republic sets aside only those financial resources determined by law for the people's republic; those which serve to implement activities, within the jurisdiction of the Republic, for assistance to cities, districts and to public agencies and business organizations which are of general interest to the Republic" (Art. 8). "The Federation has the following rights and duties ... to secure the unity of the economic system, and the planned development of the economy as a whole" (Art. 9). *Novi ustav Federativne narodne republike Jugoslavije* (New Constitution of the Federative People's Republic of Yugoslavia), (Beograd, 1953), pp. 9, 10, 11.

[5] "In order to attain self-management and to realize the individual and common interests of the working people, in order to stimulate their initiative and create the most favourable conditions for the development of the productive forces, to equalize working conditions, to achieve distribution according to work, and to develop socialist relations, the social community plans the development of the economy and the material foundations of other social activities. Planning is done in the working organizations by the working people as the bearers of production and of socially-organized work, and by the social-political communities in the performance of their social-economic functions." *The Constitution of the Socialist Federal Republic of Yugoslavia,* 1963, Basic principles III, English translation published by the Secretariat for Information of the Federal Executive Council (Belgrade, 1963), p. 6.

"In order to secure conditions for the most favourable economic and social development, to equalize general conditions of work and the acquisition of income, to determine general standards of distribution, to realize the principle of distribution according to work, and to develop socialist social relations, the Social-political Communities shall undertake, in accordance with their rights and duties, measures to develop a unified economic system, to plan economic development and the material bases of other activities, and to this end they shall adopt social plans. In order to achieve the relations determined by the social plans, the Social-political Communities shall pass regulations and other general decisions, set up social funds and social reserves, and undertake economic and other measures." *Ibid.,* Art. 26, p. 20.

[6] In this way the overall investments devised by the federal plan were overreached by 40 percent in all plans of republics and communes taken together in 1962.

[7] By *social integration* we mean the degree of connectedness between the dispersion of outputs and the specialization of inputs.

[8] This pressure was put on by the local planning agencies immediately above enterprise level. Although responsibility had been delegated to them by the central authorities, these authorities had not delegated the funds but kept them for their own purposes. Thus the local authorities tried to make good the loss by global levy on the enterprises. They had been given the authority but not the funds to carry it out.

[9] Statement of V. Bakaric, *Borba*, July 24, 1966.

[10] Nevertheless there were exceptions to this 6 percent burden which was too big for certain branches of industry (for example, agriculture or those with a very large capital investment, such as waterpower stations). Finally this capital reached an average 2.7 percent. It was reduced by the reform to 4 percent.

[11] As recently as 1963 the high tax on sales of textiles—introduced during a clothing shortage—was reduced in order to lower the price of the already over-expanded production of textile goods.

[12] The Programme of the League of Communists, "Yugoslavia" (Beograd, 1958), pp. 158–59.

[13] *Yugoslav Survey*, No. 20, p. 2907.

Benjamin N. Ward
University of California
Berkeley

Capitalism
vs. Socialism:
A Small-Country Version[1]

Empirical comparisons between capitalism and socialism are surprisingly rare. The principal systemic pair that has been given the comparative treatment is, of course, the United States and the Soviet Union.[2] Each is a dominant representative of its type, but each suffers badly from atypicality if one is interested in the relevance of their history and performance for the prospects of currently developing countries. Size, resource base, and such initial conditions as the extent of agrarian overpopulation all reduce the likelihood that propositions about the differences between these two countries that can be related to differences in their systems are transferable. Much the same thing can be said about other popular duos, such as India and China or China and Russia, with additional questions as to what can be learned about the properties of success from knowledge of the properties of lack of success.[3] Other comparisons have been attempted, especially within areas such as Latin America, but here there is a dearth of socialist countries to serve as a comparative basis.[4]

The comparison in this paper is between Greece and Yugoslavia. Each has had at least two decades of functioning as an undoubted representative of its type, initial conditions are somewhat similar and reasonably representative of a broad spectrum of developing countries on a number of dimensions, and each has had the standard credential of economic success over the past decade: an average rate of growth of output of no less than 7 percent a year. These facts, the paucity of appropriate alternative pairs, and the special interest that this problem still holds for many have provided the motivation for the attempt.

The procedure will be, after a brief introduction to the condition of these two countries in the first half of the postwar period, to develop a limited series of comparative statements dealing with structure and performance and to assess the systemic relevance of differences that emerge. Though in a sense representative, these two countries are not at all typical of their kind. Each represents more or less successful performance, so the comparison is between "best practice" in the two types of economies. Furthermore, existing data and studies do not permit definitive descriptions of structure or performance in either case, so that the conclusions are inevitably speculative. In particular, it is very difficult to separate systemic and nonsystemic determinants of the states of the two economies, so again the question of the transferability of the results is debatable. Hopefully they will add some modicum of understanding of a few major issues.

I.

Interwar Greece and Yugoslavia were representative Balkan states in their primarily agrarian economies, unspectacular economic progress, and political instability. Each possessed a minimal railroad network, abysmal roads, and very high infant mortality, and each was a net food exporter and importer of manufactures. Remittances and tourism were important items in the balance of payments. Yugoslavia had its regionally based nationalities problem and Greece its problem of settling refugees from Turkey. Yugoslavia had achieved, largely with the aid of foreign capital, some development of its mineral resources, whereas Greece had, in Athens, the largest and most cosmopolitan city in the Balkans.[5] The depression, World War II, and civil wars in both countries were catastrophic in their impact on the population and the economy. Recovery was slower in Greece, partly because the civil war there ended only several years after the end of World War II and partly because Greek political disorganization in the early fifties contrasted sharply with the monolithic regime of Marshal Tito, which brought substantial economic recovery to Yugoslavia quickly and with an iron hand.[6] However, further progress in Yugoslavia was delayed for several years by the Cominform break, during which time the economy was essentially stagnant. Thus it was not until 1953 or 1954 that recovery and return to some sort of normalcy was achieved in both countries. Table 1 measures various aspects of economic structure in Greece and Yugoslavia, both relative to one another and to the rest of the world, near the beginning of the period of "normal" development. The data refer to 90 to 130 countries depending on the property measured, including developed, underdeveloped, and newly developed (in 1955) countries. The location of the property in the table shows the position of Greece in relation to these other countries, and the signs on the left indicate in how many categories Yugoslavia ranks above or below Greece. Because of the unreliability of the data, numerical rankings have been replaced by the fivefold categorization. The higher a property lies in the table, the more like a developed country Greece is. Thus the fact that birthrates and physicians and dentists per capita are in the upper quartile means that the birthrate is relatively low in Greece, although the number of doctors and dentists per capita is relatively high. The signs indicate that Yugoslavia ranks one category below Greece for both these properties, or in the second quarter of the world's countries.

It is striking that Greece appears in 1955 to have been the world's median country with respect to a number of key developmental properties. In yet another respect Greece was a rather typical country. In terms of structure of income originating, and in particular the proportion originating in industry as correlated with per capita gross national product, Greece fits very well the typical pattern of development.

In Table 1 the economic quality of Greek human resources seems to be well above the median, but the quality of her natural resources is below the median. For Yugoslavia the situation is just the reverse with respect to Greece, and perhaps also with respect to the rest of the world. Even by 1955 Yugoslavia probably had a relatively larger share of income originating in industry than was typical for her level of per capita gross national product.[8] Thus both Greece and Yugoslavia in 1955 offered a not-so-untypical picture of the economic present for some developing countries and of the not-too-distant future for others. Perhaps the most important atypicalities are on the one hand the relatively large size of both population and resource base in Yugoslavia and on the other hand the ethnic homogeneity of the population of Greece.

TABLE 1. *Relative rankings of properties of Greece and Yugoslavia on a scale of economic development for 1955*

YUGOSLAVIA RELATIVE TO GREECE	GREECE RELATIVE TO OTHER COUNTRIES
	Upper quartile
—	Birthrates
—	Physicians and dentists per capita
0	Percentage of population in secondary and higher education
	Second quartile
—	Infant mortality
0	Calories consumed per capita
—	Proportion of active population in agriculture
—	Proportion of population in cities over 20,000
0	Adult literacy
0	Proportion of children aged 5–14 in primary school
	At or very close to median
+	Cultivated land per capita
+	Gross national product
+	Per capita gross national product
+	Per capita energy consumption
++	Energy potential
	Third quartile
+	Per capita energy potential
+++	Proportion of raw materials among exports

Source: Derived from data in Norton Ginsburg, *Atlas of Economic Development*, Chicago: University of Chicago, 1961. Some data refer to earlier years, e.g., energy potential. See text for comments.

Unfortunately there are no simple schemata that can give a clear picture of comparative organization and institutions. It is true that Yugoslavia has nationalized nearly all the means of production in industry and trade, whereas in Greece private property is the dominant mode of ownership of productive assets. It is also true that Yugoslavia has a one-party political system, with the Communist party dominating political decision making, whereas in Greece there is a multiparty system with the polls serving on occasion as an effective means for changing political power balances. However, agricultural land and other types of productive assets are privately owned in Yugoslavia, whereas some industries are nationalized in Greece and there is government participation in others. The Yugoslavs have their unique system of workers' management in industry and use markets in allocating producers' goods, whereas the Greek government constructs economic development plans and intervenes extensively in agriculture. Of course, some of these features are divergences from idealized conceptions of capitalism and socialism rather than from typical actual practice, but the reader should bear in mind the problems involved in drawing general conclusions from this two-country sample.

II.

Table 2 displays some aggregative measures of the performance of the two economies in recent times, all of them very crude as comparative measures. Yugoslavia grew somewhat more rapidly than Greece, but both had exceptionally high growth rates over the decade. Greece had a slightly lower population growth rate, its own being just under 1 percent, so the per capita rates are about 7 and 6 respectively.[9] At these growth rates, real product takes eleven years to double in Greece, nine years in Yugoslavia.

The dollar figures are exchange-rate comparisons, that is, they convert the local product estimates in local currency values to dollar values by simply dividing those estimates by the dollar-to-local-currency exchange rate. This often leads to very misleading results, as can be seen by comparing the 1963 results of Table 2 with those for 1955 in Table 1. In 1955 Yugoslavia had a higher per capita GNP than Greece, whereas in 1963, after growing more rapidly for eight years, her per capita gross social product was 40 percent lower. The 1955 dollar exchange rate for Yugoslavia grossly overestimates the value of the dinar, the dinar in that year having on the average perhaps half the purchasing power implicitly ascribed to it by the official dollar exchange rate of 300 dinars.[10] It seems clear that the relative overvaluation of the dinar compared to the drachma in 1955 was substantially greater than it could have been in 1963.[11]

The casual visitor to these two countries would probably be surprised to hear that GNP per capita was 40 percent higher in Greece

TABLE 2.   Greek and Yugoslav Aggregates

	YUGOSLAVIA	GREECE
Annual growth rate of gross domestic product, 1955–1965	8%	7%
Gross domestic product 1963 (factor cost)	4832 bln. di.	111.9 bln. dr.
Gross domestic product 1963 (factor cost)	6.4 bln. $	3.7 bln. $
Gross domestic product per capita 1963	$337	$447
Gross domestic product per capita 1963 Ratio of Greece to Yugoslavia	1.32	
Personal consumption as % of gross national product 1963	45.2	71.0
Gross investment as % of 1963 GNP	36.6	21.4

Sources: Taken or calculated from OECD Economic Surveys: Yugoslavia, Paris, 1966, 35; and Statistical Yearbook 1964, 473.

than in Yugoslavia in 1963, as the figures in Table 2 indicate. It might be noted that from 1963 to 1966 Greece had a somewhat higher growth rate than Yugoslavia, and that Yugoslavia, but not Greece, has had a 67 percent devaluation, therefore current (1966) figures will not be more favorable to Yugoslavia. One difficulty with inferences from this kind of data may be noted here. Yugoslavia's high investment ratio means a much smaller consumption ratio out of product than in Greece.[12] Thus the exchange-rate comparison puts personal consumption of goods and services per capita in Greece at almost twice the Yugoslav level in 1963. However, this grossly overstates any advantage Greece may have in this respect. Dollar-equivalent prices of key consumer goods in urban Greece were higher by some large amount, perhaps 70 to 80 percent or even more than in Yugoslavia, so that the apparent advantage is largely, perhaps completely, destroyed.[13] Because of large differences in prices and budgets among segments of the populations of the two countries and the very different distribution systems, a precise aggregative measure of consumption differences can probably not be constructed, certainly not on the basis of the evidence presently available in published statistics.[14]

The above comments, plus a number of other considerations that have been passed over, suggest a great degree of skepticism in interpreting the comparative statements directly derivable from data like those in Tables 1 and 2. Perhaps it will be acceptable to say that the data suggest that both countries have performed rather well, and over the last decade they should have significantly improved their relative rankings on the world development scale.

During the past dozen years or so Yugoslavia has increased its educational facilities more than Greece. This is particularly noticeable with respect to higher education where Yugoslavia has one of the world's highest percentages of college-age population in institutions of higher learning, about twice as many as Greece. The figures may be a little misleading because of the very many Greeks who receive their education abroad; however, from the point of view of national development this phenomenon must be discounted because a large number of those educated abroad do not return.[15]

There has been large-scale emigration from both countries, especially to Western Europe. In 1963 there were perhaps one hundred twenty-five thousand Greek workers in Western Europe, over 90 percent of whom resided in West Germany. There were slightly more than half that many Yugoslavs with work permits, most of them in West Germany also, though over a quarter of the total were in France. Emigration from Greece in the late fifties may have been removing over a quarter of the new active population from entry into the national labor force, the figure for the first half of the sixties being much higher; Yugoslavia is losing a much smaller but increasing percentage.[16] This substitution of foreign exchange (remittances) for labor force can serve to increase the growth rate of countries having both unemployment and balance-of-payments problems, at least in the short run. However, a careful assessment of the economic costs and benefits has yet to be made, and there is a widespread tendency to view the population loss with apprehension.[17]

III.

We turn now to a consideration of some major economic policies and the systemic elements in differences that emerge.

Having been an avowedly Communist country throughout the postwar period, Yugoslavia has adopted economic policies that are broadly consistent with those of other Communist countries. She has allocated a very high proportion of national product to investment, the investment ratio rising from around 30 percent in the mid-fifties to 35 percent and even higher in the early sixties. An unusually large portion of investment has been assigned to heavy industry. There has been great emphasis on increasing the share of manufactures in total exports as well as export development. Regional industrial development has also been emphasized so that all over Yugoslavia small industrial towns have sprung up. By and large the orientation has been strongly toward rapid growth of output, and policies in other areas have tended to be adapted to the implications of this goal as these implications were conceived by the leadership.[18]

Economic developments in Greece have been less dominated by public policy than in Yugoslavia. During most of the period from 1953 on the Greeks adopted "the German way," emphasizing a securely stable exchange rate as the cornerstone of economic policy. Though the government provided some assistance to industrial development, its orientation was rather passive in effect. The gross investment ratio did rise from about 15 percent in the mid-fifties to slightly over 20 percent in recent years, reflecting a stronger government interest in directly stimulating rapid growth. However, during most of the last dozen years the leading sector in Greek development was urban housing, though this was not a primary developmental goal of government policy. Thus market demand and supply factors that were to a considerable extent autonomous with respect to government were much more important in resource allocation decisions in Greece than in Yugoslavia. During the decade from 1953 to 1963 the securely stable exchange-rate policy was successful, and there were no serious balance-of-payments difficulties. However, another consequence of relative government passivity (plus biases in existing legislation) led to a very heavy concentration of new economic activity in Athens and to a lesser extent in Salonica, the two largest cities in Greece. Smaller industrial towns were for the most part in a state of stagnation or absolute economic decline during this period.[19]

During the postwar period both Greece and Yugoslavia have received very substantial amounts of foreign economic assistance. Through 1964 each country had received just under $2 billion worth of nonmilitary aid, of which one-third to one-half was associated with reconstruction. Greece, however, had received $1.3 billion in military aid, or some $700 million more than Yugoslavia; much of this difference represents U. S. support for government forces toward the end of the civil war. Except for PL 480 food programs, mostly to Yugoslavia, and military aid to Greece, the aid program has been at a low level in the sixties.[20] Thus over the entire period Greece received on a per capita basis as aid (loans and grants) more than twice the (restricted) dollar command of foreign resources than did Yugoslavia. In general, the cumulative aid total to Greece approximates her gross domestic product of about 1960, that to Yugoslavia her gross domestic product of perhaps a decade earlier. Though aid continued to be important in the sixties, it was perhaps no longer a decisive factor in maintaining economic growth.[21] The favoritism the United States showed for Greece over Yugoslavia, as represented by these figures, is no doubt related to differences in the politico-economic systems of the two countries and may in fact reflect an "advantage" that one type of economic system has over another in the present world.[22] A related difference that may also reflect a systemic advantage is the policy toward economic integration. Greece has joined the Common Market, though on the present timetable it will not be until the late seventies that substantial lowering of tariff barriers will become a fact, whereas neutralist-socialist Yugoslavia is a member of neither major trade bloc, though she is an active trader in both and a member of such international organizations as GATT and the IMF. However, so far no substantial advantages or disadvantages have accrued to either country as a result of this difference in policy orientation.

There have been noticeable differences between the social policies of the two countries over the fifties and early sixties. The Yugoslav emphasis on increasing the education and skills of the population has already been mentioned. Family supplements and wage controls have been adopted to control income distribution, at least over the broad mass of the urban population. Greece has lagged notably in skill development and does not have a family allowance policy. However, medical care for many urban workers and their families, a widespread pension system that includes an increasing number of rural families, and an income tax with some limited progressiveness in its structure represent a modest equalization policy. Farm income supports are a notable contrast to those of Yugoslavia where the agricultural population has borne a major share of the burden of the high investment ratio.[23]

The different orientation toward investment allocation is partly reflected in the structure of income originating, as shown in Table 3. Yugoslavia's relatively large manufacturing sector and relatively smaller agriculture and service sectors are a clear manifestation of differences in sectoral investment allocations.

Finally, it should be noted that over the last three years or so some of these policy differences have been greatly reduced in importance. The Yugoslavs are reducing their investment ratio at a time when Greece is increasing hers and is beginning to experience serious balance-of-payments problems not unlike those of Yugoslavia. There is considerable discussion in Greece of putting more emphasis on industrial development, with import substitution as well as export development in mind, whereas in Yugoslavia the claims of agriculture and the service sector are being given more attention. A policy of regional development is being given increasing implementation in Greece, whereas in Yugoslavia regional development is being somewhat muted by a policy of greater emphasis on profitability as a criterion in new plant location decisions. Also, there has quite recently been a substantial increase in educational expenditures in Greece, as well as an increase in farm price supports, whereas Yugo-

TABLE 3. *Sectoral Structure*

	YUGOSLAVIA	GREECE
Income originating as percent of gross domestic product, 1963:		
Agriculture, forestry, fishing	23.7	27.8
Mining	3.6	1.2
Manufacturing	29.1	19.2
Electricity, gas, water	2.4	1.8
Construction	9.0	6.0
Services	32.1	44.0

OECD Economic Surveys: *Yugoslavia*, Paris, 1966, 35; and *Statistical Yearbook 1964*, 473.

slavia has been tending toward relatively greater reliance on market values in its incomes policy. Thus it is becoming harder to find clear systemic differences associated with differences in public economic policy. We shall return to this point later.

IV.

Many of the comments on policy in the preceding section can be summarized by a statement about structure. A more rapid rate of growth in Yugoslavia was constrained by balance-of-payments difficulties, whereas a more rapid rate of growth in Greece was constrained by the limited availability of domestic savings. The framework and *ceteris paribus* assumptions that must accompany this statement are derived from the Chenery-Strout approach to describing growth possibilities.[24] A detailed study has been carried out for Greece but not for Yugoslavia, which supports the domestic-savings-constraint thesis for Greece.[25] However, the frequent overheating of the Yugoslav economy with its concomitant inflation and consequent growth slowdown offers strong if casual empirical support for balance-of-payments constraint in Yugoslavia.[26] This *structural* difference in the two economies can be clearly associated with system-related policy difference. In the Yugoslav case, rapid growth is a central tenet of Communist ideology. In the Greek case, the relatively low propensity to save was related to the poor organization of the capital market, the short time horizons of many Greek businessmen, and, over much of the postwar period, uncertainty as to the stability of the drachma. The instruments that the government might have used to siphon more savings would probably have hit primarily the middle and upper classes, and this was perhaps considered politically infeasible.[27] However, as was noted also in the preceding section, these structural-policy differences do not seem to be immutable features of either system, judging from changes over the last three or four years in each country.

V.

In this section we list a series of important differences in the economic structure of the two countries which seem to have important systemic roots. These must constitute the heart of any argument that the type of economic system has important consequences for the way an economy operates and the kinds of results it produces. Further discussion as to how fundamentally capitalist or socialist the various differences are is postponed until the next section.

1. The use of fiscal instruments by the state is restricted in Yugoslavia more by technical considerations, in Greece more by social and political considerations. In Yugoslavia, flexibility of monetary-fiscal response is limited by the absence of markets for the debts and equities of enterprises. This is a consequence of the nationalization of the means of production and therefore it is a systemic difference. Its effect is to bring much more strongly to the fore the supply of money as a major indirect control instrument, and also for the pressure of circumstances to work toward direct credit controls. During most of the period of use of market allocation for producer goods, direct control of credit by sector and even by enterprise has been the dominant form of monetary control. This has not been a very successful approach because of informational problems, a certain amount of "real bills" type thinking in banking circles, and the ability of enterprises to shift the burden of controls in various ways. There is however under consideration (as there has been several other times in the last dozen years) a reform that will convert the supply of money into the primary monetary control instrument.[28] The possible difficulty of obtaining fine control of the economy through this single device has occurred to Yugoslav economists, leading to some discussion of permitting enterprises to buy and sell bonds. The possibility of direct foreign investment in Yugoslav productive activity also raises the question whether some sort of capital market may not be desirable.[29]

In Greece the poor organization of the capital market has already been noted. The stock exchange mediates deals in the shares of only a handful of concerns, whereas informal family arrangements are of crucial importance in determining access to capital. This market underdevelopment makes fiscal manipulation by the government much more difficult than in countries with more developed markets. In addition, hoarding of gold has served to make life more difficult for central bankers during a fair portion of the postwar period. However, it should be noted that a higher level of economic activity will probably in itself produce a higher degree of organization and development of the capital markets. *Ceteris paribus*, further growth should mitigate this problem in Greece, but not in Yugoslavia.

2.   Political constraints set important limits on feasible tax policy in both countries, though to date they have probably been more serious in Greece than in Yugoslavia. The Greek difficulties in this area have already been mentioned. In Yugoslavia limits are set by the existence of an agricultural sector that is not nationalized and is much less effectively controlled by the government. Thus excessive taxation or other control of agriculture leads peasants to hold back from the market or reduces peasant incentives to increase output, which immediately puts strains on the balance of payments. On the other hand, a good crop year puts money into peasant hands and creates strong domestic inflationary pressures. A flexible policy for controlling agriculture indirectly without seriously damaging incentives has yet to be devised.

In Yugoslavia's industrial sector similar incentive considerations have set limits to the state's ability to siphon resources from enterprises. In addition, there have been strong political pressures to subsidize high cost operations in the interests of equity among workers and regions. However, on balance the Yugoslavs probably have a wider feasible range of choice with respect to tax policy than have recent Greek governments.[30]

3.   Greece and Yugoslavia both have relatively small domestic markets for most goods, and especially in manufacturing there are likely to be few sellers of any given product. Both countries have protected much of their industry against foreign competition, thus creating an environment in which monopoly power can be exercised. The peculiar decision processes of the Yugoslav worker-managed enterprise may even tend to exaggerate the monopoly-induced higher product prices, as compared to the usual capitalism-based market behavioral assumptions.[31] The Yugoslavs, much more extensively than the Greeks, have resorted to price control as an instrument for dealing with this problem, no doubt in part because of their greater power to manipulate enterprises, which in turn stems from social ownership of the means of production. Their task is facilitated by the much greater flow of information on enterprise operations to the government in Yugoslavia. Business secrecy in certain areas is permitted—and there are *de facto* pressures toward withholding or distorting information flows to the government for the usual reasons—but it is quite clear that a Yugoslav planner has available to him much more detailed information about profits and wages, operating levels, plant capacity, and so forth, than his Greek counterpart.

Nevertheless, judging from complaints in the Yugoslav press, it does not seem that this information permits effective control of the exploitation by enterprises of monopoly-induced opportunities. It is difficult enough to estimate the competitive price for an industry in practice; the procedure for estimating the appropriate second-best price is probably not even known in principle. In addition there are a variety of political pressures setting limits to the ability of the government to select the price it may believe appropriate. It is doubtful that Yugoslavia could be described as an example of the successful use of price controls as an anti-inflation instrument.

The greater information and greater political power of the Yugoslav government are reflected in yet another area: its ability to engage in rather frequent reorganization of markets as an instrument of policy. Property rights and interest-group pressures set sharp limits to the Greek government's range of choice with respect to this instrument, but in Yugoslavia such constraints as exist are obviously much weaker. A decade or so ago, wholesale trading enterprises were completely reorganized with a view to taking advantage of economies of scale while insuring some measure of competition in each major urban market, a reform that should be rated a success. More recently there has been a government-sponsored integration of enterprises in a number of industries whose aim, among other things, was to improve the ability of Yugoslavia to compete effectively in world markets. There have also been some recent attempts, so far apparently not too successful, to integrate firms in developed regions with corresponding enterprises in the less-developed regions as a device to improve the internal operation of the latter. And of course with its far higher rate of industrial growth, the Yugoslav government has a much greater ability to influence market structure by choosing appropriate properties for new enterprise.[32]

4. Both countries produce five-year development plans, though Greece only began in 1960 (ignoring a reconstruction plan dating from 1949) and Yugoslavia was without an integrated longer term plan during the early fifties. The formal documents in both cases project sectoral trends and larger scale individual projects and are of approximately comparable length. Both governments devote a fairly substantial number of technical man years to the effort, though the latest Greek plan was largely the result of a crash program of a few months duration and did not have a comparable background of detailed feasibility studies that were available to the Yugoslav planners.[33] However, the striking difference in longer run planning in the two countries is in implementation. In Yugoslavia the plan is taken seriously as a proposal for further development, and implementation is fairly closely geared to achieving its targets. This certainly cannot be said of Greek planning.

One important reason for this difference is the direct control exercised by the Yugoslav government over investment. It has been estimated that in recent years at least 80 percent of all projects required central government approval because of its participation in financing.[34] The link between the Federal Planning Institute on the one hand and the General Investment Fund and the Investment Bank on the other was close enough to assure a serious attempt at implementation of the main lines of development described in the plan. In Greece, however, most investment was private, and when there was public participation either the controlling agencies were themselves ineffectual (as was the case with the investment financing agency, OVA) or they were dispersed throughout government in ways that did not support overall control in accord with a plan.

A second possible reason lies in the nature of the bureaucracies of the two countries. Yugoslavia, having been through a revolution that substantially reduced (though it did not come close to eliminating) the influence of members of the inherited bureaucracy and university system, seems to have been able to introduce concepts of merit into the criteria for selection and promotion of members and to provide the members with an education that has been substantially adapted to preparing them for their careers. Greece of course has not been through this experience. The universities provide a very traditional, humanistic education, entrance requirements for both university and public service emphasize the ability to write an archaic form of Greek, and the technical prerequisites for many jobs seem to be largely ignored. Though there are many good Greek bureaucrats and many bad Yugoslav ones, and this relative assertion is based on very limited experience, it does have at least a certain a priori plausibility.[35]

Whatever the relative quality of personnel may be in the two bureaucracies, it is clear that the Greeks are at a disadvantage with respect to the Yugoslavs in terms of quantity and quality of information available. This applies not only to information about enterprise but also to information about resources and even about the current operations of other sections of the bureaucracy. Many kinds of information about the current state of the economy were available much sooner in Yugoslavia than in Greece, and much more information about various aspects of the economy was published in Yugoslavia. As a consequence, not only the bureaucracy but also public opinion were better informed about the economy in Yugoslavia.

In terms of tables of organization there is, if anything, an advantage to the Greeks in terms of ability to control broadly outcomes in the economy. The Greeks adopted the French system of organization, with strong central control over the provinces and a ministry of coordination superior to the other economic ministries and with broad powers. Yugoslav administration, with its American-inspired emphasis on the separation of management and administration, its frequent reorganizations, and the many lines of influence from various agencies to operating units seems by contrast subject to failure by overadministration. However, the importance in both countries of informal lines of influence casts doubt on the significance of these formal differences.

5. Unfortunately there is no satisfactory global basis for comparing income distribution in the two countries, though a few rather limited comparisons are possible. In both countries agriculture is dominated by small peasant freeholds, and large estates play a small role in producing total agricultural output. Thus there is not a highly skewed distribution of agricultural incomes. However, in both countries there has been much agricultural underemployment,[36] and the poorer farmers live in extreme poverty by any international standard. Both countries seem to have possessed urban *industrial reserve armies* over most of the period, and urban unemployment, though poorly measured, may have averaged 5 percent or more in both.[37] Casual living standard comparisons are notoriously unreliable but, for what it is worth, it appears to this observer that real wages of blue-collar workers are at a comparable level. The Greek worker is probably better housed, requires less clothing and heat, and has a dollar income that is perhaps half again as large as that of his Yugoslav counterpart, but he faces prices for many key items of food, clothing, and household durables that are 50 to 100 percent higher in dollar equivalents. The Greek worker's children have less easy access to secondary and higher education, and though medical and social insurance is provided it excludes many workers as a result of capriciously complex administration. On the other hand, many Greek peasants but no Yugoslav peasants are covered by social security, and the Greek government, in striking contrast to the Yugoslav, has an income support policy for agricultural producers.[38]

Middle-class employees in Greece are probably better off than their Yugoslav counterparts, and upper-middle-class professionals and managers are substantially better off. At the very top where wealth and power are closely intertwined in both countries, comparisons are much more difficult to make, though the Greek elite would seem to be substantially more numerous than its Yugoslav counterpart. A very important aspect of income for the top 10 percent or so of the income distribution is security of expected income, and here the Greek family's access to the protection of the laws of private property are no doubt equivalent to a substantial increment in current income. Paradoxically, the Greek population may be comparatively better off at both the top and the bottom of the income pyramid, with climate, the agricultural incomes policy, and emigration providing the relatively greater real income at the lower end of the scale.

Perhaps the most decisive difference with respect to the middle and upper reaches of the distribution is the institution of profit sharing in the Yugoslav enterprise. This has the effect of diffusing over the entire work

72

force of an enterprise profits associated with market windfalls and monopoly structure. The remaining portion of such gains is diverted into the state budget or into enterprise investment, but this should not contribute to increasing skewness.

6. The strikingly different organization of the enterprise and the different situation of the trade unions have a considerable effect on the status and welfare of industrial labor in the two countries. Observers seem to be generally agreed that the system of workers' management produces at least a good deal of worker participation in those aspects of enterprise decision making that directly relate to the workplace, such as wage differentials, performance norms, and safety conditions. It also provides a widely effective machinery for adjudicating grievances. The nature and effectiveness of worker participation in other managerial decisions are more controversial, but even here one can find many individual examples of effective worker influence. The effect of all this is to politicize the enterprise, to force technical management to engage regularly in fence mending in its dealings with the workers, and to be able to defend its policies effectively when challenged. The workers' councils in principle have full access to information on the operation of their enterprise, and in the larger enterprises they usually have subcommittees of the council assigned specialized tasks of supervision and research.

Nothing remotely resembling this exists in Greek enterprises. Top union officials must be politically acceptable to the government, which by and large prevents the appointment of representative officials since the working class in the two major urban areas is overwhelmingly leftist —and probably at least nominally Communist—in its political attitudes. In other areas of traditionally strong unionization, the Greek workers have been without an organization that can even formulate and present its proposals to management. The blue-collar–white-collar distinction seems to be quite strongly felt in both countries, but not less strongly in Greece, and Greek workers for the most part have far less effective defenses against abuses by management.

On the other hand, the greater freedom of the press in Greece has meant much greater diversity in the views presented in the mass media that are aimed at the nonintelligentsia than is the case in Yugoslavia. Of course this need not reduce the sense of alienation of Greeks from their environment, indeed it may well increase it. But in the long run, especially as the divisive effects of the civil war on participants and victims become weaker, the greater diversity of information may itself generate new political pressures.

7. It is very difficult to characterize interest groups in the two countries in a way that permits clearcut comparisons of the different ways in which they influence economic decisions. However, it is probably safe to say that in neither country do socialization and social cohesive-

ness interfere fundamentally with the material interests of the individual and his family; generally participants in both societies exhibit rather strong drives toward acquiring a higher material standard of living for themselves. The ways in which these drives find expression through the interaction of groups is a much more difficult question.

In Greece the political system produces political parties, and though the individual parties have generally proved to be highly unstable, in the postwar period the Left-Center-Right trichotomy is useful in describing policy orientation. Because of the various catastrophes that have shaken Greece in the twentieth century there is little or no "old money"; in general the founders of present fortunes are still administering them today. Though there is a royal family there is no hereditary aristocracy, and agrarian structure does not include a significant number of large agricultural estates. Partly at least for these reasons (and partly no doubt because after 1950 communism was no longer a serious threat to their power) the political leadership of the Right has been willing to provide a reasonably favorable environment for economic development, in effect attempting to buy stability with social welfare legislation and even agreeing to the eventual opening of Greece's doors to the winds of competition from Western Europe.[39] Its principal supporters have been the army, most of the higher income groups, and a large segment of the peasantry. During most of this period the Center has consisted of several small parties in occasional coalition, representing urban and small-town middle class, some portion of the urban working class, and competing with the Right, at times successfully, for a good part of the peasant vote. As for the Left, the Communist party is outlawed in Greece; however, newspapers and magazines with an orientation very similar to that of West European communist parties have been published in Athens and Salonica continually over the last decade and have supported the leftist party, EDA, which garners about 15 percent of the popular vote, largely concentrated in those two urban areas in most elections. The Center stands for more public spending of a social welfare nature, particularly in education; for more rapid growth, even if drachma stability may be somewhat threatened; and for a less Western-oriented foreign policy. The Left's policies are less clearcut—no doubt in part because they have had no serious expectations of coming to power in recent years—but they are generally oriented toward public ownership of the means of production and improved relations with the socialist countries.

Because Greek political parties have tended to center around single strong personalities and their supporters, and because they have not in general been able to develop strong permanent organizations, coalitions have been highly volatile; for example, one leading political figure was successively aligned wtih Right, Left and Center in elections over a five-year period.[40] Political discussion in Greek newspapers and casual political discussion among Greeks seem inordinately concerned with the interpersonal relations of public figures, apparently to the detriment of careful public discussion of the alternative policies that may be at issue. This seems to be particularly true with respect to economic policies during most of the period. Judging from the media, one can hardly avoid the impression that a Yugoslav urban dweller has a much better opportunity to become well informed both as to the state of the economy and alternative policies under current discussion than his Greek counterpart. This may seem a rather strange judgment when it is also true that it was risky to express opposition to established policies in Yugoslavia, and any sort of fundamental opposition was very strongly sanctioned; nevertheless it is this observer's impression.[41]

Admission to regular participation in the Yugoslav political process requires the participant to accept formally the general orientation of the Yugoslav League of Communists. This is much easier for an urban worker than for a peasant. It can pose serious conflicts for a member of the intelligentsia also, though there seem to be a considerable number of such people who are genuinely dedicated to the proposition that, generally speaking, the Yugoslav Communist way in terms of economic policies and organizations is the best possible way for Yugoslavia. And the number who accept the broad lines of Yugoslav foreign policy is no doubt much larger.

Nevertheless there are substantial conflicts over policy that have some institutionalized base. The most striking of these pits the more-developed against the less-developed sections of the country. The subsidizing of the less-developed regions by the more-developed ones, including operating subsidies for inefficient factories and social welfare provisions beyond the capacity of these regions to finance independently, has been a continual cause of discord. There is also considerable overlap of this conflict and that over the appropriate degree of centralization of economic decision making, in which the more-developed regions tend to favor greater emphasis on the market test of performance of enterprise, both established and new. When added to these differences is the fact that ethnic differences tend to coincide with policy differences, the conflict can have explosive implications.

Interest groups of this sort cannot compete for predominance through the system of elections in Yugoslavia. Rather they are expressed by somewhat veiled public discussion and intense debate behind the scenes. Since the League of Communists is organized regionally with, for example, Croats dominating the party apparatus within Croatia, the differences do emerge in decision making within the League. As a consequence, an element of compromise tends to enter into the ultimate decisions taken by the leadership, whose authority has not yet been made subject to any effectively institutionalized limitations.

75

These various regionally based interests are by no means monolithic. For example, there are many Serbs who are liberals—there are also many Serbs who have lived for generations in Croatia, and there is a certain amount of interrepublican migration which in time should serve to weaken the force of ethnic considerations on these issues. And it should be noted that there has been a good deal of repression of leftist political activity in Greece, including the beating of candidates for Parliament and harassment of political workers attempting to circulate papers and pamphlets. Though, unlike Greece, Yugoslavia has not yet in the postwar period met the test of using established political processes to carry out a peaceful transfer of power, there is enough political tension in both countries so that it cannot be confidently asserted that one rather than the other is more likely to meet the next test successfully.

VI.

The points discussed so far by no means exhaust the list of major economic differences between the two countries. However, I believe that they do cover the major differences that can be substantially attributed to the capitalism-socialism distinction. For example, the pattern of regional growth of cities and regions is very different, with the Yugoslavs having a much wider dispersal of industry and a much more rapidly growing number of middle-sized cities. But this is mainly due to policies based on reconciliation of differences in nationalities in Yugoslavia, and perhaps partly to the centralized regional administration of Greece, neither of which is peculiar to the type of economic system existing in these countries. However, the discussion to date has concentrated on differences which *may* be attributed to systemic factors. Equally interesting but more speculative is the question as to which differences *must* be attributed to these factors; that is, what are the minimal substantive differences in structure and performance that are likely to persist as a consequence of the basic systemic difference?

It is quite conceivable that the right answer is *none*. This is all the more true if property rights are understood to be the basic differentiae of the two systems. Perhaps this can most plausibly be defended by offering a scenario of possible developments over the next few years in both countries. It should be emphasized that a scenario is not a prediction and that this scenario is not very likely to occur in fact. It merely offers a projection which at this moment is by no means impossible and which is based on extrapolations from some recent events in each country.

In Yugoslavia, the already existing right of urban and rural dwellers to purchase land for noncommercial uses is continued, and price controls on urban housing are gradually weakened. The new autonomous commercial banks put a significant portion of their portfolios into real property mortgages, and a well-organized market for residential land and housing begins to develop. Enterprises acquire the right to sell bonds to other enterprises and restrictions on the sale by enterprises of capital equipment are also relaxed, so that another sector of the capital market begins to develop. Government and union controls over wage differentials are also relaxed in response to foreign competition for Yugoslav skilled workers and professionals and the relatively free conditions for emigration. Internal interrepublican migration increases rapidly as a consequence of the more rapid development of the larger cities of the north and west, and the nationalities problem tends increasingly to be localized and to lose its primarily interregional character. Government policy remains oriented toward rapid growth, but at a slower pace and with an investment ratio reduced to between 25 and 30 percent. Local governments and enterprises are the promoters of a rapidly increasing proportion of new investment, and passing the market test becomes the primary qualification for implementation of nonsocial investment. Direct foreign investment becomes acceptable; workers' management continues to prevail in enterprises in which foreign capital participates and even where it is dominant. However, in each case there is a negotiated agreement on profit sharing and the setting of certain restrictions on the workers' council's rights to make decisions unilaterally, which would substantially alter the character of the enterprise. The political opposition is gradually becoming institutionalized, though the right to advocate fundamental changes in the polity continues to be circumscribed. The development of a formal two-party or multiparty system is delayed as long as regional differences remain the basis of political conflict.

In Greece a left-of-center Parliament continues the policy of more rapid growth based on a higher level of social expenditures and various forms of support for industrial development, including government participation and in some cases outright ownership. The economy overheats from time to time, threatening moderately the stability of the drachma, but not enough to discourage the continued high rate of foreign investment. Emigration slows down as a result of higher wages in Athens and Salonica and the somewhat greater security of much of the rural population as a consequence of the incomes policy of the government. The investment ratio rises from about 20 percent to perhaps 25 percent. Higher educational facilities are expanded and their quality improved, especially as a result of competition from the new University of Patras and government support. Government-imposed rules for foreign investment insure a large and growing Greek-national participation in the management and operation of foreign subsidiaries in Greece. Greek foreign policy leans toward neutralism; and support for the development of competitive exports becomes a major concern of government. Trade unions become dissociated from the ministry of labor and develop effective collective bargaining procedures in major industries.

The realization of this scenario would leave Greece and Yugoslavia still formally capitalist and Socialist respectively. There would also be many differences in the ways in which various decisions were made. Price control might still be more widespread in Yugoslavia, workers there might still have more responsibility for investment decision making, large property accumulation by households might still be more likely in Greece, and so forth. Around the edges, the quality of life could still differ substantially for many groups. But with respect to the major areas surveyed in the preceding section, the similarities would surely be more striking than the differences. The Yugoslav monetary-fiscal policy would become relatively more flexible, income distribution relatively more skewed, capital markets relatively more developed, and foreign influences relatively stronger. Greece would grow relatively faster, inflation would be a more persistent threat, and public services would develop more rapidly. In both countries political freedoms would be widened, though in different areas.

The scenario above was designed to indicate that the small-country version of the capitalism-socialism comparison may be at least as favorable to the convergence hypothesis as the large-country versions. With the preceding text, it also suggests that evolution and revolution can produce very similar products. However, it is important to avoid slipping into any sort of deterministic theory of trends. Perhaps the most striking feature of the contemporary world as it is presently understood is its indeterminacy, the significant possibility that any of a very wide number of scenarios may turn out to be the right one. For example, a very different scenario could be written for either Greece or Yugoslavia, one that has the centralizers winning in Yugoslavia, and one that has the more conservative elements centering around the crown winning in Greece. Very striking differences between the two countries could develop and, persist in this scenario, though we shall not pursue the possibilities here.

In conclusion, a word about the possible applicability of the Greek and Yugoslav paths to other countries may be in order. One cannot help but be impressed by the importance of rather unique events to the economic success of both countries. First, massive foreign aid seems to have been a key ingredient in both countries; second, the Yugoslavs introduced workers' management slowly in a sort of revolution from above that kept the government in substantial control of broad lines of industrial policy during the first fifteen years of operation of the new system. In Greece, the repatriation of Greeks and part of their fortunes from Egypt, the assistance of Greeks living abroad in the development of Greek shipping, and even domestic industry were factors of considerable importance;

78

whereas remittances, the unique tourist attractions of the country, including its unpredictable but important jet-set fashionableness, helped development and must be considered autonomous factors. Also, both countries had proceeded some distance up the development ladder before our period opened, so that many of the prerequisites relating to organization, skill, and attitudes of the population had already been achieved to at least a minimal extent. Finally, Yugoslavia is not an archetype of all socialist countries with its market system, or is Greece of all capitalist systems with its relatively progressive and growth-oriented political elite. Each of these factors was probably essential to the achievement of steady and rapid growth in both countries.

Epilogue

This paper was written in January 1967, some three months before the military coup in Greece. Up to the present time, the junta has succeeded in keeping civil disorder and threats to its own existence to a virtually imperceptible level, excepting only King Constantine's unsuccessful coup. However, though it has not inspired much violent reaction against itself at home as yet, the junta still does not appear to have established a firm alliance with any major political group in Greece other than a segment of the officers' corps. This situation, plus the shortage of reliable current information, leaves the writer unwilling to predict the future but unable to resist a speculation or two.

Of course, the probability that Greece will, in the near future, follow the *liberal* scenario of the preceding section has been substantially reduced. Fred Riggs has argued that there is an intermediate stage on the modernization spectrum, called *prismatic,* which may be very difficult for currently modernizing nations to break out of.[42] Keith Legg has presented convincing evidence that Greece is now in this prismatic stage.[43] The coup might be described as one of the devices by which a prismatic society, in effect, defends itself against the social, political, and economic encroachments of modernization. This line of argument suggests that Greece may be in for a period of economic stagnation.

On the other hand, Yugoslavia, as a consequence of the continued struggle of its leadership against some of these more or less premodern influences, may have been able to break through the prismatic barriers and to proceed along the path of the liberal scenario toward entry into the group of modern developed countries. Some recent developments, including the 1966 ouster of Rankovic and the downgrading of the secret police, thus seem to increase the probability of this path being followed.

However, there are two key imponderables which tend to reduce the confidence with which one may hold to this line of argument. The first has to do with the new Greek government's economic policies. There is no strong reason to believe at the present time that they will result in economic stagnation. Economic growth can be related to political support, and the junta seems to have some measure of flexibility in deciding which interest groups to co-opt in developing a broader political base. For example, the properties of a new constitution, including the determination of which groups are to have some influence in formal representative bodies, are subject to substantial manipulation by the present government. The *prismatic barrier* thesis is much less plausible if it cannot be shown that it at least slows down the economic growth process.[44]

The other imponderable is the stability of the Yugoslav polity. It has not yet been subject to the crucial succession test, and political tensions have been rather high in recent years. The fact that differences have a strong regional component further complicates the problem of resolving fundamental issues, such as the name and authority of Tito's successor. Thus it is not entirely out of the question that political changes will in the next few years be a stronger depressant on economic growth in Yugoslavia than in Greece.

As a final word, the coup in Greece does serve to point up a gap in the convergence thesis. The consequences of power seizures, indeed of many simple shifts in power balances, are extremely difficult to predict, but in many of them a slowing down and even a reversal of many previous trends is certainly not excluded. Until they can be excluded by a plausible and tested theory, one should not be too surprised if convergence stops well short of structural *equivalence*.

Footnotes

[1] The author would like to thank Milan Mesaric, Gregory Grossman, and other members of the Faculty Seminar on Communist Societies for critical comment, and Michael Rabbitt for research assistance, without committing them to any of the judgments or assertions contained in this paper.

[2] The major comparative effort, by a group of American economists working in loose collaboration, is well represented by Abram Bergson and Simon Kuznets, eds., *Economic Trends in the Soviet Union* (Cambridge: Harvard University Press, 1963). For a more or less comparative study of trends in capitalism and socialism, representing a very different viewpoint, see Paul Baran, *Political Economy of Growth* (New York: Monthly Review Press, 1957).

[3] For example, Wilfred Malenbaum, "India and China: Contrasts in Development Performance," *American Economic Review*, Vol. 49, 1951, and Donald Treadgold, ed., *Soviet and Chinese Communism; Similarities and Differences* (Seattle: University of Washington Press, 1967).

⁴ For example, Wolfgang Stolper, *Structure of the East German Economy* (Cambridge: Harvard University Press, 1960).

⁵ Defining away Istanbul as Asian.

⁶ Agriculture and consumption standards recovered much more slowly, but available consumer goods were probably less unequally distributed than before the war. Dr. Jozo Tomasevich, "Postwar Foreign Economic Relations," in F. J. Kerner, ed., *Yugoslavia* (Berkeley: University of California Press, 1949), pp. 387–426; Ekonomski Institute FNRJ, *Privreda FNRJ 1947–1956* (Belgrad, 1957).

⁷ H. B. Chenery, "Patterns of Industrial Growth," *American Economic Review*, Vol. 50, 1960, 624–54, and Andreas Papandreou, *A Strategy for Greek Economic Development* (Athens: Center for Economic Research, 1962–63). The exclusion of Communist countries from Chenery's calculation probably lowers the estimated share of manufacturing for each level of income.

⁸ The GNP data on which Table 1 was based are exchange rate comparisons. As will be noted this probably overstates Yugoslavia's relative GNP for 1955.

⁹ When only a decade of growth is being evaluated, the question of distinguishing systemic from nonsystemic factors becomes especially difficult. For example, the average (compounded) growth rate obtained from output data for initial and end years can often vary substantially by advancing or retarding the two dates by a year or two. It can be said that a one-year advance or retardation has a small effect on the present comparison. Indeed, so long as the starting point goes no further back than 1952 and a period of at least eight years is included in the calculation, neither economy can be made to grow by less than 5 percent, according to the official statistics.

¹⁰ Before 1961 Yugoslavia used a complex multiple exchange rate system combined with direct controls, so that the official rate was an extremely unreliable indicator of average relative values between Yugoslavia and the rest of the world. For traded goods an appropriate average rate on the dollar might well be closer to 600 than to the official 300 dinars. However, for many consumer goods, dollar prices were very low even at the official rate (this was also true for Greece). Cf. *Statisticki godisnjak FNRJ 1958*, Belgrad: Federal Statistical Office, 228–31.

¹¹ Another difficulty with the 1955 comparison works the other way. Ginsburg's figure for GNP can be derived from official Yugoslav data by dividing the 1955 gross social product in current market prices by 300, the official dinar-dollar exchange rate. Market-price gross social product is known to understate the appropriate GNP estimate, the amount varying from one estimate to another but probably lying in the 10–15 percent range. This amount of understatement is clearly dominated by the exchange-rate overstatement. A recent Yugoslav re-estimate of Yugoslav product according to United Nations concepts puts Yugoslav gross domestic product at market prices 13 percent above gross social product in 1956, with comparable differences in other years. Gojko Grdic, "Uporedni proracun naseg dohotka po jugoslovenskoj i metodologiji ujedinjenih nacija," *Statisticka revija*, Vol. 9, 1959, 12–25.

¹² The investment and personal consumption ratios of Table 2 probably

overstate the appropriate Yugoslav figure for the former ratio (and understate the latter) because of the inclusion of some services that are marketed in Greece under public consumption in the Yugoslav data, for example in the areas of housing and education and health. Unfortunately, a detailed description of the OECD calculation was not accessible to me.

[13] A recent international comparison of per capita consumption puts Yugoslavia slightly ahead of Greece for 1960, the former having 22 percent, the latter 21 percent of the United Kingdom's per capita consumption in that year. The procedure was to correlate consumption of a few key items with careful international consumption estimates for a few countries, and then to use the estimated coefficients in predicting Greek and Yugoslav (among others) total consumption from their consumption of these few items. The procedure avoids explicit use of prices in the compared countries. However, the presence of steel and cement in the estimating equations would seem to bias the results strongly in favor of Yugoslavia. See W. Beckerman and R. Bacon, "International Comparisons of Income Levels: A Suggested New Measure," Economic Journal, Vol. 76, 1966, 519–36.

[14] Probably exchange rate comparisons exaggerate the "international" value of services in both countries, but what sort of relative bias for Greek-Yugoslav comparisons this may create is unknown to me.

[15] In the 1962–63 school year there were about thirty-five thousand Greeks and one hundred sixty thousand Yugoslavs in national institutions of higher learning. Stat. god. 1965, 325; Stat. yrbk. 1964, 159. The numbers have been increasing rapidly in both countries, in both secondary and higher education, though private secondary school enrollment was growing more rapidly than public in Greece in the late fifties and early sixties.

[16] "European Migrant Workers in Western Europe 1961–1963," Migration News, Geneva, Vol. XIII, May–June 1964, 33–36; S. Agapitidia, "Emigration from Greece," Migration, Geneva, Vol. I, January–March 1961, 53–62.

[17] An extreme version of this reaction is represented by Fausta Bellini, "L'émigration des Travailleurs Grecs," Les Temps Modernes, XXIX, June 1966, 2185–230. A similar but more moderate interpretation of Yugoslav emigration was made by George Bailey, The Reporter, New York, January, 1967.

[18] For a discussion of economic policies in Yugoslavia see for example the discussion by a number of Yugoslav economists in Ekonomist, Belgrad, Vol. 16, No. 1, 1963; Dennison Rusinow, "Yugoslavia's Problems with 'Market Socialism,'" American Universities Field Staff Reports Service, Southeast Europe Series, Vol. 11, No. 4, 1964; and Benjamin Ward, "Economic Development in Yugoslavia," in A. Pepelasis et al., eds., Economic Development (New York: Harper & Row, Publishers, 1961), pp. 523–62.

[19] A good description of recent Greek economic development policy has yet to be written. Some information can be found in the Five Year Programme for the Economic Development of Greece 1960–1964 (Athens: Ministry of Coordination,

1960); and *Shedion Programmatos Oikonomikis Anaptyxis Tis Ellados* (1966–1970) (Athens: Center for Programming and Economic Research, 1965).

[20] See USGPO, *Proposed Mutual Defense and Development Programs FY 1966*, Washington, 1965, 226–34. The non-AID economic assistance was cumulated from 1946 and so includes UNRRA deliveries, which were relatively much more substantial to Yugoslavia, the other totals being cumulated from 1948.

[21] Yugoslavia has been promised Soviet bloc aid of several hundred million dollars since World War II. According to Joseph Berliner, *Soviet Economic Aid* (New York: Frederick A. Praeger, Inc., 1958), p. 33, $444 million in non-military credit agreements were signed between 1953 and 1957. However, a large part of this total was never actually made available as a consequence of political conflicts; indeed, when the effects of the Cominform blockade of 1949–54 are taken into account, the Soviet bloc's net contribution to Yugoslav postwar economic development may well be negative. Cf. Robert F. Byrnes, ed., *Yugoslavia* (New York: Frederick A. Praeger, Inc., 1957), 25–26, 33–34, 206–8. For 1961–65 the Soviet bloc–Yugoslav trade balance was approximately zero. *Stat. god. 1965*, 234. Soviet aid to Greece 1954–65 amounted to $84 million, according to Leo Tansky, "Soviet Foreign Aid to the Less Developed Countries," U.S. 89th Congress, Joint Committee Print, *New Direction in the Soviet Economy*, Washington, 1966, 974. Thus taking account of Soviet aid would not substantially change the picture presented in the text.

[22] Because of its sensitive international political position and deliberate policy of trade development, Yugoslavia may be said to have exploited the more nomic possibilities of its political environment more intensively than the more passive Greek governments, and this difference may have some limited systemic relevance.

[23] For types and amounts of public assistance see *Statisticki godisnjak FNRJ 1965*, 306–7; *Statistical Yearbook of Greece 1964*, 102–7.

[24] Hollis Chenery and Alan Strout, *Foreign Assistance and Economic Development*, AID, 1965; and *American Economic Review*, Vol. 56, 1966, 679–733.

[25] Irma Adelman and Hollis Chenery, "Foreign Aid and Economic Development: The Case of Greece," *Review of Economics and Statistics*, Vol. XLVIII, February, 1966, 1–19.

[26] There was a devaluation of the dinar in 1961 and again in 1965. Both of these were years of slow or zero growth and were preceded by a year or more of rapid growth culminating in strong inflationary pressure. The ratio of exports to imports reached a local minimum in the time series in the year preceding each reform. The same applies to the year 1958; however, there was more talk than action and no formal devaluation in that year. *Stat. god. 1965*, 125; *Petit Manuel Statistique de la Yougoslavie 1966*, Belgrad, 1966, 71.

[27] For a discussion of capital market organization and tax policy in Greece see Howard Ellis et al., *Industrial Capital in Greek Development* (Athens, Center for Economic Research, 1964); and George Break and Ralph Turvey, *Studies in Greek Taxation* (Athens, Center of Economic Research, 1964).

[28] For a survey of monetary policy cf. Nikola Miljanic, *Novac i kredit*, Zagreb: Informator, 1964; on recent policy proposals see N. Miljanic, "Regulation of Total Liquidity in the SFR of Yugoslavia," mimeographed, 1966.

[29] Yugoslav enterprises have been permitted to sell the right to use socially owned means of production under their management to other socialist enterprises. However, these sales are under strict control and are not supposed to produce any profit directly for the seller.

[30] For a recent discussion of political aspects of Yugoslav tax and subsidy decisions see Dennison Rusinow, *op. cit.*, and George Bailey, *op. cit.*

[31] For an analysis see Benjamin Ward, *Socialist Economy* (New York: Random House, Inc., 1967), Chap. 9.

[32] The freedom with which Yugoslav authorities have used reorganization of decentralized economic decision units as an instrument of economic policy is indicated by the survey of reforms during the early years of the new economic system in Benjamin Ward, *From Marx to Barone: The New Socialism and the Industrial Firm in Postwar Yugoslavia* (unpublished Ph.D. diss. Berkeley, 1956), Chaps. 6, 7. For more recent organizational policy see Rudolf Bicanic, "Some Aspects of the Policy of Workers' Income in Yugoslavia," in E. Stiller, ed., *Lohnpolitik und Vermogensbildung* (Frankfurt, 1964).

[33] As a consequence of a change of government, this Greek plan has not been adopted by the government.

[34] Drago Gorupic, "Problemi sistema kreditiranja investicija," *Ekonomski pregled*, Vol. 13, 1962, 779–800, trans. in *Eastern European Economics*, New York, Spring, 1964.

[35] For an interesting discussion of the impact of urbanization on Greek attitudes see Karl Pfeffer and Irma Schaffhausen, *Griechenland, Grenzen wirtschaftlicher Hilfe für den Entwicklungserfolg* (Hamburg: Weltarchiv, 1959); Ernestine Friedl, "Lagging Emulation in Post-Peasant Society," *American Anthropologist*, Vol. 66, 1964, 569–86; and Keith Legg, *Political Recruitment in Greece* (Ph.D. diss., Berkeley, 1967).

[36] Peak-season labor shortages occur in both countries, and in many areas of Greece these are becoming acute, with emigration playing a major causal role.

[37] *Stat. god. 1965*, 104, 115; *Stat. yrbk. 1964*, 218, 230.

[38] *Stat yrbk. 1964*, 102–7; *OECD Economic Surveys: Greece*, Paris, 1966, 18, 33–35. The complexities and limited financial reporting of the Greek side make comparisons of the money expenditure on social services impossible with available information. This does not necessarily mean that the Greek coverage and expenditure per capita is less than the Yugoslav. In 1963 Yugoslav rural households received about 4 percent of their net income in the form of pensions, family allowances, and other forms of social insurance payments. If the price support policy is taken into account, Greek rural households probably received a higher share of income from state support.

[39] Former premier Karamanlis, of the rightist ERE party, while in office supported Greece's entry into the Common Market.

⁴⁰ Cf. Grigorios Dafnis, *Ja Ellinika Politika Kommata* (Athens: Galaxia, 1961).

⁴¹ The range of alternatives being given serious public consideration was probably wider in Greece, and fundamental revision of economy and society could be discussed publicly in Greece with much greater freedom.

⁴² Fred W. Riggs, *Administration in Developing Countries* (Boston: Houghton Mifflin Company, 1964).

⁴³ *Op. cit.*, Chaps. 2, 3.

⁴⁴ It might be argued alternatively that the coup was a product, among other things, of a weakness of Greek political structure which is more a consequence of civil and cold war than of a domestically prismatic state. This weakness came about because the army had acquired a power and influence in government that far transcended its popular support, so that continuation of democracy was inconsistent with continuation of strong military influence in government. This might better fit Riggs's exoprismatic category, in which case modernization is less likely to be blocked.

Harvey Leibenstein
Harvard University

Some Notes on
Economic Development Planning
and the Rate of Interest
under Multiple Sovereignties*

The motivating idea behind this foray into the theory of planning is that economic planning is likely to involve multiple sovereignties and multiple

* This is a revised version of an unpublished paper written a decade ago. Special note should be taken of the paper by Jan Drewnowski, "The Economic Theory of Socialism: A Suggestion for Reconsideration," *Journal of Political Economy*, August 1961. Although there are some similarities between our papers, there are also significant differences. The emphasis here is on the significant difficulties involved in interpretation and consistent implementation of the dominant preference function under multiple sovereignties.

behavioral systems. The special case of socialist planning in which most of the productive units are publicly owned, and the multiplicity of behavioral systems involved, is likely to be a major aspect of the planning problem. Such systems involve technical problems that for the most part have neither been recognized nor solved. It is the purpose of this essay to examine in part the nature of these problems.

The approach to this aspect of planning will be considered on a highly abstract level. Although there is no space to go into details, it should be evident as we proceed that the examination is applicable to two basic issues: (1) the interpretation and analysis of the operation of existing planning systems, and (2) the design of economic planning. As a shorthand way of expressing things symbols are used but no basic mathematics is involved.

Special attention will be given to the role and meaning of the interest rate in determining resource allocation under conditions of economic growth and at least in part *dictatorially determined* economic decisions. The word *dictatorial* is used in a general and formal sense and is not intended to imply anything about the political structure of the country. By *dictatorial* we refer to any method of making economic decisions other than on the basis of consumers' sovereignty. Economies in which decisions are made in this manner may or may not be political dictatorships.

1. The Allocation Problem and Dictatorial Values

In conventional static theory the interest rate, in part, serves the same function in the time dimension as transportation cost does in the space dimension. Just as in the latter case transport costs enable us to evaluate all activities as though they occurred at one point in space, so an interest rate enables us to consider all events, and decisions regarding such events, as though they occurred at one point in time. Rational calculation is facilitated by utilizing the interest rate to reduce all values to present values. Capital goods are transformed into value equivalents of consumer goods through discounting the future stream of services that the capital good yields.

A convenient way of looking at the problem is to note that in the pure-competition–consumers' sovereignty model the interest rate plays a part in three of the following four steps for achieving a rational allocation: (1) The interest rate transforms the value of future flows in terms of current flows, (2) The interest rate and the marginal efficiency of investment transforms capital goods into consumer goods value-equivalents, (3) Proper allocation involves allocating inputs to equalize the value of

87

various current flows at the margin, and (4) Consumers' preferences determine the relative values of current flows, and they also determine the interest rate that enables us to obtain an equivalence between current and future flows. It is important to note that steps (1), (2), and (3) are independent of the system of valuation between present and future goods and between different present goods. Any scheme of relative valuations obtained from and consistent with any set of preferences can lead to a proper allocation. Conversely, every allocation implies one (or more) relative valuation schemes. These notions and their implications may be clarified if we treat the matter more formally and illustrate these ideas for specific dictatorial objectives.

We define *rational allocation* as one that is consistent with a stated objective. The objective may be the maximization of consumer satisfaction given certain constraints, or some other. Consider the following sequence: (a) Every objective implies a rule of choice between alternatives, or a set of such rules consistent with the attainment of the objective, (b) The rule(s) of choice plus the relevant preference maps of the decision-making entities determine the specific choices that are actually made, (c) For given factor availabilities the application of the preference maps and the rule(s) of choice yield sets of relative valuations for the factor flows in their various uses and for the commodities produced by the factor flows, and (d) Given the relative valuation among commodities there is usually one (or more) allocation(s) of factors among alternative uses consistent with the attainment of the objective. Although the initial preference map and the relative valuations between commodities may be related to the objective, they are not necessarily determined by it. Therefore, we may say that the objective and its implied rules of choice operating on the valuation scheme lead to a certain allocation, and if all these elements are consistent it is rational allocation.

For our purposes we shall assume that the rules of choice are correct for the objectives considered *if information was complete and accurate*—that is, they are rules that when applied do lead to the objective. For want of a better term we shall call such rules of choice *optimizing rules*. Given the alternatives open to the decision-making units in the economy and some other data, the application of the optimizing rules leads to a set of choices one of whose results, in the aggregate, is the allocation of resources. Of course, a knowledge of the optimizing rules alone is not sufficient to make a choice. It is commonplace that a set of relative valuations of some entities that can enable one to determine, directly or indirectly, the relative valuations of the alternatives are needed, in addition to a knowledge of the optimizing rules, in order to make an intelligent choice. In actuality, the decision processes and the other elements of the economic processes that determine the resource allocation are a much more complicated affair. But for our purposes it is convenient to concentrate on the essentials and omit the intervening elements that may be involved. With this in mind let us write O_a for the set of rules consistent with object a.[1] V_a is a vector of values whose elements are prices of factors and commodities including the interest rate(s); and A_a represents the final allocation whose elements are those quantities of capital goods and consumer goods that result as a consequence of the operation of O_a on V_a, given the resources. We write this relationship as follows:

$$O_a(V_a) = A_a$$

For purposes of discussion it is simpler to speak of an objective in the singular. We shall do so throughout this paper since this simplification is unlikely to affect the points we have in mind, although we recognize the possibility that the discussion can also be carried forward in terms of *objective functions*—that is, sets of multiple objectives that can be reconciled in some fashion.

With respect to our equation, we expect the following relationships to hold. Every objective (and related optimizing rules) combined with a set of relative valuations implies a resource allocation, which may not be unique. Further, every set of optimizing rules and consequent allocation implies a related set of values, although there may be more than one set of valuations that fits these conditions. Finally, and most important for our purposes, every allocation (assuming it to be a rational one) and set of values implies a set of optimizing rules and an objective, although the latter need not be unique.

We consider two such relationships:

(1) $O_a(V_a) = A_a$
(2) $O_b(V_b) = A_b$

where (1) represents the situation under consumers' sovereignty, and (2) represents the situation under some dictatorial objective function and dictatorial values. Now, suppose the rules O_a are permitted to operate. Then the dictator's problem is to find a set of values V_c so that

(3) $O_a(V_c) = A_b$

From this we obtain $V_c - V_a = T_c$, which is a vector whose elements are the necessary taxes and subsidies that give the dictator his desired allocation.

The point of this is that from the dictator's view the entire scheme as visualized in equation (3) is perfectly rational, but from an outside observer's view none of it would seem to make any sense. The operation of O_a may give the impression that the objective is maximum consumers' satisfaction. Not knowing O_b, $\mathcal{V}_c$ certainly seems to make no sense to the observer. But even if O_b could be guessed at on the basis of other evidence $\mathcal{V}_c$ would still not make any sense since $\mathcal{V}_b$ is not known.

An observer's attempt to understand the rationale of the allocation process would be confounded if the rules of choice O_a were not of the type to which competitive conditions have accustomed him. The problem for both the observer and the dictator is really somewhat more complicated than we have just indicated. The reason is that the economy is likely to be subject to dual or multiple sovereignties. Consumers' choice may be permitted in the consumer goods market, but the firms may have to operate on another basis. Let us see what happens if the dictator tries to use the price system as an allocative mechanism under such circumstances.

We divide O_a into two parts. Let O_a' represent the behavior rules of consumers and O_a'' the rules for the firms. Commodities are of two kinds, producer goods $\mathcal{K}$ and consumer goods C, so that the final allocation flow $A = C + \mathcal{K}$. The relationship that determines the dictator's allocation reads $O_b(\mathcal{V}_b) = C_b + \mathcal{K}_b$, or for each sector separately we have $O_b'(\mathcal{V}_b') = C_b$, and $O_b''(\mathcal{V}_b'') = \mathcal{K}_b$. The dictator's problem is to find $\mathcal{V}_c'$ so that $O_a'(\mathcal{V}_c') = C_b$, that is, a set of prices that results in the consumption of exactly C_b. This last yields $\mathcal{T}_c'$, the vector of taxes and subsidies on consumer goods that permits C_b. Once C_b is determined, finding $\mathcal{V}_c$ presents no special conceptual difficulties since it is the set of prices that clears the market for the given quantities. But the problem in the other sector is more complicated.

The dictator would like to see the result $\mathcal{K}_b$ in accordance with his objective and values relationship $O_b''(\mathcal{V}_b'') = \mathcal{K}_b$. But finding a $\mathcal{V}_c''$ so that $O_a''(\mathcal{V}_c'') = \mathcal{K}_b$ becomes a very difficult matter if the price mechanism alone is used, since calculations for investment choice by the firms depend on prices of consumer goods $(\mathcal{V}_c')$ that do not reflect the valuations of the consumers or of the dictator. It is not a matter of setting prices that will clear markets to final consumers. To choose between investment alternatives, firms have to calculate the value of the output stream of different types of producer goods. If the firms use current prices they would use either $\mathcal{V}_c'$ or $\mathcal{V}_c' - \mathcal{T}_c'$, but neither of these would yield the result $\mathcal{K}_b$ and hence would not fit in with the dictator's objective. Similarly, the dictator cannot instruct firms to use $\mathcal{V}_b'$ since this would not give the right result because the firm's objective is O_a'' and not O_b''. One way out is simply to instruct firms to produce $\mathcal{K}_b$. Considerations of this sort may explain the use of output targets in an economy like the Soviet rather than reliance on the pricing mechanism. Another solution is to instruct firms to make economic choices in accordance with O_b, and to give firms planning prices $\mathcal{V}_b$ to work with.

The major implication of this discussion from our point of view is that the degree of rationality of dictatorial decisions cannot be determined unless we know the dictator's objective and the dictator's values. The reason for this is that there is a degree of freedom between interest rate(s), factor prices, and commodity prices. Where prices (or values) are arbitrarily determined, there is some set of prices combined with a zero interest rate that will yield the same allocation as some other set of prices and a positive interest rate.[2] Or, conversely, the interest rate is meaningful only in relation to other prices but not apart from them. Whatever allocation can be achieved by a positive interest rate can also be achieved by a zero interest rate if we are permitted to manipulate all other prices including future prices.

It may be argued that when we speak of a zero interest rate in this context we are not really talking about a zero interest rate as we usually understand that term, but only of a hidden interest rate that is disguised by the freedom to manipulate all other prices. But this is consistent with our main point. Under dictatorial values the interest rate need not have any meaning in the usual sense. The interest rate has meaning only in relation to known objectives, related optimizing rules, and a known scheme of price determination.

Let us stop for a moment and reinterpret some of our ideas. The first equation may be looked upon as representing actual operating rules and people's actual objectives. In any economic system some of the units are likely to operate in terms of the motivations developed for these units. The dictator has to realize that he cannot dictate behavior in every respect. There are essentially three basic choices that exist: (1) The dictatorial planning agency may try to issue specific commands, that is, to indicate in detail the inputs and outputs and activities of every operating unit, (2) Another scheme is that which parallels the operation of a free enterprise system in which the working units pursue their own ends but their objectives are deflected through the introduction of a system of taxes and subsidies, resulting in different allocations than would occur without taxes and subsidies, or (3) the dictator can issue rules of behavior to operating units as well as necessary parameters, such as shadow prices, and have the operating units follow these rules. Of course, combinations of all three procedures are possible.

The first approach, using dictatorial command, is either technically impossible in detail or highly inefficient. The second approach is especially interesting since it is the one most likely to be recommended by economists.

Here we return to the problem mentioned earlier. The dictator wants an output of capital goods different from that produced on the basis of the derived demand of the expected output of consumer goods. (We need not consider why the dictator wants a unique output of capital goods. One possibility is that he has in mind a future stream of consumption goods quite different from that which would be produced under consumers' sovereignty.) The basic question is whether a set of prices exists consistent with the equation

$$(4) \quad O_a''(V_c'') = K_b$$

First, we should note certain differences between this and the consumer goods case. In the consumer goods case, a set of subsidies and taxes clear the market for the quantities desired by the dictator. In the capital goods case this does not work. A set of subsidies and taxes can possibly induce firms to produce the dictatorially desired output of capital goods, given producers' motivations. However, these prices inclusive of subsidies and taxes are not the prices at which the output is wanted by the firms that purchase capital goods since their demand is determined by the costs and subsidies for the production of consumer goods. Thus we need another set of subsidies and taxes to determine the purchase of the capital goods produced for each *use*. A given commodity could sometimes be used either as a consumption good or a capital good. Hence, buyers who have multiple uses for such goods will have to be policed to make sure that the goods they buy at a given price inclusive of a subsidy are put to the appropriate use.

Additional difficulties enter when decreasing cost industries are involved. In such circumstances taxes have to be imposed that increase with the quantity of capital goods produced so that the dictatorially desired amount is realized. To do this correctly would require a knowledge of the details of the production functions of all plants. A similar problem arises if the dictator has different trade-offs between the present and different dates in the future. In this instance firms should take different interest rates into account in determining the output of capital goods of different durabilities. It is possible that a complex set of taxes and subsidies would induce firms to produce that output of capital goods of durabilities desired by the dictator. The point to be stressed is that to calculate the appropriate taxes and subsidies requires much more knowledge than is likely to be available. Since the appropriateness of the decisions is likely to be known only to the dictator in the future, there is no present test (such as clearing the market) for the levels of taxes and subsidies employed.

Two more basic difficulties enter the picture. First, taxes and subsidies produce incentives for the creation of black markets. Obviously tax avoidance leads to the possibility of personal gain by some members of producing firms. It is likely that the output of capital goods that does not go through the tax system is more profitable for both sellers and buyers than one that does. For example, some firms would buy some capital goods produced by others without taxes, but they might find it profitable to produce these goods themselves if in this way they could avoid taxes. Once again the problem and costs of policing the system enter the picture.

A second difficulty is that the level of *directed* effort by workers and managers may be very different under a system of publicly owned firms than under private ownership. This may also hold true for various systems of taxes and subsidies in the sense that they divert efforts either toward black market activities or toward record-keeping and other administrative techniques necessary to police the system.[3]

Finally, we must consider the possibility that the dictator will not use only taxes and subsidies but may wish to impose rules of operation on firms. This is most likely to occur where the firms are publicly owned and where the motivation system is not really understood. However, it involves the problem that the rules of behavior imposed on operating units will probably not be those they will want to follow. It is one thing to legislate rules of choice, but it is quite a different matter to have the units themselves follow such criteria. The degree to which rules are followed will depend on the motivating system, and if the rules do not follow the self-interest of the agents to a great degree there is likely to be considerable deviation from these rules. The main point is that we visualize a difference between actual behavior and prescribed behavior. Of course, it is recognized that prescribed behavior will influence actual behavior. Using our previous notation we can visualize the following relations:

(5) $\quad O_a(\mathcal{V}_b) \neq \mathcal{A}_b$

(6) $\quad O_{ab}(\mathcal{V}_b) \neq \mathcal{A}_b$

The interpretation of these expressions is that the actual objective a under the given set of valuations dictatorially desired $\mathcal{V}_b$ will not yield the desired allocation $\mathcal{A}_b$. Furthermore, firms pursuing objective a but told to operate under prescribed rules b will also *not* yield the desired allocation $\mathcal{A}_b$. Thus, the dictator has to guess which new set of valuations will yield the desired allocation, if such a set is available. If not, then the next stratagem may be to impose a set of *pseudorules* and/or a set of *pseudovalues*. By *pseudorules* we mean those that, combined with normal incentives, will lead to the results that the planners desire. But this stratagem probably goes too far. It is most unlikely that the planners know enough about the motivations of organizations and individuals to determine the correct set of pseudorules and pseudoprices. In fact, planners are frequently unaware that this problem exists. Hence, it is not surprising that the targets that planners have in mind are frequently not realized and that their aims are frequently frustrated. This aspect of the problem has been ignored in the discussion of the Lange-Lerner prescription for socialist economies since in that discussion it was implicitly assumed that any prescribed set of rules would be followed. Experience with actual organizational behavior would indicate that this is a false premise on which to operate.

II. Allocation Criteria and the Interest Rate under an Aggrandizing Dictator

For purposes of this essay we shall consider two extreme types of dictatorial objectives. For want of better names, we shall refer to one as that of the *aggrandizing* dictator and to the other as that of the *benevolent* dictator.

In the aggrandizing dictator we visualize one who attempts to maximize the *growth* of the productive capacity of the economy, that is, he attempts to maximize the growth of *all* productive factors. He wants as large an economic domain as possible. This objective would appear to be reasonable for the power-seeking dictator. The value of any factor other than inventories of final goods is imputed from their productivity, but the value of final goods is determined by dictatorial values. The dictator may permit some consumer goods to be valued in accordance with consumers' preferences, but others, for example military goods, would be valued on the basis of other priorities.

In the benevolent dictator we visualize one who wants to maximize *per capita* consumption. His focus is on the productivity of labor and its relationship to per capita consumption. The valuation of current consumption goods may be on the basis of consumers' preferences, but the valuation of future outputs of consumers' goods would not be.

We shall see that the allocations under these two types of dictatorial decision functions are quite different, and consequently the role of the interest rate is also quite different.

Maximizing the rate of capital accumulation will not yield the desired solution for the aggrandizing dictator if the allocation of resources is in any way a determinant of the rate of growth of any resources other than capital. Since this is the case, it follows that increases in capital accumulation, given the full employment of all resources, will be at the expense of the rate of growth of some other factor.

Consider the example where there are only two factors and two commodities: labor and capital, consumer goods and capital goods. In this situation, under the assumed dictatorial objective, the nature of consumption goods differs from that in the nondictatorial case. They now become a factor in the production of the resource labor. To the extent that an increase in consumption affects fertility rates, mortality rates, or current health (and hence the productive efficiency of the labor force), consumption goods may be looked upon as investment in labor. Thus,

94

the opportunity cost of a unit of capital is measured by the extent to which it decreases the total labor force. The interest rate may be measured in terms of the marginal productivity of consumption goods. Maximization of all resources is achieved by an allocation of current output in such a way as to equalize the marginal productivity of all goods produced.

At this point something must be said about the meaning of the marginal productivity of consumption goods. We assume that there is a determinable relationship between a dollar expenditure on consumption goods and an increase in the labor force. A unit increase in the labor force will yield an increase in the stream of goods in the future, and the discounted net revenue of this stream represents the marginal productivity of consumption goods. In computing the discounted net revenue it is necessary to maintain this additional unit of labor in perpetuity, that is, the labor equivalent of repair, maintenance, and replacement of capital.

Under these circumstances, to determine the allocation between current consumption and investment the appropriate interest rate is the marginal productivity of consumption goods as it has been defined in this context. Equating the marginal productivity of capital with this interest rate will yield the optimum rate of accumulation of capital for the aggrandizing dictator. The next problem is to find the appropriate discount rate in obtaining the present value of the stream of goods attributable to any factor. Under consumers' sovereignty the interest rate that determines the allocation between capital goods and consumer goods is also the appropriate rate to be used as the discount rate of the future stream of goods. In both cases it measures simultaneously consumers' sacrifice and hence the rate of substitution between present goods and future goods. Under the aggrandizing dictator's objective the interest rate determined by the marginal productivity of consumption goods becomes, in a similar fashion, the appropriate discount rate in determining the present value of the output stream. Here too the interest rate so defined measures the rate of substitution between present consumption goods and future consumption goods. Labor, in this context, may be looked upon as stored up consumption goods that have the power of producing other consumption goods. Adding to the capital stock is essentially a means of increasing the future flow of consumption goods at the expense of the current flow. The extent to which these two flows are substituted for each other at the margin is measured, of course, by the marginal productivity of consumption goods. In a sense, we substitute the marginal productivity of consumption goods under this objective for their marginal utility under consumers' sovereignty. However, the two interest rates implied by these two alternate objectives are by no means likely to be the same.

It is of interest to note that our *simplified* model of the aggrandizing dictator is the same as the von Neumann model of an expanding economy.[4] Two characteristics of the von Neumann model and of our model are of interest. First, in equilibrium the allocation will yield the greatest rate of expansion of all possible allocations. Second, in equilibrium the rate of interest is equal to the rate of expansion. Neither of these properties holds for the consumers' sovereignty model or for the Lange-Lerner type of socialist economy model. Thus, employing the interest rate implied in either of those models will not yield a maximum rate of economic expansion. We may note also that once an economy of this kind gets into equilibrium the standard of consumption is constant over time if the technological parameters, as well as the parameters determining mortality and fertility rates, remain the same.[5]

For some, the interesting case from the point of view of economic growth may not be the equilibrium position but rather the course of development prior to the achievement of the equilibrium expansion path. If we consider the nonequilibrium case and drop the assumptions of no fixed factors and of all goods entering into all production processes, then we must modify our conclusions. Under such circumstances we would not expect all factors to expand at the same rate. We are given a dictatorially determined system of values for all stocks (that is, for both human and nonhuman assets) and the commodities in all *investment* uses (using investment in the broad sense of adding to both human and nonhuman stocks). Under the optimum allocation a dollar's worth of any commodity adds a dollar's worth of value to some stock. The rate of interest, viewed as the opportunity cost of capital, will therefore be equal to the momentary rate of expansion in the *value* of total assets. But in this nonequilibrium and less restrictive case, the interest rate will not be one that will maintain itself through time. It would be noteworthy for some purposes to work out all the implications of the nonequilibrium case, but for present purposes it is sufficient to observe that in this instance the interest rate is equal to the momentary rate of expansion in the value of total assets, whereas under other objectives the interest rate varies inversely, or is unrelated, to the rate of expansion.

In the previous two-commodity example we assumed that consumers' goods were productive in the sense that they added to the productive capacity of the economy. We now expand our considerations to include nonproductive consumers' goods. We shall refer to these nonproductive consumer goods as *luxury goods*—although they need not be luxuries as the term is commonly understood. They may be civilian goods that do not add to longevity or work capacity; or they may be military goods, memorials to the dictator, and so forth. What properties does the rate of interest have in this case? The answer to this question depends on whether or not, with respect to changes in investment, luxury goods are produced in a given proportion to consumers' goods. That is, if there is a 10 percent decrease in the output of capital goods will this result—given the dictator's demand schedule or preference schedule for luxury goods—in a proportional increase in both luxury goods and productive consumer goods or not? Consider the situation in which changes in output in consumer goods and luxuries are proportional. The opportunity cost of a unit of capital is a set mix of consumer goods and luxuries. Luxuries may be looked upon as a cost to entities that can be used in the expansion of the economy. Luxuries bear an opportunity cost but are of no value from the point of view of expansion. The new rate of substitution between present goods and future goods is the expansive power of a unit of a consumer goods mix (including luxuries), which is lower than it was when there were no luxury goods by the amount of expansive power foregone in producing luxury goods instead of productive consumer goods. Thus, the interest rate is lower than it was in the previous case. In equilibrium the interest rate is still equal to the rate of expansion of the economy, but it is lower than the rate of expansion of all resources in the no luxury goods case. If we think of luxury goods as military goods, this analysis implies that in the expanding equilibrium one of the properties of this solution would be a constant ratio of military goods to manpower.

If the proportion of productive consumer goods in the consumer goods mix changes over time, there is little reason to expect the rate of interest to be equal to the rate of expansion of all factors. Suppose that, given the dictator's demand function for luxuries, the proportion of productive consumer goods in the mix decreases with increases in the labor/capital ratio. In this situation maximizing the rate of expansion would call for substituting capital for labor, and we would expect the capital stock to grow at a faster rate than the labor stock. Conversely, if the proportion of productive consumer goods in the mix increased with increases in the labor/capital ratio, we would expect labor to increase more rapidly than capital. Although the interest rate would not be equal to the rate of expansion in the productive capacity of all resources, in equilibrium the interest rate is equal to the rate of growth of stocks if stocks are measured by the extent to which they contribute to expansion. Consider the situation in which the ratio of productive consumer goods in the mix decreases as labor increases. Therefore every unit of labor is less effective as a growth-contributing factor as labor is added. Labor, or what is the same thing, the productive consumer goods that produce labor, must not be permitted to grow to the point at which their growth-contributing power falls below that of the capital that could be produced by the same amount of resources. Therefore, labor grows less rapidly than capital but at the margin, in equilibrium, the growth-contributing power of labor and capital is equal, but the rate of increase of the quantities of these two factors is not.

Thus far, in referring to the rate of interest we considered only the *real* rate of interest that is consistent with the dictator's objective and values. In other words, we assumed that $O_b(V_b) = A_b$. But now suppose that consumers' preferences are permitted to operate in the consumer goods market. In this instance prices of consumer goods would not be equal to what they would be under V_b. It is unlikely that consumer demand would be in proportion to what the "demanded" commodity adds to the expansibility of the economy. A dollar expenditure by a consumer need not add one dollar's worth of labor force. Thus, the prices necessary to clear consumer goods markets (part of V_o) would not be equal to the productivity of consumer goods. The *operating* interest rates employed would depend on the prices that firms and planners use in making their calculations. Therefore, the operating interest rate need not reflect the rate of expansion. In other words, we have to distinguish between the *real* interest rate that depends on the dictator's objective and relative valuations and the *operating* interest rate imposed on various decision-making entities, because these entities calculate on the basis of valuations determined by consumers' preferences rather than by the dictator's preferences. If any interest rate is observable it will be the operating interest rate. Of course, the operating interest rate will appear to be irrational from the point of view of consumers' sovereignty. Also, the observed operating interest rate may seem irrational if it is examined *only* in the light of the dictator's objective.

III. Allocation and Interest
under the Benevolent Dictator

What the problem looks like for the benevolent dictator will be sketched only briefly.

There is a variety of related entities that the benevolent dictator can choose to maximize. We assume that the dictator wants to maximize the rate of growth in per capita consumption, subject to certain constraints, such as setting certain minimum standards for the present population.

The basic decision for the economy is to choose between present consumption per capita and future consumption per capita. From the point of view of the benevolent dictator the value of capital depends on the extent to which it can increase consumption per capita which, in turn, depends on the effect of investment on (a) increasing the future flow of goods, (b) increasing or decreasing the size of the population, and (c) the consequences of the interaction of these flows. This will depend on the extent to which labor and capital are subject to decreasing or increasing returns. Suppose labor is subject to decreasing returns and capital is not. In this instance an additional unit of investment increases future per capita consumption in several ways. First, investment decreases current consumption and leads to a higher mortality rate and therefore a slower rate of population growth. Second, if the rate of investment is larger than the rate of population growth the stock of capital per individual increases, and as a consequence we would expect that normally output per capita would increase accordingly. On the other hand, if the rate of investment is too small to overcome the rate of population growth, the choice is between present consumption and preventing declines in future consumption per capita. The opportunity cost of capital lies in the loss in current per capita consumption, just as the gain from capital lies in potential future gains in per capita consumption. The rate at which the current loss and future gain are substituted for each other depends on the dictatorially determined rate of sacrifice of current for future gains. Thus the interest rate is arbitrarily picked by the dictator, and it represents that rate of discount at which the future consumption standard is substituted for the present one.

How does this differ from the consumers' sovereignty case? First, the dictator picks the rate of substitution; it is not based on the consumers' desire to save. Second, the revenue stream of investment that is to be discounted is the net addition to *per capita* consumption and not the net value of the stream of outputs attributed to this unit of investment. This implies that the effects of investment decisions on population growth are considered. It is clear that the investment decisions on this basis would be different from those under a regime of consumers' sovereignty.

In this instance the interest rate is not equal to the rate of expansion of the economy. Indeed, the real interest rate varies inversely with the rate of expansion of per capita output.

Here too we are faced with the problem of dual sovereignties, depending on the latitude given consumers and firms in the determination of economic decisions and on the objectives firm managers are presumed to pursue. We would therefore expect the operating rate of interest to be quite different from the real rate consistent with the dictator's objective.

IV. Conclusions and Summary

Under the dictatorial objectives assumed above, the criterion for the allocation of resources and the allocation of investment turned out to be quite different from the marginal productivity criterion under consumers' sovereignty as that term is usually defined.

Suppose that the dictator is interested in "forcing" the development of the economy. In that situation an allocation on the basis of the conventional marginal productivity criterion will not maximize what the

dictator may want to maximize. Maximizing the value of the future output stream as it is valued under consumers' sovereignty (where the discount rate equals the interest rate that reflects consumers' time preference) is not what the aggrandizing dictator or the benevolent dictator wants. For the aggrandizing dictator, maximizing the future output stream as valued under consumers' sovereignty will not maximize the rate of growth of the capital and labor stocks, and hence of the output capacity of the economy. Nor for the benevolent dictator will maximizing the future output stream maximize the rate of growth in per capita consumption if the rate of population growth is a function of the rate of investment and its allocation.

Once we leave the familiar and well-trodden precincts of static analysis under consumers' sovereignty, the variable we knew as the interest rate can take on meanings and values that we had not considered sensible in their former habitat. Allocations and interest rates that are rational in the context of static analysis and consumers' sovereignty may be irrational in others, and vice versa. In our efforts to analyze the role of the interest rate in such unfamiliar contexts, we found that a distinction has to be made between the *real* and the *operating* interest rate. The real interest rate is the interest rate that is consistent with the dictatorial objective and dictatorial values. The operating interest rate, which differs from the real interest rate, is the interest rate consistent with the fact that decentralized decision-making bodies make decisions in accordance with objectives and values that differ from the dictatorial objective. The real interest rate is a measure of the opportunity cost of capital *in terms of the dictatorial objective and values*. The operating interest rate reflects neither the dictatorial objective, consumers' preferences, nor any other single set of objectives and values. Rather, it is that rate necessitated by the dominance of the dictatorial objective and values over those permitted to operate in some sectors of the economy so that the net outcome of all economic activities yields an allocation approximating the dictatorially desired allocation.

To illustrate our general notions we examined the allocation problem for two dictatorial objectives. We saw that in our first example, that of an aggrandizing dictator, the real rate of interest reflects the expansibility of the economy. In the special equilibrium case where no "luxuries" are produced, the real rate of interest is equal to the rate of expansion of all factors. This equilibrium case is described by the von Neumann model of an expanding economy. In our second example, under a benevolent dictator, the real rate of interest reflects the dictatorially determined rate at which consumers sacrifice their present consumption standard for their future standard.

On the basis of such ideas it would appear that the Lange-Lerner solution for the socialist economy is, at best, incomplete. The problem does not end with the socialist state simulating the economist's idealized state of perfect competition. The Lange-Lerner simulated competitive solution misses the point that a real competitive system is not only a decentralized system but it is also a motivational system. By reproducing in some sense the decentralized part of the system, one is not reproducing the same motivation scheme. In other words, a system that possesses the informational processing capacities of a competitive system does not necessarily have its identical motivational properties. Firms with different ownership relations and different interests in the proceeds of the firms' outputs are likely to have different motivational properties. Thus a system of decentralized units plus rules imposed from above will not yield the same results as in the case where the procedural rules arise as a consequence of internally determined motivations. Also, the *raison d'être of* some types of socialism may imply objectives different from that of consumers' sovereignty, in which case the meaning of opportunity costs and interest rates change considerably. Multiple sovereignties are almost inevitable under many kinds of planning, and as a consequence special problems of pricing and interest rate determination, problems absent from the state of perfect competition, enter the picture.

This paper probably raises more questions than it answers. The bits of analyses presented should be looked upon as nothing more than primitive conjectures which, hopefully, may stimulate further research in this area.

Footnotes

[1] The optimizing rules may be (but need not be) unique for the objective. But when we write O_a we specify both the optimizing rules (O) and the objective (a). Note that by O_a we do not necessarily have in mind a single rule. O_a may be a set of rules of choice followed by the various decision-making units involved. Also, the objective may be complex in the sense that it need not involve the maximization of a single variable but may involve the finding of an optimum among variables that move in opposite directions. Although we need not belabor this point and attempt to spell out all the possibilities, it may be well to remember that O_a can be a highly complex operator involving more than a single rule that is uniformly applied.

[2] Compare E. Malinvaud: "Capital Accumulation and Efficient Allocation of Resources," *Econometrica* (April, 1953), pp. 252ff. This point can be seen intuitively if we consider the analogous rate of the transportation cost in the space dimension. Consider a country where the only significant transportation cost is along the east-west axis. Suppose that including transportation costs an even spatial distribution of production is optimal. Suppose that weight is a major distinguishing feature between the various commodities. Apart from transportation

cost, at existing prices, production of all commodities can be carried on most efficiently either at the east or the west boundaries of the countries. But if prices can be set by the dictator, it is possible for him to set factor prices so that an even spatial distribution of production is obtained even if transportation cost is formally priced at zero.

³ On the possible significance of this point see the author's "Allocative Efficiency vs. X-Efficiency," *American Economic Review*, June, 1966.

⁴ "A Model of General Economic Equilibrium," *The Review of Economic Studies*, XIII (1945–46), 1–9. See also Robert M. Solow and Paul A. Samuelson, "Balanced Growth and Constant Returns to Scale," *Econometrica*, XXI (1953), 412ff.; and T. C. Koopmans, *Activity Analysis of Production and Allocation*, pp. 98ff.

⁵ It may be worth noting that in the von Neumann model the system of prices and outputs is not uniquely determined as is the equilibrium rate of interest. There may be a number of possible systems of prices and outputs consistent with the maximum rate of expansion. Cf. D. G. Champernowne, *The Review of Economic Studies*, XIII (1945–46), 13–18.

R. A. Gordon
University of California
Berkeley

Full Employment
and Price Stability
as Goals of Economic Policy[1]

Full employment and price stability are only two of the *aggregative economic goals* that today are espoused, more or less explicitly, in both Western Europe and the United States. In addition to full employment and price stability, the aggregative goals usually emphasized are rapid economic growth and balance-of-payments equilibrium. To these we might add something that has come to be called *incomes policy*. These five goals are concerned with crucial economic aggregates—total employment, general level of prices, total output, total payments to and receipts from the rest of the world, and total money incomes. These aggregative variables are all interrelated. And they are all subject to some degree of

103

control through the two main types of aggregative economic policy, that is, fiscal and monetary policy.

When a government espouses these aggregative goals, we may assume that the policy-makers have in mind some crude notion of a social welfare function that expresses the way in which their concept of the national welfare depends on the behavior of the target variables we have just described—the policy-maker wants to make social welfare (as he views it) as large as possible by bringing about changes in the target variables. In practice, of course, this process of maximizing social welfare is very crudely approximated. Thus, when targets are set—such as an unemployment rate of 4 percent and a growth rate of 5 percent—these targets represent abbreviations of rough notions regarding the way in which social welfare is assumed to vary with changes in the unemployment rate, the growth rate, and the other target variables.

An Aggregative Welfare Function

Let us pursue this notion of a welfare function a bit further.[2] When these aggregative goals are espoused, it is implied that national economic welfare (Z) is related to the following variables or constraints:

1. The rate of overall unemployment, $\dfrac{U}{L^\circ}$

2. The rate of growth in total output, $\dfrac{\overset{\circ}{Y}}{Y^\circ}$

3. The rate of change in a country's international monetary reserves, $\dfrac{\overset{\circ}{A}}{A^\circ}$

4. The rate of change in the general price level, $\dfrac{\overset{\circ}{P}}{P^\circ}$

5. Some measure of wage restraint, for which we might write $\dfrac{\overset{\circ}{w}}{w} - \dfrac{\overset{\circ}{y}}{y}$, or the difference between the rate of change in wages and in productivity

Let us see how current debate and policy action suggest that total economic welfare is related to these variables or constraints. First, however, we have to introduce the following elements:

6. n to represent some notion of the rate of increase in the domestic price level beyond which the functioning of the domestic economy (apart from balance-of-payments considerations) becomes impaired because of, among other reasons, "loss of confidence in the currency"

7. Two additional price variables: P_d, or an index of domestic prices of

goods that move in international trade, and P_f, to represent an index of foreign prices of the same goods

The pursuit of our five aggregative goals can now be described as follows:

$$Z = f\left(\frac{\overset{\circ}{U}}{L}, \frac{\overset{\circ}{Y}}{Y}, \frac{\overset{\circ}{P}}{P}\right)$$

subject to the following constraints:

$$\frac{\overset{\circ}{A}}{A} = k \pm e$$

$$\frac{\overset{\circ}{P_d}}{P_d} - \frac{\overset{\circ}{P_f}}{P_f} = m \pm f$$

$$\frac{\overset{\circ}{w}}{w} - \frac{\overset{\circ}{y}}{y} = \frac{\overset{\circ}{P_f}}{P_f} + m \pm g$$

$$\frac{\overset{\circ}{P}}{P} \lessgtr n$$

$$\frac{U}{L} \lessgtr q$$

The expression in parentheses tells us that economic welfare changes in some way with changes in the three variables inside the parentheses. These variables relate to only three of our aggregative goals: employment, growth, and price stability. The other two goals are listed as constraints, and prices and unemployment show up again as constraints as well as variables within the parentheses.

The significance of the distinction between what is inside and what is outside the parentheses of the Z function can be expressed as follows. The variables in parentheses can vary over some range; and, given the policy-maker's rough notions about the nature of the function, he can try very approximately to maximize welfare by seeking to change the values for these *target variables*. His freedom to do so is limited by the constraints. The policy-maker is not free to vary these constraints to any significant degree as he tries to increase social welfare.

We can thus differentiate among our aggregative goals. Employment and growth are positive goals. Both can vary over some range, and economic policy can seek to change them to increase economic welfare as viewed by the policy-maker. Welfare is also related to the rate of change in prices, but in a complex way, and the nature of this relationship throws some light on the different ways the employment and growth goals have been pursued in various countries.

Price Stability as a Positive Goal
and as a Constraint

The goal of price stability influences policy in three different ways, all of which are represented in the symbols we have described.

    1. Some positive value is attached to price stability for its own sake. Hence, the rate of change in the price level appears within the parentheses of our welfare function, the assumption being that welfare is inversely related to the absolute rate of change in the price level.[3] This relationship, however, is not a simple one. Within a not insignificant range of price variation *and apart from the balance-of-payments problem,* I doubt that any Western European government would be prepared to sacrifice any significant degree of employment or growth in order to reduce the rate of change in the price level. To a lesser extent, this has also been true in the United States. The emphasis on price stability in the United States in recent years has been associated primarily with the balance-of-payments problem, although in 1967–69 a rise in the price level of about 4 percent per annum caused grave concern for more reasons than merely the balance of payments.[4]

    2. The second and more immediate way in which price stability influences policy is through its importance as an instrument of achieving balance-of-payments equilibrium. In serving in this capacity, price stability is viewed not as making a positive, independent contribution to welfare in its own right. Instead, it is viewed as a constraint. In this case it is a constraint of the second order, which is required if the first-order constraint, balance-of-payments equilibrium, is to be observed.

Here the relevant target is not stability in the domestic price level but some desired relationship between the domestic price level and that of the country's chief trading partners—between, to put it roughly, domestic and foreign price levels.

Thus we stated this constraint as being of the form

$$\frac{\overset{\circ}{P}_d}{P_d} - \frac{\overset{\circ}{P}_f}{P_f} = m \pm f$$

that is, the difference between the rate of change in the domestic and foreign price levels should not exceed an amount m—plus or minus, in the short run, a margin of error, f. Obviously this constraint does not require a stable price level. If P_f is rising rapidly, P_d may also rise rapidly. All that is required is that P_d rise at a rate no greater than $\dfrac{P_f}{P_f} + m$. The difference, m, can, of course, be zero or negative. It has been a tenet of American policy in recent years that m should be negative. The rise in the American price level should be kept below that of the European in order to improve our competitive position and so eventually restore balance-of-payments equilibrium.

Most of the countries in Western Europe have been able to permit their domestic price levels to rise moderately rapidly, since for each of them P_f was also rising and thus m could be kept close to zero. The German revaluation in 1961 represents an exception. The German balance-of-payments surplus might have been eliminated by taking m as a significant positive figure, that is, by encouraging the domestic price level to rise faster than in other countries. Instead, the mark was revalued upward.

3. Now we come to the third way in which the behavior of the price level influences policy. There is some upper limit to the rise in the price level beyond which the functioning of the economy is impaired—through speculation, the development of politically disturbing inequities in the distribution of wealth and income, and the beginnings of a "flight from the currency." This is the rationale usually offered, over that involving the balance of payments, for attempting to maintain a stable price level.

We expressed this constraint in the form

$$\frac{\overset{\circ}{p}}{p} \lessgtr n$$

The odds are that n has a higher value than is generally assumed, and it is doubtful if any country in Western Europe has encountered this constraint in the last decade. It would seem that in the postwar period n has had a lower value in the United States than in most European countries.[5]

Thus, particularly in Western Europe during the last decade, price stability as an aggregative goal has fundamentally operated as what we have called a *second-order constraint*, imposed by the need to satisfy the primary balance-of-payments constraint. As a result, the goal has taken the form not of stability of the domestic price level but of approximate constancy in the relation between domestic and foreign price levels. Stability in the domestic price level itself has entered positively—but on the whole not very strongly—into policy-makers' welfare functions. This accounts for the official statements frequently heard that the domestic price level should not rise more than about 2 percent per year. However, it is fair to say that no government would be prepared to sacrifice much employment to bring the rise in prices down from 4 percent or 3 percent per year to 2 percent if not forced to do so by the balance-of-payments constraint.[6]

Incomes Policy

Let us now turn to *incomes policy* which, of course, is closely related to the goal of price stability. Incomes policy is a polite way of referring to a policy of wage restraint with a *quid pro quo* which takes the form of some restraint on other incomes, particularly profits. In terms of our welfare formulation, we have here a negative constraint of the third order: wage restraint is needed to meet the price constraint that is a condition for satisfaction of the balance-of-payments constraint.

Emphasis on incomes policy is a relatively new development in Europe. It was paralleled in the United States by the formulation of the *wage-price guideposts.* The new emphasis on wage restraint reflects the growing inflationary pressures in most European countries and the search for methods of price restraint, from the side of costs, that would not entail the threat to the employment and growth goals that would come from relying only on restriction of aggregate demand through monetary and fiscal policy.

It is clear from the continued upward pressure on prices in most Western countries that incomes policy has thus far not provided a very effective constraint. No country has succeeded in keeping wages from rising faster than productivity. Indeed, whatever the official statements, no government has in fact tried to enforce such a stringent requirement.[7] It will be remembered that we wrote our expression for the incomes goal as

$$\frac{\overset{\circ}{w}}{w} - \frac{\overset{\circ}{y}}{y} = \frac{\overset{\circ}{P_f}}{P_f} + m \pm g$$

If foreign prices are rising, wages can rise faster than productivity, subject to whatever differential (m) between the trends in domestic and foreign prices the government wants to maintain. It has been the hope of the American government that it could maintain a negative m virtually as large as the rate of increase in foreign prices. This does imply holding wage increases down to the rise in average labor productivity. Growing balance-of-payments difficulties in the last few years have forced some European countries to try to reduce the value of m to zero or lower, and it is in this recent period that the emphasis on incomes policy has developed.

In one important respect, incomes policy stands on a different footing than our other aggregative policies. In economies that emphasize free collective bargaining, the means may not exist to implement the policy effectively. In the absence of centralized wage bargaining on a national scale, with some direct influence by government, an incomes policy is merely—as it has been characterized by the Council of Economic Advisers—a set of guideposts. But, as an OECD report has put it, "Once the guidance has been given, the problem is to get people to follow it, and to do so without damage to democratic values. Many governments have moved very cautiously on incomes policy because of their awareness of the difficulty of securing the necessary co-operation, and of the embarrassing situation which arises if they offer specific guidance which is then rejected."[8] This is true on both sides of the Atlantic.

The Goal of Full Employment

In turning to the goal of full employment, I should like to begin by making a distinction between *aggregative full employment* and *aggregative and structural full employment*. By aggregative full employment, I mean the lowest level to which it is considered feasible to reduce the overall unemployment rate, given not only some minimum of frictional unemployment but also the underlying structural factors that make some sectors of the labor force more vulnerable to unemployment than others. What we mean by *feasible* in this context will be explained later.

Given a heterogeneous labor force, some degree of *structural* unemployment will always exist at aggregative full employment. We must therefore go on to the second step in formulating a satisfactorily comprehensive statement of the full-employment objective. This second step involves an answer to the following question, How far is a government prepared to go in reducing the amount of structural unemployment that exists at aggregative full employment? The answer to this question, when costs and benefits are weighed on the scales of the policy-makers' value system, yields what we may call aggregative *and* structural full employment. In the United States, aggregative full employment today is widely assumed to imply an overall unemployment rate of 4 percent or perhaps a little less because of recent success in bringing down the unemployment rate below this figure. But it is also believed by many that unemployment might, by means of an intensive manpower policy, be brought down further to 3 percent or less at a cost that was worth incurring in terms of the benefits to be achieved.

For the time being, we shall confine ourselves to the goal of aggregative full employment. This is the goal that we try to achieve through the appropriate management of aggregate demand, primarily through the use of monetary and fiscal policy.

In Western Europe, 2 percent unemployment is the target most frequently mentioned. When translated into American definitions, this may mean an unemployment rate from below 2 percent to perhaps 3 percent as a maximum. Almost all countries are loath to announce an official quantitative target. (The United States, during the Kennedy and Johnson administrations, has been a notable exception to this generalization.)

What has been the aggregative full-employment goal in the United States? Between 1946 and 1961, official policy at least tacitly accepted a target goal of about 4 percent. But the target was not made explicit. One might say that a range rather than a single figure served as a target—the range being from an unemployment rate slightly below 4 percent to an upper limit that at times was probably close to 5 percent.

The employment goal became much more explicit with the advent of the Kennedy administration. A temporary target of 4 percent was accepted by the Council of Economic Advisers. But this was to be only an interim goal: "If we move firmly to reduce the impact of structural unemployment, we will be able to move the unemployment target steadily from 4 percent to successively lower rates."[9] This continued to be the position of the Council of Economic Advisers in the Johnson administration.

In early 1964, at the time of the reduction in income taxes, the state of employment policy in the United States might be described as follows. The 4 percent target was official policy. Social welfare was assumed to increase significantly as unemployment fell from about 6 percent to below 5 percent. But slowness in getting the tax cut, official and public concern with the balance of payments, continued worry in Congress and large sectors of public opinion regarding budgetary deficits and growth of the federal debt, and the fact that public discontent with unemployment of 5 percent or more for so long was no greater than it was—all these reasons suggest that, in the collective judgment of American policy-makers, social welfare was being maximized at an unemployment rate of more than 4 percent.

The success of the 1964 tax cut and the hopes built up by several years' experience with unemployment below 4 percent have brought about a significant change. There has been a noticeable decline in the degree of concern over budgetary deficits and a greater willingness, by Congress and conservative public opinion, to accept an expansionary fiscal policy. There is also greater sensitivity to unemployment in excess of 4 percent. As a result, there has been some shift in the collective welfare function that shapes economic policy. Marginal rates of substitution have altered so that today a decline in unemployment achieved through fiscal action is thought to entail a lower social cost and a greater social gain than existed a few years ago. As a result, the actual employment goal in the United States today, as it manifests itself in the interaction between the administration and Congress, is closer to 4 percent than it was when this figure was explicitly put forward at the beginning of the Kennedy administration.

Aggregative Full Employment
and the Welfare Function

We have defined aggregative full employment as the lowest level to which it is considered feasible to reduce the overall unemployment rate. But what is to be our criterion of feasibility?

One way of answering this question is suggested by our welfare function, in which social welfare is inversely related to the unemployment rate and the rate of change in prices and positively related to the rate of growth of output. Further, we can assume that unemployment is inversely related to the rate of growth. This means that welfare is doubly increased as unemployment declines.

This suggests a simplification of our welfare function which has been widely accepted as a basis for formulating the full employment goal. We can write

$$Z = f\left(\frac{U}{L}, \frac{\overset{\circ}{P}}{P}\right)$$

where welfare is inversely related to both the unemployment rate and the rate of change in prices. Each of the two variables in parentheses affects welfare not only directly but also through its association with other variables or constraints.

Given this simplified welfare function, we can then define the full employment target as that unemployment rate which will maximize welfare when account is taken of the welfare effects of the changes in the price level that are associated with changes in the level of unemployment.

These relationships can be illustrated in Figure 1, which is based on a similar formulation by Richard Lipsey.[10] The curve XX', which is a variant of the "Phillips curve," portrays the assumed relationship between the unemployment rate (horizontal axis) and the rate of change in prices. The lower unemployment, the faster prices rise. Only at an unemployment rate of Oe is the price level constant. This curve is drawn on the assumption of a given amount of frictional-structural unemployment.

The curves which are concave downward are indifference curves reflecting the policy-maker's *marginal rates of substitution* between a little less unemployment and a slightly faster rise in prices. Each of the

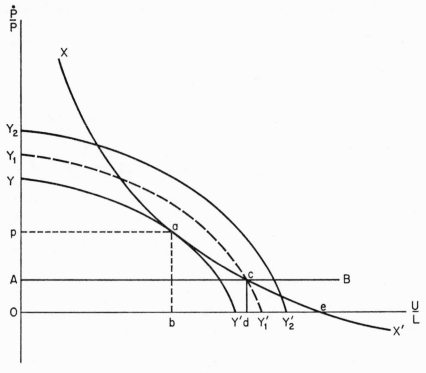

Figure 1

indifference curves represents a different level of welfare; welfare increases as the indifference curves shift to the left toward the origin. The
curve $\mathcal{Y}_2\mathcal{Y}_2'$ reflects a lower level of welfare than does $\mathcal{Y}_1\mathcal{Y}_1'$, $\mathcal{Y}\mathcal{Y}''$ reflects
a higher level of welfare than does $\mathcal{Y}_1\mathcal{Y}_1'$.

 Let us assume that no balance-of-payments constraint is in operation. Then, given the relationship between unemployment and inflation
represented by XX', the policy-maker will seek to reach point a, where
his indifference curve is tangent to XX'. Given XX', this maximizes his
concept of economic welfare, with an unemployment rate Ob and a rate
of price increase equal to Op.

 What happens if we introduce a balance-of-payments constraint?
Let us say that OA is the maximum rate of increase in the domestic
price level that is permissible if balance-of-payments equilibrium is to be
maintained. The line AB cuts the XX' curve at c, which corresponds to an
unemployment rate of Od. One can say that the policy-maker has been
forced to operate on the truncated indifference curve $Ac\mathcal{Y}_1'$. The section
$c\mathcal{Y}_1'$ is part of the curve $\mathcal{Y}_1c\mathcal{Y}_1'$ (which would exist in the absence of the
balance-of-payments constraint). This curve is to the right of $\mathcal{Y}\mathcal{Y}''$ and
represents a lower level of welfare as viewed by the policy-maker.

At least since the publication of Beveridge's *Full Employment in a Free Society*, it has been customary to define the full employment goal by relating the volume of unemployment to the number of job vacancies. For Beveridge, full employment meant "always having more vacant jobs than unemployed men." This has been criticized as going too far, and the criterion today is usually stated in terms of merely an equality between vacancies and unemployment.

This way of defining full employment is illustrated in section A of Figure 2. Vacancies are measured on the vertical axis, and unemployment on the horizontal. The 45-degree line portrays all possible situations that correspond to an equality of vacancies and unemployment. The curve VV' represents the relation assumed to exist between vacancies and unemployment as aggregate demand varies, given the factors determining the amount of frictional and structural unemployment. Point a represents a situation in which vacancies equal unemployment—that is, full employment—at an unemployment rate of Ob.

How does this relate to the price-stability criterion illustrated in Figure 1? To show the relationship, let us turn to section B of Figure 2. Here the vertical scale measures the rate of price change, as in Figure 1. On the horizontal axis we have the rate of unemployment, using the same scale as in Section A. The curve XX' shows the rate of price change associated with each possible level of unemployment. When vacancies equal unemployment at point a in section A, at an unemployment rate of Ob, we see in section B that this unemployment rate has associated with it a rate of price increase gh. Does this correspond to full employment by our previous criterion?

Not having specified the policy-maker's preference function, we cannot say. Let us assume that the policy-maker does have a set of preference functions like those in Figure 1 and that YY' in section B is the one that is tangent to XX' at point i. Then the full employment goal corresponds to an unemployment rate of $O'j$, not $O'b$, and this goal requires that vacancies be in excess of unemployment.

Let us take another possibility. Assume that balance-of-payments considerations impose the price constraint represented by the horizontal line nl in section B, so that the policy-maker is forced to accept an unemployment rate of $O'm$ ($= Od$ in section A). This gives us *full employment* with unemployment substantially in excess of vacancies.

This suggests that the relationship between vacancies and unemployment does not provide an adequate basis for defining the goal of full employment. In brief, it ignores the other related variables that affect welfare. We should also mention the practical difficulties. Reliable

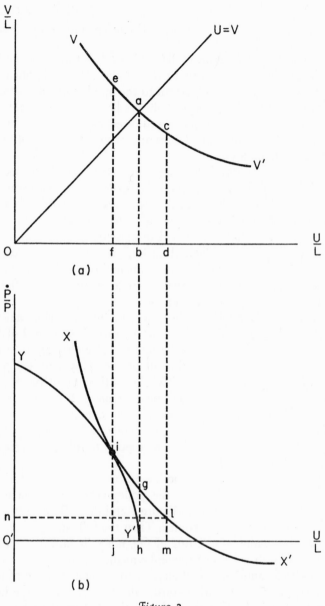

Figure 2

vacancy data do not yet exist in the United States, and there are in addition serious problems both in developing such data and in interpreting what they mean. In particular, little confidence can be placed in the specific criterion of an equality between officially reported vacancies and unemployment. Depending on how vacancies are defined and reported, the number of vacancies may or may not be approximately equal to the number of unemployed in situations generally considered to correspond to full employment.

Although the simplified welfare function illustrated in Figure 1 provides a basis for defining the full employment goal, it does not yield a *quantitative* target to serve as a guide to policy. Thus far, attempts to verify the precise relation between the level of unemployment and the associated change in prices (or wages) in the United States have not met with success. Other variables are certainly involved, and the short-run function portrayed by the curve XX' in Figure 1 shifts and changes its shape for reasons that are not yet fully understood. (In addition, the curve will shift as the volume of frictional and structural unemployment changes.) Further, there is obviously no way of giving quantitative expression to the indifference curves portrayed in Figure 1.

The setting of a full employment target must, therefore, continue to be based on very rough-and-ready procedures, in which the changing preference functions of successive policy-makers are applied to crude impressions of the (also changing) relationships that are presumed to hold between the level of unemployment and the other relevant variables. In the United States, this crude process has led to the recent official *interim target* of an overall unemployment rate of 4 percent.

Structural and
Aggregative Full Employment

It is increasingly recognized that a full-fledged employment policy must be aimed at something more than the *overall* rate of unemployment. The pattern of unemployment among different occupations, regions, age groups, and so on, is also crucially important. Increasing emphasis on the structural aspects of unemployment has been characteristic of European countries as well as of the United States. As overall unemployment has fallen to levels that seem very low by prewar and early postwar standards, European governments have placed increasing emphasis on the differentially high unemployment rates that remain for particular sectors of the labor force. Throughout Europe the labor force is much more homogeneous than in the United States. Nearly every country, however, does have some variant of a depressed-area problem, and in some countries unemployment rates are relatively high among the unskilled.

The development of an integrated labor market policy to deal with such differential unemployment rates, and more generally to expedite the adjustment of labor supply to the changing pattern of labor demand, began earlier and has proceeded further in Europe than in the United States. The most fully developed of such programs is that of Sweden, which has probably set its employment target higher than any other country in the West.

Emphasis on policies to cope with the structural aspects of unemployment has increased tremendously in the United States in the last few years with such efforts as the Public Works and Economic Development Act, the greatly enlarged program under the Manpower Development and Training Act, the Economic Opportunity Act, the new program of federal aid to education, civil rights legislation, and other measures aimed at improving employment opportunities for the disadvantaged segments of the labor force. The president is now required to submit to Congress each year not only an *Economic Report* concerned largely with aggregative economic goals, particularly that of aggregative full employment, but also a *Manpower Report*, which deals with the structural aspects of insuring that all "those able, willing, and seeking to work" can find jobs for which they are qualified.

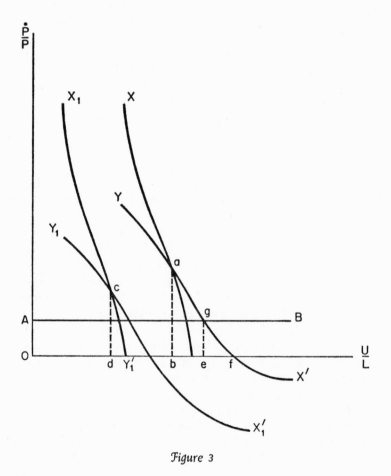

Figure 3

What is involved in giving a structural dimension to the goal of full employment can be illustrated by the use of diagrams similar to those we employed in defining the goal of aggregative full employment. Figure 3 portrays the relationship between unemployment and the rate of change in the price level under two different sets of conditions with respect to the severity of structural unemployment. Underlying structural (and frictional) factors determine how far the XX curves are from the origin and also help to determine the shape of the curves. Thus the curve XX' portrays a situation with more structural and frictional unemployment than does X_1X_1'. Under the conditions portrayed by XX', some price increase can be avoided only at the expense of an unemployment rate equal to Of. If the policy-maker's welfare function implies indifference curves such as YY', then the aggregative full employment goal will be set at an unemployment rate of Ob. If the balance of payments imposes the constraint represented by the horizontal line AB, the full-employment target will involve an unemployment rate of Oe.

Suppose that a successful manpower policy results in reducing the hard core of structural and frictional unemployment so that we move from XX' to X_1X_1'. If the policy-maker's preferences are given by Y_1Y_1', the aggregative full employment goal can be set at the lower unemployment rate of Od.

Thus, if we are to have a policy of *both* structural and aggregative full employment, we must ask the following question. By means of the various instruments of manpower policy, how far is a government prepared to go in reducing the amount of unemployment that exists at full employment? Or, in terms of our diagram, how far is it prepared to go in seeking to shift the XX' curve to the left? The answer to this question, when costs and benefits are weighed on the scales of the policy-maker's value system, yields what we may call aggregative *and* structural full employment. In the United States, aggregative full employment has been officially interpreted since 1961 as implying an overall unemployment rate of about 4 percent. But it is also the official belief that unemployment can be brought down to a lower figure at a cost that is worth incurring in terms of the benefits to be achieved. The benefits are measured less in the decline of the overall rate than in the reduction in unemployment among the groups that now have the highest unemployment rates. In this connection, it can be argued that a full-fledged policy of aggregative and structural full employment needs to have not a single quantitative target but an entire matrix of target figures—target unemployment rates for each of the important sectors of the labor force.

The relation between aggregative and structural full employment can also be illustrated by the vacancies-unemployment relationship portrayed in section A of Figure 2. VV' in this diagram represents the relationship between vacancies and unemployment under one set of conditions determining the level of structural and frictional unemployment. Here vacancies equal unemployment at an unemployment rate of Ob. If manpower policy now succeeds in shifting the curve downward to the left, vacancies would be equal to unemployment at a lower unemployment rate. A successful manpower policy permits us to set a higher goal (a lower overall unemployment rate) for aggregative employment policy.

A Cross-sectional View

In our discussion thus far, we have considered the relation between *total* unemployment and the *total* number of job vacancies. But there is yet another way of considering the relation between vacancies and unemployment. We can look at the vacancies-unemployment relation for each segment of the labor force classified in a particular way, for example, by occupation or region, at a given level of aggregate demand. We can call this the cross-sectional relationship between vacancies and unemployment. A simple illustration is provided by Figure 4.

Here we assume that the labor force is divided into four groups (for example, occupational groups ranging from the most to the least skilled). For a given level of aggregate demand, the vacancy-unemployment relation for each of the four groups is given by the points A, B, C, and D. At A, vacancies are greatly in excess of unemployment; the reverse is true at point D (presumably representing the least skilled). As we have plotted the points, total vacancies for the entire labor force equal total unemployment at point E on the 45-degree line. Thus, using the vacancy-unemployment criterion, we have a situation of aggregative full employment. But labor is in excess supply in two sectors and in short supply in the other two. Immobility prevents workers from moving from the sectors of labor surplus to those with a labr shortage.

Suppose that, through an effective manpower program, a given number of the unemployed in each of sectors C and D become qualified for jobs in the labor shortage sectors. We might then get the situation traced out by A′ B′ C′ D′. Unemployment is reduced by a given amount, with no change in vacancies, in each of sectors C and D; and vacancies are reduced by the same amount, with no change in unemployment, in each of sectors A and B. The overall unemployment rate falls from Oa to Ob, provided that there is sufficient expansion in aggregate demand to absorb the increase in output in sectors A and B.

We can visualize a wide variety of shifts that could occur in the cross-sectional vacancies-unemployment relationship. The closer to the 45-degree line manpower policy can squeeze the points A, B, C, and D, the lower will be structural unemployment; and, if aggregate demand ex-

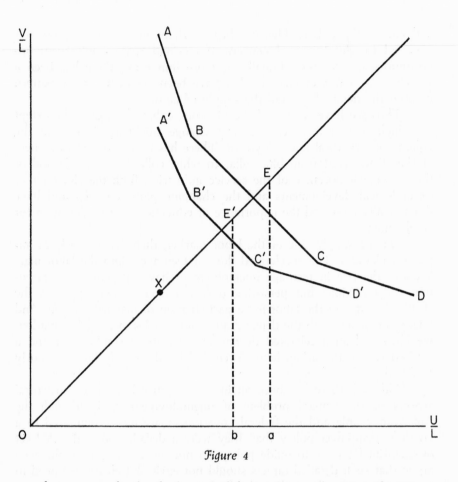

Figure 4

pands correspondingly, the lower will be total unemployment. If in Figure 4, for example, we assume that minimum frictional unemployment for all sectors can be brought down to the rate of unemployment initially in the tightest labor market (sector A), a transfer of workers to sectors A and B might conceivably go on (if enough unemployed workers could be successfully matched against vacant jobs) until all four sectors were at point X on the 45-degree line. At this point only minimum frictional unemployment, assumed to be the same for all sectors, would remain.

The New Emphasis on
Manpower Policy

As already noted, interest in the structural aspects of employment policy has grown rapidly in the United States in the last few years. There has been a shift in welfare functions—in the administration, in Congress, and among the public. This has been perhaps most dramatic, but not confined to, the increased concern about inadequate employment opportunities for Negroes, Equally or more important, there has been a growing awareness of changes that have been occurring in the pattern of both the demand for and the supply of labor.

Thus we have witnessed the vigorous debate regarding the extent to which accelerating technological change might be increasing the volume of structural unemployment. There has been growing awareness of the steady shift from blue-collar to white-collar employment and of the growing importance of the service industries. Both the character of technological developments and the changing pattern of demand have dramatically increased the importance of education as a qualification for employment.

On the supply side of the labor market, there have also been important changes. The accelerated flow of teen-agers into the labor market and the rise in teen-age unemployment have attracted wide attention. Less obvious but persisting over a longer period has been the steady increase in the labor-force participation of married women. And finally, involving both the demand and supply sides of the labor market, we have had an accelerated decline in agricultural employment and a marked rise in the urban labor force, fed by the steady flow of poorly qualified workers from rural areas.[11]

Although there has been an increased sensitivity to the structural aspects of the general problem of unemployment, and although the American people and the federal government are more committed to a vigorous manpower policy than they were a decade ago, a detailed set of quantified targets to guide policy do not yet exist. One might even argue that such detailed targets should not exist. But clearly we need to be more specific about the relation between particular unemployment rates and the overall rate and about the costs and benefits of programs to reduce specific rates by particular amounts. To ask only one question of considerable importance, Is an ultimate goal of 3 percent for aggregate full employment consistent with the best pattern of particular unemployment rates—by age, color, occupation, and education—that we can hope to achieve through the manpower programs now in operation or likely to be adopted in the years immediately ahead?[12]

The Recent Pattern of
Structural Unemployment in the United States

After six years in which the annual average unemployment rate never fell below 5 percent, the United States finally achieved the goal of a 4 percent unemployment rate in December 1965; and the rate was below

4 percent in the several years that followed—3.8 percent in 1966 and 1967, and 3.6 percent in 1968. Against this background of aggregative full employment, it is appropriate to ask what has happened to the structural dimensions of the American unemployment problem during this period of full or overfull employment. As the overall unemployment rate has fallen below 4 percent, public concern has mounted regarding the continuing high unemployment rates among disadvantaged groups, particularly nonwhites and youth. But there does not seem to be much concern about the semiskilled white adult male who, it was once feared, might be largely displaced by automatic machines, electronic controls, and the shift to white-collar occupations calling for considerable education. Nor is much attention being given to the possible relative deterioration in the position of women in the labor force.

In this concluding section, I shall briefly summarize what has been happening to the structural dimensions of the American unemployment problem during this period of aggregative full employment.[13]

Changes in labor-force composition during the preceding decade or more make any aggregative full employment goal somewhat more difficult to achieve than in the mid-fifties or even at the beginning of the sixties. Adult males account for a much smaller percentage of total unemployment than was the case twelve or fifteen years ago. On the other hand, a growing proportion of total unemployment consists of teen-agers and young women age twenty to age twenty-four. And relative to the national unemployment rate, the position of teen-agers in 1967 was worse than it had been in any previous postwar year. Although there is much concern about the unemployment rate of boys, the relative position of the unemployment rate of girls has deteriorated even more. However, perhaps some hope can be found in the fact that the teen-age share of the labor force has now stopped increasing and in the hoped-for effects of present and future manpower programs aimed at youth.

So far as unemployment is concerned, not much progress has been made in improving the relative position of nonwhites, whose unemployment rate is still about twice the national rate. (And if we allow for underreporting, their relative position is probably even worse.) During the sixties the relative position of nonwhite women has worsened, but relative gains have been made by nonwhite men. In contrast is our failure to bring down the tragically high unemployment rates for nonwhite teen-agers.

Although some recent gains have been made, we know that nonwhites are disproportionately concentrated in the less-skilled blue-collar and service jobs. It is important to recognize that, looking ahead, "the occupations in which nonwhites are now concentrated will be growing more slowly than other occupations. Thus, even if nonwhites should continue to increase their share of jobs in the higher skilled occupations at the same rate as in recent years, the present unemployment gap between nonwhite workers and white workers would not be narrowed appreciably."[14] If nonwhite relative unemployment rates are to be reduced in the future, the movement of nonwhites into the more rapidly expanding occupations will have to accelerate.

Although a steadily increasing proportion of the nonwhite labor force resides in our large cities, apparently the percentage of this urban nonwhite population in poverty areas, as defined by the Bureau of the Census, is declining. But the proportion of the nonwhite population that resides in the so-called slum areas is increasing. In addition to the desired gains from manpower, education, job creation, and other programs directly aimed at the poverty-area job seeker, we have to accelerate the movement of Negroes and other minority groups out of poverty neighborhoods and also improve housing, schools, and other public services. Much needs to be done to provide better public transportation, as well as improved training, counseling, and placement services, to facilitate the matching of job seekers in the centers of the cities with the growing number of jobs available outside the urban centers.

Among the occupational and industrial changes in the pattern of unemployment, only one needs to be mentioned here—the relative deterioration in the position of unskilled laborers in 1965–68. With respect to long-term unemployment and involuntary part-time employment, recent improvements have, on the whole, been what we should expect as the overall unemployment rate declines. In these respects as in some others, the American economy is doing better than it was in 1956 when the unemployment rate was about 4 percent, but not as well as in 1953 when the unemployment rate was only 2.9 percent.

At the time this is being written, the national unemployment rate has been at or below 4 percent for three years and at about 3.5 percent for the preceding six months. This low overall figure is the result of a rate of expansion in aggregate demand that brought a rise in prices that has proved to be unacceptable to American policy-makers and probably to most Americans. The result has been, in addition to a tight money policy that was already in effect, new restrictive fiscal action in the form of both tax increases and a proposed substantial decline in federal nondefense expenditures. The result is likely to be a moderate increase in the overall unemployment rate.

If it becomes possible to reduce military expenditures significantly because of a cease-fire in Vietnam, it will not be easy to keep the national unemployment rate below 4 percent, even if appropriate fiscal and other measures are promptly adopted. And, it can be anticipated, even a modest rise in the national rate will bring with it significant increases in the unemployment rates that are now relatively high. Thus the slackening of the economic expansion in 1967 raised the overall unemployment rate, seasonally adjusted, from 3.7 percent (in January) to 4.3 percent (in October). This resulted in an increase from 11.1 to 14.8 percent in the teen-age rate (both sexes, white and nonwhite), from 6.7 to 8.8 percent in the nonwhite rate, and from 7.4 to 9.1 percent in the rate for nonfarm laborers (all figures seasonally adjusted).

Two obvious morals can be drawn from this brief summary of recent experience. First, the job of reducing the very high unemployment rates of underprivileged groups will be made immensely more difficult if aggregate demand does not expand rapidly enough to maintain the national unemployment rate at 4 percent or preferably less. Second, manpower and other Great Society programs thus far adopted have not as yet had much effect in reducing the structural dimensions of the unemployment problem that still faces the United States.

Footnotes

[1] This is a revision of a paper that was originally presented at a seminar on economic policy in Decani, Yugoslavia, in June 1966. It is based largely on a monograph, *The Goal of Full Employment* (New York: John Wiley & Sons, Inc., 1967), Chaps. 2, 3, and 4. This volume is one in a series resulting from the research program on "Unemployment and the American Economy," carried on at the Institute of Industrial Relations, University of California, Berkeley, under a generous grant from the Ford Foundation.

[2] The following discussion is based on my paper, "Full Employment as a Policy Goal," in *Employment Policy and the Labor Market*, A. M. Ross, (Berkeley: University of California Press, 1965). See also *The Goal of Full Employment*, Chap. 2.

[3] This, for example, is the position taken in William Fellner et al., *The Problem of Rising Prices* (Paris: OECD, 1961). It might be argued that the prevailing view in most countries, particularly among those groups with some influence on policy, is that the optimum rate of change in the price level is not zero but some positive number—say, 1 percent or 2 percent per year—because the moderate stimulus thus provided to economic activity more than offsets, in its effects on welfare, the redistributional effects that benefit debtors at the expense of creditors and those on fixed incomes. Contrast this view with the unqualified declaration that "rising prices are not compatible with steady growth" in Fellner et al., op. cit., p. 75.

[4] It might be noted that American policy has had to concern itself with the problem of cyclical instability in general economic activity more than Europe has in the postwar period. Prevention of rapid price increases on cyclical upswings becomes a means of minimizing speculative excesses and other maladjustments and thus of minimizing the duration and amplitude of subsequent cyclical contractions. These considerations have obviously been important in Federal Reserve

thinking and also played a prominent role in the Johnson and Nixon administrations in 1968–69.

[5] I have suggested that the authorities in the United States place a good deal of importance on the need to restrict the rise in prices during cyclical expansions, apart from balance-of-payments considerations. This concern with the interrelations between rising prices and cyclical instability is likely to lead, at least in the short run, to placing a lower value on n than if the concern of the authorities were more vaguely conceived in terms of a flight from the currency and severe inequities in the distribution of the burden of inflation. This seems to have been the case in 1968–69, for example.

[6] A qualification is needed here. If overfull employment existed, a government would be prepared to permit a modest rise in unemployment in order to restrain the rise in prices. The labor market could be so tight that a slight rise in unemployment would be considered as adding to rather than subtracting from total welfare.

[7] Britain tried to do so in 1966–67, after this paper had originally been written.

[8] *Policies for Price Stability* (Paris, 1962), p. 35.

[9] *Economic Report of the President,* January, 1962, p. 46.

[10] R. C. Lipsey, in *Employment Policy and the Labor Market,* A. M. Ross, ed. (Berkeley: University of California Press, 1965).

[11] For a review of these developments, see R. A. and Margaret S. Gordon, eds., *Prosperity and Unemployment* (New York: John Wiley & Sons, Inc., 1966).

[12] This range of questions is considered in greater detail in my book, *The Goal of Full Employment,* esp. Chap. 7.

[13] This summary is taken from my paper, "Unemployment Patterns with 'Full Employment,' " *Industrial Relations,* VIII (October, 1968), 70–72.

[14] Joe L. Russell, "Changing Pattern in Employment of Nonwhite Workers," *Monthly Labor Review,* LXXXIX (May, 1966), 503.

George Katona
The University of Michigan

Planning
and the
Consumer Sector

The Setting

In today's affluent society each of the three major sectors of the economy
—business, consumer, and government—may exercise autonomous influence on economic trends and the rate of growth of the economy. Before World War II only business investment and government deficits or
surpluses were assigned this role, whereas the consumer sector was
viewed as a transmitter of income. It was widely assumed that consumers spent the income they received from business and government at
a fairly constant rate and neither generated income nor contributed to

capital formation. This assumption, no doubt an oversimplification in earlier days, is untenable today. The economic function of the consumer sector has changed radically during the last twenty-five years in which a mass-consumption society has developed.

The invention and the general acceptance of the automobile and of numerous household appliances, together with the greatly increased trend toward home ownership, comprise one factor responsible for the change. Many of the investment expenditures on housing and consumer durables do not stem from immediate needs; they are postponable or can be bunched at certain times. To a large extent they are made on credit, and thus consumer decisions influence the money flow.

The change in income distribution represents the second major factor that brought about the change in the role of the consumer. Not many decades ago the great majority of consumers were close to the subsistence level and their rate of spending was dependent on their income. Wealthy people influenced the economy primarily as entrepreneurs or as investors in financial assets rather than as consumers. Today we still have the poverty segment in our society as well as the small proportion of rich people. (In 1966, 18 percent of the family units had an income of less than $3,000 and received about 4 percent of the aggregate personal money income; on the other hand, 4 percent of the family units with more than $20,000 income received 17 percent of aggregate income.) But in contrast to earlier times, we also have today a very large and steadily growing proportion of families who are in a position to spend some of their income on what they would like to have rather than on what they must have. If we set the limits for the group with discretionary expenditures, somewhat arbitrarily, at $7,500 to $20,000 family income before taxes, we find that more than 40 percent of all units fell in this group in 1966. These middle- and upper-middle-income consumers received more than half of total personal income. The group of families below the discretionary income group ($3,000 to $7,500 income) consists primarily of younger people, many of whom expect to belong to and will belong to the discretionary income group when they get older and advance in their careers.

As a result of the changes just described, today masses of consumers have great discretion in action. Spending by consumers is no longer a function of income alone; discretionary spending depends both on ability to buy and on willingness to buy. Measurement of changes in willingness to buy has become an important task of economic research, both for testing hypotheses or contributing to economic theory and for assisting the economic policies of government and business. Studies of the relation of changes in consumer motives, attitudes, and expectations to changes in discretionary expenditures (primarily on durable goods) and in amounts borrowed by consumers indicate that the factors shaping willingness to buy have had substantial predictive value in the years 1950–66.[1]

Some of the insights gained from the analysis of the behavior of American consumers will be recapitulated briefly in the next section of this paper. This discussion will introduce the major task to which this paper is devoted: an attempt to answer the question of how economic policy, and planning in general, may be adapted to what is known about the factors that shape consumer behavior.

Some Principles of Consumer Psychology

Consumer behavior can hardly be called rational because careful weighing of alternatives and planning ahead have been the exception rather than the rule. But consumer behavior cannot be characterized as irrational because it is not overwhelmingly capricious, impulsive, or nonunderstandable. Although strongly influenced by habits and persistent stereotypes, irrespective of whether they are suited to changed circumstances, most consumers, much better educated than their forefathers, try to adapt themselves to substantial changes in their environment in a sensible manner. They do so—

1. by being aware that income rises with age and also with education, and by deriving optimistic attitudes from this knowledge
2. by being strongly motivated to satisfy secondary wants when primary needs for food, clothing, and shelter are no longer pressing, and by raising levels of aspiration with success and accomplishment and reducing them with failure
3. by being influenced not only by personal financial prospects but also by their perception of the general economic situation, and by requiring constant stimulation before increasing discretionary expenditures
4. by being thing-minded and security-minded at the same time, that is, desiring improvement in their standard of living as well as greater reserve funds, and using income increases for both purposes

What these characteristics of consumers add up to is that consumers in general are not inclined to excessive behavior. When good times continue over prolonged periods but new stimuli are lacking, or when expectations exceed accomplishments, uncertainty and caution set in. Similarly, recessions do not generate unlimited pessimism; satisfaction with personal financial trends on the part of many consumers sets the stage for a positive response to new stimuli. Thus consumers have contributed to stabilizing the economy during the past twenty years, and this was particularly because of their reaction to price increases. Inflation is considered an evil that restricts consumers' ability to enjoy what they believe to be the well-deserved fruits of their labor. During the years of creeping inflation when prices went up slowly and were expected to go up further to a smaller extent, consumers aware of the need to spend more on necessities tended to reduce their discretionary expenditures. Thereby they helped to contain incipient booms.

Consumer Response to the Tax Cut of 1964

What are the tasks of economic policy and what are the means at its disposal in a mass-consumption society that is characterized by great discretion in action on the part of millions of consumers? The discussion of this question can begin by a description of consumers' response to the major policy measure of recent times, the tax cut of 1964. This analysis will be extended to a study of consumer response to income increases in general, because rising incomes represent the principal feature of American economic development in the entire postwar period.[2]

In 1961 when President Kennedy took office, he and his advisers were confronted with several previous years of low rate of income growth and high rate of unemployment. Two recessions had followed each other closely; both business investment and consumer investment expenditures had stayed considerably below long-range trends. To stimulate the economy, traditional policies were used first: some increase in government spending and incentives offered for business investment. Yet no improvement occurred in 1962, except in a field not related to government policy—consumer demand for automobiles rose (primarily because of satisfaction with compact cars and fairly stable auto prices). Then in 1962 Kennedy proposed a new line of economic policy: stimulation of consumer demand by adding to the purchasing power of millions of individuals through a reduction in income taxes.

Sometimes the announcement of a new measure elicits substantial response from consumers and businessmen. This was not the case when the tax cut was first proposed. In 1962–63 most people thought that taxes could not and therefore would not be reduced. A widely perceived analogy between private and government budgets led people to believe that at a time of substantial government expenditures it would not be possible to reduce government revenues. It took a long time until a different opinion spread among the American people. Toward the end of 1963 and early in 1964 most people derived optimistic expectations from the news they heard. They learned that the tax cut would increase American purchasing power by more than $10 billion; they thought that people in general were spending-minded and would promptly use the gain in purchasing power to satisfy their desires for a variety of goods and services and would thereby bring about good times. Optimistic people increased some of their discretionary expenditures before they received any benefits from the tax cut. In January and February 1964, the last two months before the new law went into effect, purchases on the installment plan increased greatly.

Disregarding findings about anticipatory responses, we turn to the major economic question, What did consumers do with the substantial amounts of money that they saved in taxes during 1964? We note that the tax savings occurred gradually; tax withholdings from paychecks were reduced by 4 percent of wages and salaries beginning with March 1964.

It is of no use to ask people what they did with the money they saved because of the tax cut. Small amounts of money are not segregated according to their origin, and most people cannot tell how they used one or the other part of their funds. Moreover, a comparable control group that had not profited from the tax cut did not exist. But it was possible to segregate different groups of people and study their behavior. One aspect of extensive studies will be reported here.

A panel representative of all families with $3,000 to $20,000 annual income, interviewed several times in 1964 and 1965, was divided into four groups. The first group, *No Change*, was characterized by substantially stable income before taxes in the course of the year 1964; this group, of course, profited from the tax cut. The second group, *Upward Trend*, received sizable increases in wages, salaries, or profits in addition to the tax cut. Two other groups, a relatively small one with a downward income trend, and a large one with a mixed trend (both increases and decreases in income in the course of the year) will not be discussed in this paper.

Three forms of discretionary action were measured for each subgroup of the panel. In each quarter of 1964 cash outlays on durable goods and housing as well as amounts borrowed were larger among consumers of the Upward Trend group than among consumers with stable income. On the other hand, the No Change group put more money in banks and securities in the first nine months of 1964, but not in the fourth quarter or in the first few months of 1965. In 1965 the net outlays on durables of this group increased substantially.[3]

How can we explain these findings? They may be related to the following differences between the two groups:

1. Although the disposable income of both groups increased, the increase was much larger in the Upward Trend group than in the No Change group.

2. Increases in wages, salaries, or profits are often associated with a feeling of progress or accomplishment. Many people who received raises in pay felt that they deserved them because they had done a good job. Paying lower taxes, on the other hand, was not viewed as a personal accomplishment.

3. Increases in wages, salaries, or profits are often *cumulative* in that they bring about the expectation of further increases. Having attained a higher income level frequently results in striving for a still higher level. The theoretical model distinguishes three forms of income increases, those followed by (a) further income increases, (b) stable income, and (c) declining income. The Upward Trend group consisted overwhelmingly of people who expected further income increases. This was not the case for the No Change group because tax gains, though permanent, were not seen as something that would be repeated.

It appears that both immediate and delayed responses to income increases occur, depending on the time perspective and the attitudes of the income recipients. Discretionary demand rises promptly and to a large extent in response to an income increase when the increase is viewed as cumulative, whereas there will be a lagged response when the increase is noncumulative. Consumer response is adaptive to success (also to failure) and differs according to the personal evaluation of success. An increase from $10,000 annual income to $11,000 is not the same under all circumstances. Psychological considerations make a difference in people's behavior.

Policy-oriented conclusions also emerge from the studies. The success of the tax cut of 1964, the great extent to which it stimulated the economy, must be attributed primarily to the fact that it occurred at a time when a very substantial proportion of Americans had increased their income before taxes.

The importance of the second and third considerations stated previously may be demonstrated by reporting on further studies. On the basis of several interview surveys conducted with representative samples between 1963 and 1966, the American population was divided into nine groups. The first group reported that their income had gone up during the preceding twelve months and that they expected further income increases during the coming twelve months. This group, called the ++ group, represented on the average 27 percent of all family units in the recent prosperous years. Since income increases do not occur every year for all people, it is hardly surprising that the second and third group, consumers with income increases followed by stable income (+=), and those with stable income followed by income increases (=+), together represented 22 percent of the family units. Among the remaining groups, the one characterized by income stability (==) was the largest, with 22 percent. Stagnation was particularly prevalent among older people.

The greatest impact of different forms of income changes was found in the rate of purchasing of new cars, in the incurrence of new installment debt, and in expressed intentions to buy cars. The order of these forms of behavior was as follows:

GROUP

Highest frequency	++
Second highest	+=, =+
Third highest	+−, −+
Lowest frequency	−−, ==, −=, =−

Multivariate studies disclosed the effectiveness of groupings by income trend. The ++ group appeared with a substantially and significant coefficient in regression equations in which discretionary expenditures or incurrence of debt were the dependent variables and income level, age, and home ownership were held constant.

Economic Policy in
an Era of Consumer Discretion

A cumulative trend of income increases exerts a strong influence on consumers' willingness to buy. This has also been evident in the last few years. We shall turn from the discussion of the best postwar years, 1964 and 1965, to a study of consumer behavior in 1966 and 1967, when dark clouds appeared on the horizon. The Survey Research Center's "Index of Consumer Sentiment," a composite of five attitudinal and expectative questions asked of representative samples every three months, reached its highest postwar level in August and November 1965. By January 1966 the Index registered a small decline, which accelerated greatly in the following nine months. The rate of decline in this period was similar to that during the first nine months of 1957. Among the many factors that impeded consumer sentiment are the following:

1. People's confidence and optimism are dependent on their awareness of some reason that brings prosperity. Although in the preceding years people knew of powerful favorable developments—the tax cut, unusually many and substantial income increases, reduction in unemployment, rising military expenditures in Vietnam—in 1966 no new favorable factors were apparent.

2. Almost all people were aware of price increases and expected further price increases in 1966. Because of rising prices, a greater proportion of consumers expected to be worse off.
3. The great majority of people in the middle- and upper-income groups knew of rising interest rates. Since easy money was associated with prosperity, many informed people thought that tight money would affect the economy adversely.

As a result, consumer optimism weakened considerably. Yet outright pessimism did not develop. This was because the frequency of cumulative income increases remained high and represented an optimistic indicator, reducing to some extent the impact of the adverse factors. For example, news about inflationary wage settlements was viewed both as good and bad. Many consumers thought that such settlements enhanced their own chances of obtaining substantial income increases and at the same time worried about inflation.

What will be the role of economic policy under such circumstances? Early in 1966 when an overheating of the economy was indicated, an increase in income taxes was widely advocated. During the following twenty-four months of protracted discussion about a tax increase, little attention was paid to the probable response by consumers. Yet this question could have been studied. A priori there are three possible ways consumers would respond to a moderate, across-the-board increase in income tax rates:

1. Consumers might consider a tax increase an inefficient step that would not dampen the upswing in the economy. Therefore they might continue with their old rate of expenditures so that the reduction in disposable income would be absorbed by a reduction in saving.
2. Consumer expenditiures might be cut by the amount of the tax increase.
3. Consumers might cut their expenditures to a much larger extent than warranted by the tax increase alone. This possibility would take place if consumers thought that the tax increase would greatly worsen economic trends.

Surveys conducted in 1966–68, prior to the tax increase, have given some indication of consumer attitudes. The tax cut of 1964 was still well remembered at that time. Most people in speaking of a possible tax increase did not think only of the amount of money by which their own tax payments would increase. Rather, they drew a simple inference: since the tax cut was good for the economy as a whole, a tax increase would have bad effects. Even discussion of a need for a tax increase indicated to many consumers that something was wrong with the economy. Since some discretionary expenditures are postponed when overall prospects are not considered favorable, the discussion of a tax increase contributed, along with the other factors described above, to a reduction of consumer demand and a high rate of consumer saving in 1966–67. Thus the tax increase of 1968 had anticipatory effects before it went into effect. On the other hand, by the time disposable incomes were actually reduced by the increased taxes, the adverse psychological effect of the measure was scarcely noticeable.

Generally it is necessary to distinguish the direct influence of economic policy on disposable income from its psychological influence, dependent on people's perception of what is happening and their expectations of what will happen. This is true of fiscal as well as of monetary policy—and of business policy regarding capital investments and the introduction of new products as well. The effects of changes in taxes, interest rates, and prices on purchasing power, as calculated in the form of additions to or subtractions from the money flow, rarely suffice to provide a correct indication of the short-term influence of policy measures. Evidently the psychological impact is not measurable in exact quantitative terms in advance. "Iffy questions" are often misleading, and the circumstances that prevail at the time of the introduction of policy measures may alter the response. But the perception of all consumers, and of different groups of consumers (high-income investors, middle-income car buyers, and so forth), may be determined at an early stage. Continuous surveys of consumer feelings and notions may serve to provide indications of the probable response and also of the manner in which the new measure and its announcement should be shaped to promote desirable rather than undesirable reactions.

A great deal remains to be done. Studies of consumer decision making and of factors shaping consumer decisions need to be continued on an increased scale. Consumers' discretion of action has made forecasting more difficult, but not impossible. Successful planning requires the consideration of the probable consequences of policy measures. This is a point of which Carl Landauer has been well aware. He urged the construction of realistic rather than abstract models. The former must be expressed by observable variables and tested under diverse circumstances to assist economic policy and planning in general.

Footnotes

[1] See George Katona, *The Mass Consumption Society* (New York: McGraw-Hill Book Company, 1964), as well as the annual monographs, *Survey of Consumer Finances*, published by the Institute for Social Research, Ann Arbor, Michigan. The predictive value of the Survey Research Center's "Index of Consumer Sentiment" was also demonstrated in Eva Mueller, "Ten Years of Con-

sumer Attitude Surveys: Their Forecasting Record," *Journal of the American Statistical Association,* 58, December, 1963, 899–917.

[2] The discussion in the next few pages is based on the monograph by George Katona and Eva Mueller, *Consumer Response to Income Increases: An Investigation Conducted in the Year of the Tax Cut* (Washington, D.C.: The Brookings Institution, 1968).

[3] The findings reported above were confirmed by multivariate analysis in which income level, age, etc., were held constant.

Nathan Glazer
University of California
Berkeley

Some Criteria
for Programs
for the Slums and Ghettos

The American city is indicted for many failures. The beginning of wisdom in considering our urban problems is determining what are our really significant and important failures, and what, on the other hand, are perhaps only temporary problems resulting from rapid growth or simply disagreements over what is aesthetic. I believe that during the past few years we have come a long way in beginning to make these essential distinctions. Ten years ago the suburbs were attacked because they were boring or because they did not reproduce classic city patterns. Today most of us would agree that the suburbs—for those who can get into them—are a success. They provide spacious and technically quite good housing, they provide open space, they are being equipped with new facilities, public and private, and they provide environments for family life that most people seem to find desirable.

Of course there are problems in the suburbs, but we shall not find our truly depressing failures there. Many suburban problems are physical problems, which have to be solved through physical means. If we are fortunate enough in this country to be able to find problems that we can define as physical, which can be ameliorated by technical solutions, then we are not so badly off. For this is a rich country with the capacity in technical and skilled manpower and capital resources to make an impact on almost any physical problem. The great expansion of American urban areas of the past twenty years does raise serious problems of air and water pollution, of limited recreational and educational facilities, of new means and systems of interurban transportation. But those problems can in large measure be solved by building new facilities which will have some clear impact on the problem. It is true that there are many political obstacles in the way of designing acceptable legislation, getting legislative bodies to appropriate the necessary expenditures, and designating or designing the appropriate local authorities for the planning and operation of the new facilities and regulatory agencies that these new problems require. However, we already have models of various kinds of solutions, by no means perfect, that nevertheless go some way toward solving such problems of expansion. Thus, we have public corporations, special districts, and forms of cooperation between cities, counties, and states.

If we can find problems for which physical programs provide some part of the solution, we are fortunate. For we are the kind of nation that likes to build, that can afford it, that benefits from it. Our problem is to devise the political solutions that make it possible for us to give free rein to what we do best—such solutions as the interstate highway system, the college facilities building program, and the FHA, all of which help to make it possible for this rich country to use its resources to build new facilities, with benefit to large numbers and harm to only a few.

One key distinction it is necessary to make in discussing American urban problems is the difference between the problems of expanding urban areas, the suburbs, and the central cities. Another key distinction is that between problems that are and are not subject to amelioration through technical means. On the whole, these two distinctions overlap —the problems of the expanding urban areas are in large measure the technical problems of new systems of transportation, new systems to deal with air and water pollution, and new facilities of all kinds. On the other hand, the major problems of the central cities are not solved through technical means. And among the most serious of our central city problems is our persistent effort to attack what are primarily social problems with physical solutions to which they will not succumb.

Of course, the two distinctions do not overlap so neatly. There are also social problems in expanding urban areas, even if they are not serious ones—for example, the boredom of teen-agers and housewives.[1] More seriously, a remarkable and increasing degree of political effort, ingenuity, and invention is required to permit even those technical solutions that are possible to problems of expansion to operate. Thus, it is startling to realize that Japan instituted efficient, inexpensive, and technically sophisticated high-speed transport to link its major cities between Toyko and Osaka in only a few years. We in this country, attempting to achieve the same result in the Boston-New York-Washington corridor, have made little progress in seven years. The technical problems of high-speed transportation in the sea-level Boston-Washington corridor are much less complicated than those in the mountainous Tokyo-Osaka corridor, but political obstacles have prevented possible technical solutions. Finally, aside from the purely social problems, and aside from the political problems that prevent easy development of technical solutions, there are technical problems that involve far more than technical solutions and may require a complete reordering of social life. This is particularly true of the environmental pollution problems. The problem of environmental pollution may indeed be *the* problem of urban life in an affluent society and involve measures and approaches we have scarcely dreamed of, whether technical or social.

Nevertheless, at this time the problems of new and expanding urban areas are for the most part technical in a simpler sense and can be ameliorated by available technical programs of various kinds.

The same is not true of central city problems. We can divide our efforts to deal with central city problems through federal policy into roughly three historical periods. The first period, from 1933 to World War II, emphasized the clearance of slums and their replacement with sound housing for the working classes and the poor. (There was little slum clearance or building of new publicly subsidized housing in this period—but this was the *aim* of housing reformers and of federal policy, insofar as it dealt with the central city.) The second period, from the passage of the first postwar housing law in 1949 to, let us say, the antipoverty program and the first summer riots in 1964, emphasized urban renewal and slum clearance, not particularly to provide sites for new housing for low-income groups but to provide sites for new residential, business, educational, and industrial uses. It was thought that these measures would hold or bring back the white middle class, improve the tax base of the central city, and help it to compete with the suburbs. The third period, from 1964 to the present, involves our still groping efforts to deal with the problems of the ghettos, which we recognize as social and economic and moral and political, but which we still hope to assuage through physical means. The chief legislative landmarks of this period are the poverty program and the still evolving Model Cities Program of the Department of Housing and Urban Development, in which we have added a large array of social programs to a central core of physical rebuilding and rehabilitation. President Johnson placed great emphasis on this program as the major new approach to central city problems, and many cities are now engaged in planning this kind of program. It is being continued in the administration of President Nixon.

Aside from the Model Cities Program, various programs aiming at the physical renewal of the city, which began with some degree of enthusiasm and commitment from many sources, have ended in a disappointing way. They continue, but they are subject to intense criticism, and few see in them the major instrument for a decisive attack on our central city problems.

Studies have shown that public housing is unpopular with many of the people eligible to live in it and for whom it is designed. It is unpopular with the people who don't live in it but who pay for it. It is unpopular (though to me this is the least significant of its defects) with architects, planners, and urban designers. Those who go into the job of building and managing public housing are generally not our more imaginative public servants. It is very expensive to build and often expensive to maintain. Of course, many public housing projects are popular with those who live in them, but any bargain representing the kind of money saving to tenants that public housing does is likely to find some popularity. And many of the people most eager to get into public housing are those who are so poor or meet such discrimination that they are grateful for anything.

The local and federal programs that encourage the rehabilitation of the slums have also been failures to a great extent. They are expensive and incapable of creating strong and lasting commitment or lasting improvement.

There is the urban renewal program, and while a good number of people would argue it has been a success in some terms, no one would argue that it has been successful in changing the slums or the inhabitants of the slums.[2]

It has often been argued that public housing and urban renewal are good programs, but the problem has been that they have been mounted on too small a scale. It is scarcely necessary to deal seriously with this argument today when the roofs of public housing projects turn out to be ideal locations for snipers, and when urban renewal in its classic form of bringing back the middle class and private investment has in so many cities stopped abruptly as it becomes impossible politically to acquire new large sites for clearance. Would a *bigger* public housing program or urban renewal program have mitigated in any serious way the urban crisis or would they instead have exacerbated it?

The beginning of wisdom in dealing with the American slum is understanding that its problems are only partially and in a limited way physical problems, that is, problems of poor housing and poor public facilities. Of course, housing is poor and public facilities are old or lacking, but it is not this that makes the slum an explosive danger to the city. When European experts are shown through our slum areas they are horrified, and they find it impossible to understand why a country richer than any in Europe cannot provide better housing for its poor people. And it is true that, as we understand slums in this country, there are no slums in some European countries. It is easy to spring then to a physical solution.

But this is an error. If we look at the statistics of this nation and of the European nations whose experts are horrified with our slums, we will discover that according to various measures of housing quality our housing, even in many cases our slum housing, is better than the common run of working-class housing in Europe. Thus, only 11.5 percent of American housing units had more than one person per room occupancy in 1960, compared with 48 percent in Sweden and 39 percent in the United Kingdom. Even crowding among urban nonwhites is less than in developed foreign countries. Bathing facilities for exclusive use are found in 85 percent of American housing units, compared with bathing facilities in 61 percent of housing units in Sweden and 73 percent in the United Kingdom.[3]

Not only is American housing better than that of other advanced countries that do not have our overwhelming urban problems but improvement in our housing seems to do nothing to ameliorate our urban problems. Public housing in this country is technically good housing. It is not crowded, since the management can assign rooms according to the size of the family. However, when people talk about slums and slum problems in this country, they often do not make a distinction between public low-cost housing and private low-cost housing. In New York, for example, public housing is often called *high-rise slums*, and we know that riots can break out in housing projects as easily as in slums.

It is said that although public housing is technically good housing, it is also inhuman and institutional because of the way it is designed and administered, and therefore those living in it have as many, if different, grievances as those living in the privately owned slums. Thus it is for these reasons that our investment in good low-cost housing is not rewarded with satisfied tenants. Improvements in design and administration are certainly possible. And yet the publicly subsidized low-income groups in all advanced nations increasingly live in similar high-rise developments —as do indeed more of the middle class, whether publicly subsidized or not, under similar restrictions that density and expensive high-rise rental quarters seem to require, but without the same social consequences. In our cities, the new housing is considered socially no better than the old and is labelled *slum* indiscriminately with the old.

Steady and indeed massive improvement in the housing of those worst off has not been accompanied by any sense that our urban problems are being met. Although we have been successful in reducing the proportion of substandard housing in our cities since World War II, this has had little effect on urban problems or on public consciousness of them—almost everyone believes that the slums have grown, and everyone knows that our problems have increased. Between 1960 and 1966, the quantity of substandard housing occupied by nonwhites dropped 25 percent, from 2,263,000 units to 1,691,000 units. The standard housing occupied by nonwhites increased 44 percent, from 2,881,000 units to 4,135,000 units. Obviously this has had no discernible impact on our urban problems.[4]

Our slum problems are not primarily physical problems; they are complex social problems because the slums in our cities are increasingly inhabited by Negroes, who suffer from extreme prejudice and discrimination. When foreign visitors comment on our slums, they are reacting only partly to their physical condition—they are reacting more to the sight of men standing around without employment, children playing without supervision, youth lounging about without any apparent occupation. They are reacting to a social as well as to a physical scene. Even the *physical* aspects of the slums are in large measure determined by the social and economic problems of those who live in them. If the maintenance is poor, it is because homeowners are too poor to make repairs, tenants too disorganized to require landlords to make repairs, families and the neighborhood community too involved in immediate problems to uphold a reasonable standard of civic cleanliness.

Compared with other countries and other times, our slum problem is not primarily a problem of specific facilities but a problem related to the existence in this nation and in our cities of a large depressed population, which has suffered from discrimination, segregation, poor education, and other disadvantages. Our slums have always varied, depending on who lived in them. We have had German slums, Irish slums, Jewish slums, Italian slums. We are now living in an age of Negro slums. Each group has created an environment that to some extent reflected its experience. Now we have a group that has suffered from the worst experience, with the worst effects, and this is reflected in the environment it has helped to create.

It is thus understandable that we should move from an emphasis on physical programs to an emphasis on social programs. There are programs created by the Office of Economic Opportunity, and there is the program combining physical and social efforts in the Model Cities legislation. It seems to make sense, if the problem is social, to spend more money on social programs. But the matter is not that simple. If we have physical problems, we can spend money and we will have a fairly good chance of contributing to the solution of the problem. The highway may be in the wrong place, the sewage plant may not be the most efficient one, the school may not be well designed, but for the most part some contribution to solving the problem has been made. But when we come to social problems, we can have radical disagreements as to how to spend the money, for what, and with what effect. And it may turn out that considerable expenditure has not affected the problems at all. Furthermore, whereas it is generally the experts who disagree about physical programs, the experts and everyone else disagree about social programs.

The history of programs that attempt to control juvenile delinquency is a good example of this. We have had programs that emphasize psychological therapy, work with groups, or total community and neighborhood programs, but we do not know how to reduce juvenile delinquency though we know how to spend great sums of money. Thus when we say, let's solve the social problems of the slums, we really do not know what will work, and we do not know what it will cost.

Crime falls into this category. Education falls into this category. Making good neighborhoods falls into this category. If *making good neighborhoods* means improving street layout, building playgrounds, improving transportation, building new schools, and so forth, we can estimate the cost. But if it means transforming a neighborhood so that people feel better and are happier or so that social problems are reduced—violence, dependency, delinquency, illiteracy—it is not clear just what we should do.

Under these circumstances, three criteria of social programs for central cities have become popular. The first comes from the argument that experts, legislators, administrators, and people of good will don't really know what to do. Therefore we must involve the people of the slums themselves. We must ask them what they want and what they need, and we must give them some of the power, personnel, and funds to carry out their goals. This approach has been used infrequently in the urban renewal program and more often in the Community Action Program of the Economic Opportunity Act, and it is part of the Model Cities Program.

There is a second general criterion for action which has become popular. It too recognizes that the problem is complex and then goes on to say that the solution must also be complex. Since everything is involved in the problem of the slums—education for children, work training for youth, jobs for men, recreation for all, organization to make the voice of the people effective, media of communication—everything must be worked into a program for the slums. Eventually this will mean complex approaches with an emphasis on planning and coordination of a great variety of programs.

The third criterion emphasizes concentration on specific areas within cities—since the problems are so great and unmanageable, our complex urban social programs should first be designed only for target areas.

Although the three criteria need not be linked, in practice they have been. In the Community Action Program, we have asked the poor in selected target areas to participate in the construction, formulation, and administration of a complex and many-sided program. In the Model Cities Program, we have also selected certain neighborhoods and have made a place for the people to participate in formulating these complex programs to transform poor areas.

All three criteria are in large measure misguided, and all three, affecting our current thinking on how to deal with our critical central city problems, have helped contribute to the ineffectiveness of our recent urban programs, to the rising frustration of our slum and ghetto populations, and thus ultimately to the terribly dangerous situation that now faces American cities.

The attempt to put complex social programs directly in the hands of those affected by them has in general led not to the amelioration of the problems of the slums but to an enormous increase in conflict and in opportunities for conflict in the cities. The attempt to create complex and many-sided programs involving the coordination of many different types of approaches has led to enormous confusion. The concentration on problems of specific areas has prevented us from giving full attention to those basic national programs that seem essential in any advanced and complex society. The poor of a modern society cannot be raised through their efforts, in their neighborhoods, through the coordination of programs and resources that are themselves inadequate.

It is easy to consider both the conflict and the confusion as necessary first stages in the creation of a better form of government of urban affairs, and this is indeed one possibility, but I think a closer analysis of the recent developments will suggest that we are neither on the right course nor are we emphasizing the right things.

The first problem is that these complex programs place an enormous strain on available planning and administrative capacities. Both in the Community Action Program of the Office of Economic Opportunity and in the Model Cities Program we ask that a plan be worked out that will demonstrate how all the social efforts to improve the poor neighborhood will work together. In granting funds, we place emphasis on ingenious new programs and ingenious mechanisms for coordination. We then find such ironic developments as the rise of consultant firms, into which the few people capable of developing these complex programs to the satisfaction of federal officials gravitate. The consultant firms themselves generally include former federal officials who understand these complex requirements for coordination. Thus programs that, according to the intent of Congress, are supposed to reflect the needs and character and capacities of individual cities are themselves very often the product of a small group of experts, who have generally gained their expertise in the federal government. At each step in the development of these complex programs the cities need the guidance of federal officials and the aid of increasing numbers of consultants.

When any approach to social problems takes a form in which the ordinary talent available to staff city services cannot manage it or manage it well, it is time to take another look. Up to now our approach in helping the cities to handle these complex coordinated approaches has been to appropriate more money for planning and to increase the number of steps at which there is federal supervision. In other words, our approach is to increase the demand for increasingly scarce and specialized individuals.

We have also never asked the question whether coordination of social services, to the extent these new programs demand, is either possible or necessary. This question must be raised when we consider the varied origins of various programs, the varied relations of federal, state, local, and private agencies in conducting them, the varied statutory and administrative requirements each must meet, the varied professional and other interests that are often behind the different statutory and administrative requirements, the varied lead times that different programs require, and so forth. All these make the task of coordination and planning enormously difficult, and often an exercise in showing good faith to get the money that bears little fruit.[5]

One wonders why this American emphasis on local coordination and planning is not found to the same extent in other countries that have, it is generally agreed, more adequate social services. The main reason undoubtedly is that they have a simpler political and social structure, permitting coordination at the level of law-making and central administration. We cannot unfortunately create this simpler structure overnight—or probably at all—and thus the need for coordination and planning at the local level must always be greater in this country. But there is another reason why other countries require less planning and coordination, and this is because their major social services are themselves more adequate to their major tasks. When a country has inadequate child welfare services, low levels of public welfare maintenance, few public housing programs, and weak agencies for enforcing housing codes, one approach is to condemn each agency for its bureaucratic ineptness and inefficiency and to create a higher coordinating and planning agency. But another approach would be to strengthen each branch of social service that is contributing to welfare and to place less priority on the task of coordinated planning.

When in addition to the demand for coordinated planning we insist that in the planning of these programs, which are already beyond the capacities of most mayors and their staffs to fully understand or fully develop, the people of the poor neighborhoods be involved, we compound our difficulties. Conflict is valuable when it leads to some decision, conclusion, or reorganization of power, with some degree of coherence. It is not valuable when what is fought over are dark and murky and rapidly developing and scarcely comprehended new complex programs. Under these circumstances, conflict, which can certainly be healthy, leads only to confusion and frustration. After desperate struggles to control a community action program, the winners may discover they have gained not much more than dust because of the complexity of the program, the inability to define it in clear and comprehensible terms, and its low level of financial support. One reason for a low level of support, if not an important one, is that Congress does not know what programs of this complex type do or are supposed to do.

The emphasis on local participation and control, just as the emphasis on coordinated social planning, has been a distinctively American development. There is some good justification for it, particularly in view of the make-up of the American population. The significance of racial and ethnic groups creates needs for kinds of representation that more homogeneous countries do not require. But it is also true that local participation and control, just as coordinated planning, tends to be a substitute for adequate national programs. There would be less demand for local participation and control if public assistance, child welfare services, normal city services, work training and placement programs, and the like, were more adequate.[6]

Our new Model Cities Program shares a number of important characteristics with Community Action Programs. Only the federal administrators and the consultants really understand what it is about and how it is supposed to work. The battles of the poor to gain an increasing control over the program will finally result in their greater frustration. And the city administrators will go along because it will be yet another way to get federal funds, not because it is the method they might have chosen or because it will provide funds in the most efficient way.

It would be pointless to criticize our best considered approaches to solving the problems of the slums if one did not have alternatives to suggest. The alternative I would propose is the creation of new institutions of urban government and services and the strengthening of old institutions in ways that clearly meet specific needs and involve not the creation of new and ambiguous professions but new branches of government service. I can best illustrate this approach by describing what has happened to the programs of the OEO.

Initially, a great deal of emphasis in the poverty program was placed on the Community Action Program which was an earlier version of Model Cities, but with fewer resources and a larger component of local participation. It also emphasized the selection of poor neighborhoods, a local determination of what programs might help the area most, and a complex and lengthy planning and coordinating process, which was not a one-shot affair but continuous. Great problems developed in making the CAP viable—the conflicts over representation, types of service to be included, ultimate locus of decision-making power, and so forth. It was as if a hundred communities were living through a period of constitution making, with a considerable shortage of founding fathers of vision and authority.[7]

But after all this turmoil, some of the most successful programs were those that had not been originally envisaged as playing any important role in overcoming poverty in the neighborhoods. The three that have been unexpected successes are Operation Headstart, the legal services program, and the comprehensive neighborhood health centers. What do I mean by success? I mean that a substantial consensus in the community at the local and national levels accepts these programs as good and valuable, and the chances of their continued funding as a regular part of government service are good. One cannot define them as successful in terms of overcoming poverty, but then what would qualify as success in these terms?

What the people in the slums need is not more planning and participation but a number of services that are at present poorly handled or not handled at all. We should institute or invent new services for a variety of long-range problems. We can set some criteria for such programs:

1. We have to define a clear need in simple and unambiguous terms, which is felt as a need by those for whom the service is designed.
2. We have to define some action, either a service or a physical facility, that clearly meets that need.
3. Our definition of need and service or action must be such that it is politically acceptable to enough citizens to be instituted.
4. There must be personnel available to carry out the need or service.

These are not simple criteria, but they are important ones. They explain why Operation Headstart, legal services, and neighborhood health centers are a success, and why the Community Action Program is a failure. They also suggest some problems that the Model Cities Program will have to face and possible ways of improving it.

What new institutions of government could we establish in the slums?

Admittedly the task of setting criteria on the basis of the experience of the past is easier than predicting the institutions that must emerge and will emerge in the future. If we look at our cities of 150 years ago, we find that there were no police services, no regular sanitary services, no professional firefighting services, no public health services, no public education. In time all these services were established and became the backbone of city government. Our problem is to create institutions that twenty years from now will seem perfectly natural—they will fill a need, they will be accepted, they will get budgets, and they will be run by regular city governments, or metropolitan governments if these replace them. I doubt that any of them will be totally original—they will be extensions of old services, as Operation Headstart is an extension of education services, legal aid an extension of public defender services, and neighborhood comprehensive health centers an extension of well-baby clinics and hospital outpatient departments. But politically that will be their virtue. The totally new is always difficult to establish. New services are most easily established in connection with a commitment that society has already made—the service expands or fulfills the commitment.

Following this line of analysis, the most valuable role of the Model Cities Program will be to discover, by accident or design, new services and means of expanding old services—just as this was the most valuable part of the poverty program. It is part of the inevitable dilemma of social change that we cannot design dependable institutions in advance. We know that we need better schools in slum areas. If Model Cities helps support experiments in this area, experiments that can then become the model for a new type of school or school system, good. If Model Cities can devise new means of assuring safety in the slums—the involvement perhaps of youth as police trainees, the development of new community-service-oriented police, good. If Model Cities can show us how to improve our housing inspection services and our incentives for improving housing maintenance and repair, that will be good, too. If Model Cities can aid in expanding means of bringing better health care to the slums— and here we need inventiveness if we are to overcome the ingrained opposition of the organized medical profession to most of the obvious solutions—that will also be good. The object of Model Cities should not be a permanent service of planning and coordinating city services to the poor, for that is properly the task of city government, but the creation of new institutions that will make city government in these areas better.

In summary, we have placed too much of our hope on programs that require complex skills of coordination and planning that do not yet exist and may never be instituted in the forms in which some of us envisage them. The pattern of government in the past—an organized service providing a program to a clientele—is still a model that can teach us a great deal about how to improve life in the slums. Our problem is to define politically acceptable new services for the cities that can provide clear and immediate improvement in some conditions of life, that can be staffed by personnel without exotic and complex qualifications, and that can be instituted without endless conflict. For the past few years we have experienced much confusion from the argument that the poor want power and participation. Of course they do—as any citizen does. But even more they want income and services. It is along these lines that we should try to improve the slums and the central cities.

Footnotes

[1] Herbert Gans, *The Levittowners* (New York: Pantheon Books, 1967).

[2] For a general review of American housing programs, see Nathan Glazer, "Housing Policy and the Family," *Journal of Marriage and the Family*, XXIX:1, February, 1967, pp. 140–63. For the major critiques of urban renewal, see Herbert Gans, *The Urban Villagers* (New York: Macmillan-Free Press, 1962); Martin Anderson, *The Federal Bulldozer* (Cambridge: Massachusetts Institute of Technology Press, 1964); Scott Greer, *Urban Renewal in American Cities* (Indianapolis: The Bobbs-Merrill Co., Inc., 1965).

[3] European figures from D. V. Donnison, *The Government of Housing* (Baltimore: Penguin Books, Inc., 1967), pp. 50, 54; U.S. figures from the U.S. Census of Housing, as presented in an unpublished RAND paper by Ira S. Lowry.

[4] *Social and Economic Conditions of Negroes in the United States*, U.S. Department of Labor, Bureau of Labor Statistics, No. 332, October, 1967, p. 55.

[5] On some of the problems in the planning and coordination of a range of social problems, see Peter Marris and Martin Rein, *Dilemmas of Social Reform* (New York: Atherton Press, 1967).

[6] I discuss some of these characteristics of American social services at somewhat greater length in " A Sociologist's View of Poverty," in *Poverty in America*, ed. by Margaret S. Gordon (San Francisco: Chandler Publishing Co., 1965), pp. 12–26.

[7] On issues of local participation and control, see Earl Raab, "What War and Which Poverty," *The Public Interest*, III:1, Spring, 1966, pp. 45–56; Daniel P. Moynihan, "What is 'Community Action'?", *The Public Interest*, Fall, 1966, pp. 3–8; and Nathan Glazer, "The Grand Design of the Poverty Program," *New York Times Magazine*, February 27, 1966.

Politics cannot but have priority over economics.
To argue differently—means to forget the ABC
of Marxism.

Lenin, 1921

Andrzej Brzeski
University of California
Davis

Social Engineering
and *Realpolitik*
in Communist
Economic Reorganization*

In contrast to most utopias, from Plato to Bellamy, the doctrine of "scientific socialism" contained no detailed prescriptions for the eudae-

* An earlier draft of this essay was read to the Seminar on Comparative Study of Communist Societies at the University of California (Berkeley). I am grateful to the participants, and especially to Gregory Grossman, Chalmers A. Johnson, Jerzy F. Karcz, Howard R. Swearer, and Benjamin N. Ward, for their enlightening criticism. I am also much indebted to Henry Y. Wan, Jr., my colleague at the University of California (Davis), for his helpful comments and to Catherine Mulholland for editorial assistance. Naturally, I alone bear the responsibility for all errors and misconceptions.

monic community of the future. Yet, with a boundless faith in the potentialities of social engineering, it implied that postcapitalist society would be able to create the prerequisites for individual growth, social harmony, and economic abundance. "With the seizing of the means of production by society ... man's own social organization ... becomes the result of his own free action," wrote Engels in *Anti-Dühring*. Least of all did the founders of Marxism expect serious hindrances to a rational reorganization of the economy.

The Russian Revolution put the problem on the historical agenda. But despite Stalin's boast at the Eighteenth Party Congress that Russia "has proved in practice ... quite capable not only of destroying the old system but of building a new and better socialist system,"[1] the task has been elusive. The experience of nearly half a century has not borne out Marxist optimism in matters of social engineering. Far from realizing the ideals of Engels's "Kingdom of Freedom," the various organizational measures instituted by the Communists, whether in the Soviet Union, Eastern Europe, or China, have been tainted by irrationality and conflict.

The various stages of communist economic reorganization have been carefully chronicled and analyzed; they warrant no further description here. Rather than once again traversing a familiar terrain, this essay deals with one aspect of the problem, the interplay of economic and political factors in organizational change.

Marxian dialectics—the much-cited passage from a letter to Bloch[2] notwithstanding—treats politics as an epiphenomenon of the "mode of production." The record of communism suggests a different, more erratic historiosophy. Contrary to the implications of Marxian theory and contrary to those analysts who tend to interpret communist politics in terms of substantive policy issues, such as economic reorganization, policy appears to have been an outgrowth of peculiar "politburo politics." Lenin's slogan which I adopted as the motto has thus become prophetic.

Carl Landauer once observed that organizational innovation could logically be considered, along with technology, a codeterminant of history in the Marxian scheme of things.[3] With respect to communism at least, I propose to go beyond this Schumpeterian revision by including the constitution of the body politic as an independent, and perhaps decisive, variable.

The Hypotheses

Explicitly or implicitly, most students of communist reorganization have interpreted the reshuffling of institutions as a quest for the organizational forms most suited to achieving such objectives as "efficiency," "growth" and "industrialization." A popular notion holds that the recent movement toward economic reform reflects the increasing difficulties experienced in operating a complex industrial economy through centralized command.[4] Arguments of considerable subtlety have been advanced in support of this position. Frank and Waelbroeck suggest that the "growing impracticability of Soviet type planning" may be due to the so-called square law (according to which the number of possible input-output coefficients varies with the square of the number of products).[5] Thus—to use the tripartite conceptual framework introduced by Campbell—the reorganizations in Soviet bloc countries are perceived as an adjustment of the administrative system (Structure II) to the system of production possibilities (Structure I).[6] This kind of explanation, which is fashionable with critics and apologists of Soviet-type socialism alike, has a certain affinity with Marxian theory. Summarily, the hypothesis can be described as *technological determinism.*

Another common explanation of communist economic reorganizations links the reforms to a shift in policy goals. According to this, Stalin's "command economy" was specifically (and perhaps aptly) designed to launch a poor agrarian society into an industrial takeoff. By contrast, the experimenting with profits and markets (to which the communist countries seem to be inclined) provides an organizational setting suited to a consumer-oriented policy in more affluent economies. To quote again from Frank and Waelbroeck, "multiplication of objectives has changed in a profound way the character of the problems encountered by Soviet planning, endangering the ability of traditional methods of running the economy to continue to work in a satisfactory way."[7] Again, in Campbell's terminology, reorganization when thus explained (changes in Structure II) aims at establishing a closer connection between the nonisomorphic Structures I and III (the system of production possibilities and the normative economic model).[8] This hypothesis of reorganization may be labeled *policy determinism.*

Whether reorganization occurs in response to changes in the production structure or as a result of policy reformulations or both, it fits the concept that organization is a mere instrument for achieving economic objectives.[9] But another possibility exists too. Perhaps, as Wiles suggests, the communist leaders as "specialists in taking political power ... treat all economic thought as a means to the end ... viewing the base not as an object of unbiased study in itself, but solely as the foundation of their political position."[10] If so, organizational changes in the economy would come about mainly for reasons connected with communist *realpolitik.* Such a hypothesis seems quite plausible in some instances of reorganization. *Gosplan's* demotion vis-à-vis the ministries in the Voznesensky affair is a good case in point.[11] The *sovnarkhoz* reform may also have been largely an interfactional maneuver.[12] Similar maneuvering can be suspected in other measures too. Quite obviously, power politics alone may be inadequate to explain *all* organizational changes, but it is nearly always relevant in accounting for *lack of change* (organizational rigidity). The *kremlinological* hypothesis of reorganization stems from such considerations.

"Kremlinology," as I interpret it, derives from a Machiavellian perception of the political process. Given the conditions in the Soviet Union and Eastern Europe there is much to render this view realistic.[13] But the power maneuvers of competing cliques, which try to utilize organizational means for their own interest, can also be put in a broader socioeconomic framework.[14] Thus, for instance, the removal of Bukharin by Stalin may be seen as the final victory of the urban elite, bent on rapid industrialization, over the peasantry. Similarly, the Khrushchev-Malenkov contest may be interpreted as one involving party cadres and managerial technocracy. And Khrushchev's struggle against the "anti-party group" (Molotov, Kaganovitch & Co.) may be looked upon as an attempt by the provincial power groups to challenge the absolute rule of the Moscow bureaucracy. How the conflicting forces of the society at large operate and in what way they find leverage on the *verkhushka* ("top") is an intriguing question for a political sociologist. Here, all the explanations entailing the importance of social conflict in reorganization will be subsumed under the generic term *societal hypothesis*.

Logically, the four explanations of organizational change could be mutually exclusive. At another level of interpretation, this need not be so. Indeed, the different hypotheses can be tied together in a theory of a higher order. Marxism, or neo-Marxism, would neatly integrate the two "determinisms" with the "societal hypothesis," as in Trotsky's analysis of the Soviet state.[15] Furthermore, by accepting the dialectic of "the last resort" everything can be reduced to "technological determinism." Even "kremlinology" could be somehow fitted in if, with a twist of Plekhanov, the personalities of leaders are treated as tools of "historical necessity."

An examination of the different hypotheses both from a logical and from an empirical stance leads to some important insights into the problems posed in this essay. But first I must take a detour through some rudimentary ideas on organization and reorganization.

Economic Organization
and Reorganization

Very abstractly, organization may be conceived of as a system of receiving, processing, storing, and transmitting messages. According to Wiener, "the information carried by a set of messages is a measure of organization."[16] But as yet there have been few examples of *social* organization usefully described in cybernetic terms. The oldest and probably the most successful of such attempts is the competitive model of the economy. Otherwise, realistic models have only begun to be constructed by management science for microentities,[17] but not for the society (or economy) as a whole. Therefore, even though I incline to the view that "to develop a generally useful theory of the administrative economy . . . the specialists on the Soviet economy should take mass leave, and study cybernetics together,"[18] the treatment here will be taxonomic.

Although it may be "easier, and probably more useful, to give examples of . . . organizations than to define the term,"[19] the working definition adopted in this essay will be as follows: *Economic organization consists of the devices by which production, exchange, and distribution of goods are determined and coordinated.* The vague term "devices" will be given a more precise meaning below. At this point, I wish to draw a distinction between economic *organization* and economic *system*. In my terminology, the latter is a broader concept embracing policy goals in addition to "economic organization" proper. The question of how much (or what kind of) change in goals gives rise to a new "system" must be left aside, lest it result in philosophical hairsplitting. The criterion of differentiation should be intuitively clear in most cases of practical importance. Thus, for instance, I would speak of a change in the Soviet economic "system" if, all other things (including "organization") being equal, the priority of growth versus current consumption were to be reversed. To complete this excursion into terminology, I might add one more concept: the *economy*. As used here, it is more inclusive than the "economic system" because it also encompasses the physical components of Campbell's Structure I "technology . . . and resource limitations."[20]

Since there is no possibility of entering here into a specification of all the "devices" that make up the Soviet-type economic organization, I restrict my taxonomy to a few broad categories.

1. Partitioning

A Soviet-type economy, in addition to the usual *household* and *public service* sectors, comprises the following structural components:
Firms, specialized by process and/or purpose, carry out the activities of production and the purchasing and selling of goods.
Agencies in charge of firms direct the activities of groups of the latter.
Bureaus in charge of activities direct and/or supervise a particular subset of activities across the economy.
Central authority directs the activities of agencies and bureaus and, through them, of the entire economy.

2. Channels

Communication channels are *vertical* and *horizontal*. The first link the center with the firms through *industrial* and/or *territorial* hierarchies of agencies and bureaus. The second link agencies (bureaus) with other agencies (bureaus) and, on a lower level, firms with other firms.

3. Content

Messages from "above" to subordinate units may be called *directives* and *permits*. There are two kinds of directives: commands and rules. *Commands* are addressed to specific units to carry out certain activities. Their general form is: "X, do y!" In this group are all sorts of obligatory targets, limits, and allocation quotas. Similarly, the orders to keep records, file reports, and hire and fire personnel are in the nature of a command. *Rules*, in contrast, prescribe a manner of doing things: "y should be done in such and such a way"; for instance, "price (cost, tax, bonus, and so forth) should be calculated as follows" or "output should be expanded until marginal cost equals price." The distinction between "rules" and "commands" is somewhat arbitrary and not very rigorous, but to an economist it conveys meaning. Permits, as suggested by the term, relay the consent of the authorities to subordinate units' requests (see below).

Messages from "below" to higher echelons can be classified as *reports* and *requests*. The first relate past activities. The second pertain to future activities, in particular they may ask for clarification and/or change of directives.

Messages sent along horizontal channels will be called *elaborations* when they pertain to interunit relations arising from directives. Otherwise, the most important class of horizontal messages, for instance in market transactions, will be termed after Hurwicz *proposals*, to describe "a set of visible actions ... that might conceivably be taken by some units."[21]

Any economic organization consists of formal and informal elements, but a characteristic feature of socialism (even à la Lange-Lerner) is the preeminence of bureaucracy. The economic organization of the Soviet bloc countries is bureaucratic par excellence. The organs making up its hierarchical structure are created by administrtive fiat. Their authority, function, and responsibility are specified by law. The channels and modes of communication are routinized. The rules of behavior, the rewards, and the sanctions are prescribed in minutiae. Consequently it is possible, at least in principle, to draw up for the economy as a whole a chart detailing the procedural and substantive coordination of activities, whether carried out "by plan" or "by feedback." Upon a closer examination some loose ends are discovered in this highly formalized "structural expression of rational action."[22] But this will be discussed later.

Economic organization (however defined) embraces the *internal* arrangements within the various units. These arrangements are disregarded throughout here; like the economist's mythical "firm," all the entities making up the overall organizational structure are treated as "black boxes." This gross oversimplification is partly vindicated by circumstances. First, the generic peculiarities of "socialism," as we know it, lie in its macro- rather than in its micro-organization. The internal structure and operation of the firm, whether socialist or capitalist (with the possible exception of Yugoslavia), display a good deal of similarity. Analogously, the internal setup—if not the authority and function—of a socialist govermnent office is not unlike that of its capitalist counterpart. Second, the differentiation of the genus "socialism" into national species can be most clearly observed, for the Soviet bloc at least, in its macro-organization. Since the introduction of one-man management decades ago, the changes in internal organization of firms and administrative units have been anything but spectacular. Not so, however, the overall organization of Soviet bloc economies, which, in this respect, have exhibited variability over a wide range of relevant dimensions.

In any case, speaking of *reorganization* (or, synonymously, of organizational change), I have in mind only such rearrangements that affect the three major categories mentioned above: the partitioning of the economy, the channels and the content of communication. The prevalent bureaucratic *modus operandi* of socialism makes formal reorganization the main vehicle of change. Still, informal rearrangements (for example, the rerouting of communications outside official channels or unauthorized extension of command) are not uncommon. Naturally, such processes —in contrast to reorganization by decree, whether piecemeal or wholesale—are gradual. The forces that make for informal organizational change only produce discernible results over longer time periods. Consequently, it is convenient to refer to this process as *organizational evolution*, reserving the term "reorganization" for formally instituted change.

Traditionally, the *theoretical* interest in the reorganization of the Soviet-bloc economies has focused rather heavily on its centralization versus decentralization aspect. Quite apart from the ambiguity of these concepts, which have still to be precisely and meaningfully defined,[23] this emphasis ignores a whole gamut of organizational dimensions. Reorganization, like organization itself, has many facets of which the "degree of centralization," whatever its measure, is not necessarily the most important. This has been properly recognized in the *empirical* research on communist countries.

For every economy, even in the short run, there is more than one feasible arrangement of components and their communications. If one thinks of each of the possible organization setups as codified in a separate book of rules, there exists, figuratively speaking, a collection of such books at any given time. The feasible range of reorganization expands with the time horizon, that is, the number of rule books in the "library" increases with the length of the period during which the changes are considered. In the long run—a period sufficient to allow: (1) for investment in such infrastructure as communication media, computational facilities, and buildings and/or (2) for retraining of personnel—the possibilities for reorganization become almost inexhaustible.

The Economics of Reorganization

That *organization affects economic performance* is a truth that dates back to Adam Smith's celebrated observation of the benefits of the division of labor, if not earlier. Contemporary organization theory, management science, and system engineering are all based on this fact. In simple situations, as exemplified by Adam Smith's pin factory, the bearing of organization on quantitative and qualitative indices of performance is often self-evident. It is less so in a more complicated setting, although simulation techniques do offer some possibilities of assessment.[24]

Whether the relationship between organization and output is purely "technical" and direct or of a roundabout "sociopsychological" nature[25] is inconsequential: in either case the state of organization could be legitimately introduced as an explicit variable (of shift parameter) in the production function. If this is sometimes overlooked in the economist's standard formulation of the problem, it is presumably because organization is treated as fixed or because its variability is subsumed under input and/or technology changes. Many economists, as Schumpeter, stress organizational innovation as a separate propellant of economic growth.[26] Organizational improvement is also often accounted for in econometric factor productivity studies.

Even though there is little doubt that the adoption of a different "book of rules" will usually have some consequences for output, growth, and/or other facets of an economy's performance, the praxeology of reorganization is extremely involved.

Several factors must be reckoned with in *any* rational decision to reorganize an economy:

First, reorganization generally entails the use of resources: additional personnel and facilities, outlays on plant modification, rearrangement of files, and so forth. Hence, one might speak of the *installation cost* of an organization (the expense involved in adopting a particular "book of rules").

Secondly, an old organization, decreed out of existence, may have a certain *salvage value*, reflecting the opportunity cost of retrievable resources—personnel, facilities, files, and the like. Conceivably, some of the elements making up the salvage value of a scrapped organization can be negative (not unlike the cost of junking an old car stalled on the highway).[27] The difference between the installation cost and the salvage value is the net *changeover cost* of reorganization.

Thirdly, a newly installed organization does not operate from the start "at full capacity." It takes time to break it in. This can be accounted for by a *learning function*. Conceptually, one can distinguish two aspects of the organizational learning process. The first is the mastering of a new way of doing things, that is, learning proper. The second is the overcoming of resistance to change.[28]

Finally, organizations designed to perform specific tasks (for example, to maximize output) within a given environmental context tend to deteriorate with the passage of time. This may be expressed by a *decay function*. By analogy with biological and economic phenomena, the organizational decay may be notionally broken down into two processes. Insofar as the environment (of which narrowly defined technology constitutes a part) changes, as it ordinarily does, any established organization becomes *obsolete*. The alleged impairment of Soviet-type planning and management by the "square law" falls into this category. Or, to give an example *pro domo sua*, the persistence of the "Keynesian syndrome" (unemployment due to excess saving, sticky interest and wage rates, and so forth) could be interpreted as an obsolescence symptom in the private market economy. In addition, the erosion of organizational efficacy over time may occur because of *depreciation*. What I have in mind is depreciation of *morale* rather than *moral* (or physical) depreciation. There is now universal recognition of human imponderables as an organizational resource.[29] But as organizations age, their participants' morale tends to decline. Several forces are at work in producing this result. Defects and malfunctioning become noticeable as experience in running an organization accumulates, especially when obsolescence is far advanced. Eventually this breeds dissatisfaction and, wherever possible, criticism and demands for change. Gradually the desire for novelty outweighs the security of familiar circumstances. The Schumpeterian description of the decline of capitalist civilization fits this paradigm.[30] Likewise, the current ideological and cultural crisis in the Soviet Union undermines the morale essential for successful operation of the organizational framework established by Stalin. Informal organizational change (evolution) may counteract some of the influences that erode the efficacy of the established institutions (for instance, *blat* and *tolkachi* are a saving grace for the overly centralized supply system), but they cannot entirely eliminate organizational decay so long as the formal arrangements are still observed.

A special kind of "decay" (which is due neither to "obsolescence" nor to "depreciation") may set in when organizational changes are frequent. In this case, familiar to the observer of Soviet-type economies, the cynical disbelief in the permanence of institutions, procedures, and positions can lead to impairment of all organizational functions. The learning processes are slowed down and, in extreme situations, such as that of war communism, organizational structures disintegrate and the most vital activities are paralyzed.

Admittedly, all these concepts are too abstract to serve as a practical guide to reorganization. Nonetheless, they refer to phenomena that cannot be disregarded in truly enlightened social engineering. Theoretically, the problem is analogous to dynamic equipment programming.[31] At all times the decision makers face an array of (what they consider) feasible organizational variants. They have to choose from this collection that also includes the existing state of organization. The decision, which should ideally be made for the whole sequence of replacements, has three aspects: *whether, how,* and *when* to reorganize. To answer these questions, the *verkhushka* should have an idea about the "productivity" of the different organizational setups, their breaking-in characteristics, viability, and net changeover cost. Quite apart from the "objectivity" or "subjectivity" of the premises, a calculated choice of action presents great difficulties.

Even for the simplest social welfare function, and on the most convenient assumptions, the mathematics of a "rational" decision is cumbersome. Moreover, the dynamic optimization problem may have no solution, except for a *predetermined* sequence of reorganizations. This would be the case of optimal timing of specific measures in a long-term reorganization program, as in the timetables for certain East European reforms. Of more interest would be a situation where the organizational changes under consideration are few, and the time horizon is short (for example, when the leaders do not look beyond their political tenure). In such a realistic setting, an optimal reorganization strategy could be determined by trial and error.

Whatever the case, communist leaders would be justly dismayed at the suggestion that formal "model building" ought to guide their organizational reforms. For the praxeology of reorganization has as yet remained an "empty box." Not only do the decision makers lack the required information about organizational variants—their productivity, breaking-in characteristics, decay, and changeover cost—but the acquisition of such data is virtually impossible. Since each reorganization is conducted once and for all, under unique circumstances, the economic terms on which organizational alternatives are given cannot be validated *ex ante* by cross-national or historical comparisons. Direct experiment, short of actual reorganization, is also inapplicable. Thus, a major organizational overhaul is nearly always a gamble with unknown odds or, as Popper describes it, a "holistic experiment."[32] This is why Carl Landauer's skeptical view of communist planners' knowledge and ability to make rational decisions[33] applies with special force to reorganization. If organizational changes in the Soviet Union, and elsewhere in Eastern Europe, were at all economically "rational," they were so only in a trivial, tautological sense—each successive arrangement *must have seemed* superior to the previous state. To claim more for their design would be an imposture.

The substantive rationality of the reorganization decision is unequivocal only on those relatively rare occasions when the established institutions are breaking down and *must* somehow be replaced by different arrangements, for example, Russian war communism and the advanced commune in China had to be abandoned to avert national catastrophe. This can be likened to a weak version of "satisficing" behavior.[34]

The unpredictability of results in large-scale social engineering is exemplified by the failure of the *sovnarkhoz* and the disappointments of the Czech reorganization of 1958. For the Communists, however, the most instructive lesson followed from the revamping of the Yugoslav economy during the early 1950s: the Soviet bloc experts were convinced, at the time, of an imminent collapse of Tito's new institutions. The survival of market socialism should have proved to them how little is known about the workability and efficacy of macro-organization. On the Yugoslav side, too, there was total uncertainty. Tito had little more to go on than vague hopes and a prospect of massive financial assistance from the West.

The economics of reorganization, as I see it, yields little in the way of explanations, predictions, and practical norms. But it sheds some light on the problems raised in this essay.

Regardless of the state of organization, most of the time there are some valid economic grounds for considering changes. The symptoms of organizational decay may be marked, particularly in an economy passing from a preindustrial to an industrial stage. Besides, over time, organizational evolution may give prominence to informal arrangements that must be either eliminated by appropriate reforms or ratified. For one reason or another, there is always the lure of possible improvements to be achieved through reorganization. This is counterbalanced, however, by the economic arguments against reorganization: the changeover cost, the anticipation of continued learning within the existing arrangements, and, more generally, the extreme uncertainty of the results of any change. Whereas the cost and the benefit, incalculable as they are, cannot be equated at the margin, the opposites are easily perceivable and open to debate. Thus, almost always, *there are legitimate causes for an economic controversy over reorganization.* The debate can be suppressed indefinitely, as during Stalin's reign, for political and ideological reasons. Or it can come to the surface, as in the Soviet Union during the 1920s and, most recently, throughout Eastern Europe. It can be public or conducted *in camera* by the bureaucrats. But it never lacks for arguments from both sides.

The issues at stake are many. Economic performance is not judged according to a single yardstick even in private corporations. There are various goals and, consequently, various criteria of evaluation. In the Soviet Union and Eastern Europe, this multitude of goals goes far beyond the competing desires for growth, stability, and distributive justice. In the absence of valuation and coordination through the market mechanism, the bureaucratic "social welfare functions" become disaggregated to the point of absurdity. Hence, there is the notorious profusion of "success indicators" measuring the accomplishment of component units.[35] A variety of partial criteria (and of derivative incentive schemes) applies to physical outputs and inputs, finance, technology, and so on. Both current flows (production, cost, profit) and certain stocks (inventories, debt) are involved in this multiple evaluation. Naturally, the ranking of such diverse dimensions of economic performance is difficult and often impossible. And in the case of conflicting objectives (for instance, quantity versus quality or unit cost versus output size), it usually diverges in various parts and on different levels of the organizational structure. The literature on communist economies abounds in relevant illustrations.[36]

The disappointing scores achieved in one respect or other continually provide arguments for some kind of reorganization. In this way, the fragmentation of economic criteria magnifies the ever-present potential for organizational debates. However, if remedial measures are taken and happen to be successful in rectifying a particular defect, the causes of dissatisfaction change rather than disappear. For each successive stage in the chain of reorganization breeds its own evils.

In reorganizations concerned with the partitioning of the economy, mergers along production lines, through increased scale and diversification of activities, create an opportunity for more flexible utilization of plant and personnel. This improves some facets of performance and, in particular, can be very helpful in inflating, by an appropriate manipulation of assortment, such decisive indicators as the value of gross output or total profit. But inevitably there are some diseconomies of scale that adversely affect cost, quality, or other dimensions of performance. Besides, the simplification of external (intercomponent) networks of communication achieved through such mergers is coupled with greater complexity of communication within the enlarged units. Different problems are bound to arise when bureaus are joined or incorporated into agencies. This type of merger simplifies communication networks throughout and usually facilitates internal coordination, but often at the expense of slackened control over an activity that was previously singled out for special attention.

The net outcome of repartitioning measures is something one cannot generalize about, yet the unending chain of reforms shuffling and reshuffling the communist economic organization testifies to the existence of the cross pressures generated by each move.[37]

This push and pull is also apparent in the rechanneling of communications. Rearrangement of routes (often but not always correlated to changes in the partitioning of the economy) has posed some very real dilemmas. Industrial hierarchies impede regional cooperation between firms, boost transportation costs through cross-hauling of freight, and, more generally, promote inefficient vertical integration. The "empire building" of industrial agencies (deriving its rationale from the overriding importance of supply reliabilty in a seller's market) illustrates vividly the clash between micro- and macro-rationality in communist economies. But if the territorial principle prevails, other undesirable tendencies come to the fore. "Localism," that is, the striving for autarky and preferential treatment of regional needs, may become pronounced. In consequence the overall coordination of activities suffers and central directives, mainly concerning technology and interregional capital transfers, are vitiated by a region-centered administration. The palliative of combining the two principles of organization has never been able to resolve the conflict which, to a greater or lesser extent, has plagued all communist economies. Due to sheer size, the Soviet economy has experienced the greatest difficulties which have, from time to time, prompted pendulumlike swings from industrial to territorial emphasis. The *sovnarkhoz* reform of 1957, which brought in its wake a creeping "re-ministerialization" and, eventually, the reestablishment of the industrial hierarchy in 1965, is the most striking example of the cross pressures at work. But, less dramatically, the same phenomenon has been characteristic of Soviet economic organization since its inception.

A predominant, synthetic criterion, such as profit in the private market economy, would perhaps reduce the potential for institutional instability insofar as it permits a more consistent evaluation of organizational performance. With multiple gauges of success, the incentives for partial or overall reform are strong but confusing and at times result in erratic moves. The organizational dilemma is most pronounced in measures involving changes in the content of messages. Highly specific directives, particularly the commands, are instrumental in concentrating resources in priority sectors. But, as everybody knows nowadays, detailed commands stifle managerial incentives and lead to rigidity in supply and to inefficient production. The substitution of rules for commands makes for more flexibility in day-to-day operation and, with proper pricing and incentives, eradicates much of the waste. Yet, it also unavoidably undermines the effectiveness of central preferences and is incompatible with the all pervasive *ex ante* coordination of activities so long identified with communist planning. If the reliance on rules is associated—as it must be to make sense—with a significant extension of the price system, "marketization" can bring socialism closer to the production frontier, but not without a certain risk of impairing the desired growth, stability, and income distribution. The East European debates have taken notice of these and of other hazards of the market. The Yugoslav experience has demonstrated them in practice.

Today, in East European cafés, socialism is jokingly defined as "the shortest way from capitalism to capitalism" and, for reasons still to be discussed, it may very well be that notwithstanding the risks the communist leaders will eventually "go market." But the halfheartedness of the East European reforms in this direction shows that the road is not clear yet.[38] The Kremlin has shown the greatest reluctance to institute fundamental changes. As one writer concluded, analyzing the recent Soviet reorganizations, "what happened is nothing more than yet another timid adjustment of the existing system of administrative planning . . . masking . . . refusal to face radical reforms."[39] This conservatism should not be ascribed to political factors alone, although politics may indeed be crucial in the process of organizational change. The degree of uncertainty involved in overhauling the entire economic organization is sufficiently high to warrant caution and thus provides the strongest defense for the adherents of the *status quo*. The deeply ingrained mistrust of synthetic performance criteria, together with the proliferation of success indicators which is its logical consequence, obscures the perspective and nurtures the sources of disagreement over reorganization.

The Politics of Reorganization

After the Poznan revolt of June 1956, the future of Soviet-type economic organization in Poland seemed doomed. From Gomulka's famous October speech acknowledging that the "immutable in socialism can be reduced to the abolition of man's exploitation by man,"[40] it was commonly understood that the new leader had pledged himself to the fundamental reforms for which the Poles were clamoring so vehemently. His subsequent actions have only brought disillusionment and belied the openmindedness he professed in matters of organizational detail. Changes have been relatively insignificant; practically speaking, the economic organization installed in the early 1950s remains intact today.[41]

The economic rationale of such delaying tactics has already been discussed. But the story of organizational conservatism does not end there. The truism that economics occupies a "limited place among human interests at large"[42] is singularly pertinent to decisions concerned with economic reorganization. The transition from Soviet-style economic arrangements to, say, "Libermanism" or "Titoism" can hardly be a matter of political indifference. Indeed, within the structure of the communist polity, any but a trivial reorganization constitutes a political issue. By this I mean more than a subject of political disagreements (any issue can be fought over, should there be a debate). Economic organization (and reorganization) has *in itself* a direct bearing upon the nature, distribution, and balance of political power.

The role of economic controls in securing the basis for communist political power has been stressed by various writers, among them Carl Landauer.[43] In fact, its importance is programmatically acknowledged by the Communists themselves. Yet the problem is complex and interesting enough to merit a few additional comments.

The assumption underlying the preceding discussion of organizational engineering is that of the so-called goal model of organization. The sociologists have been increasingly critical of this approach and convincingly so. Instead, they see organizations of every kind primarily as entities striving for survival.[44] Paradoxically, depending on circumstances, this dominant concern for survival may account for contrasting attitudes toward organizational change: seemingly "irrational" conservatism and rigidity on one side and open-minded flexibility on the other. At any rate, it has serious repercussions on the question of reorganization decisions.

The sociologists have also discarded the idea (still lingering in economics) of intraorganizational harmony of interests. It is now acknowledged that in any organization there is rivalry and conflict and that organizational cohesion is always a balance of competitive and cooperative relations. In formal, highly centralized organizations, a truce can usually be enforced, but even then a mutual exchange of services is necessary for the stability and workability of the institutional arrangements. Should the central influence weaken, for whatever reason, imbalances and conflicts come into the open, setting off a process of dislocation and readjustment.[45] That this fully applies to the communist economic organization is quite obvious to all observers of the Soviet Union and Eastern Europe. Constituents of the organizational machinery —planning commissions, ministries, central boards, trusts, firms—have conflicting interests and at all times compete, openly or *sub rosa*, for power, status, and income. Besides, personal rivalries are as ubiquitous and strong as in the corporate world of the West.

In communist societies, as elsewhere, the antagonists in intraorganizational struggle seek external support and legitimization, the more so since they are public officials. Groups competing for tangibles always purport to speak *pro publico bono*, that is, in the interests of efficiency, justice, and so on. Their objectives can best be achieved through reorganization. The top bureaucratic echelon may resist change to keep the contenders in their place or to promote it. Indeed, the same highest echelon can use the device of reorganization to weaken those who challenge the *status quo!* This need not be done aboveboard. Even in a political environment where there is acquiescence in the arbitrary decisions of the directorate (a *politburo* or presidium), public relations may require pretense. Like Samuel Butler's Erewhonians, who often "do not believe or mean things which they profess to regard as indisputable," communist leaders may obfuscate the actual meaning of a move. Thus, for instance, as a result of the *sovnarkhoz* reform the provincial party cadres have in all probability gained the upper hand over the aspiring managers, although the measure was heralded as (and had some appearance of) yielding to the managers' demand for more independence from bureaucratic controls.

Since latent or open conflicts within the economic organization are an everyday occurrence, the existence of grounds for a legitimate controversy (discussed in the preceding section) is most welcome to at least some of the participants. Whenever an appropriate opportunity presents itself, the adversaries readily enter the contest, as in the four-way battle between the planning commission, ministries, central boards, and firms that raged in Poland in 1956–57. That the intraorganizational conflict over reallocation of functions and rewards may genuinely coincide with the requirements of "progress" (improved performance) is of no concern here (although it is the crux of Marxist interpretations). What is important is the availability of forces that are always ready to press for *some* sort of organizational change. Reorganization does not take place, however, at least no major reorganization, unless it is ushered in by a political rift.

Earlier, I intimated my inclination toward the old-fashioned "kremlinological" view of communist politics. Like Robert Conquest, and for similar reasons, I believe that a student of the Soviet Union, or of Eastern Europe, is well advised to follow "the tradition of Suetonius and Procopius and Tacitus, of Machiavelli and St. Simon and Abulfeda,"[46] that is, to interpret events in the historiographical categories of biographies of rulers, court intrigues and camarillas, usurpatory takeovers of power, and the like. That this approach can be as meaningful today, when applied to post-Stalin "collective leadership," as it was when the "personality cult" ruled supreme has been shown in a startling reinterpretation of the Polish October.[47] Most recently, the circumstances of the "anti-Zionist" campaign, which is still going on in Warsaw, point to a classical palace revolution with Caesarist overtones. And despite all the theorizing by the reporters, so does Novotny's fall.

Yet even in the Byzantine milieu of a *politburo*, the realities of economic organization do matter and, therefore, speculations on the politics of reorganization are not out of place.

Simply described, the pragmatic features of communist regimes lie: (a) in the wide and penetrating control over society by a monoparty,[48] and (b) in the subordination of the party to its directorate. To all appearances, the latter is the completely autonomous locus of power. An enormous apparatus of repression safeguards its political monopoly. Ideology, interpreted *ad usum delphini*, serves as an instrument of its legitimization. The interlocking party and state machineries, through a hierarchical chain of command and such "transmission belts" as the unions, youth organizations, and the like, reach into every cell of the society. More mundane means are used, too, to strengthen the hold. The directorate, by narrowing down the scope of direct bargaining between economic units, occupational and functional groups, and regions, reserves the arbitration of conflicts to the party hierarchy. The emergence of interest groups is obstructed so that the hierarchy, as the principal granter of benefits, can more easily manipulate the atomized society. Furthermore, personnel matters at all levels are open to party intervention. The juxtaposition of "red" and "expert" has now lost much of its original sharpness, but a form of economic patronage has replaced earlier revolutionary criteria in selecting executive and managerial personnel. The peculiar institution of *nomenklatura* ("the list of jobs and personnel") secures for the hierarchy the exclusive right to make appointments to key posts throughout the nation. The *nomenklaturnye* cadres (not all of them party members) are moved at will across the board: from job assignments in industry to overall planning, education, military, diplomacy, or . . . sports. Since they can be revoked without notice, favors thus distributed tend to keep their recipients in line. Moreover, the directorate's privileged clientele forms an extensive network of personal identifications and loyalties without which no leadership can operate effectively. In this manner, the ruling group's vested interest in the suppression of dissent and the prevention of political challenge is internalized as a "survival value"[49] by large numbers of dependent personnel.

However, neither the directorate nor its auxiliary hierarchy is a self-contained monolithic entity. For one thing, only too humanly, they are internally divided by personal animosities, competitive ambitions, and differences of opinion. More fundamentally, despite the tremendous power they wield, the directorate and the party hierarchy are not extraneous in their relationship to other segments of the socioeconomic organization. Directly or indirectly, they are a part of it—within rather than above the organizational bureaucracy.

Regular supervision of the various links of economic organization by party delegates, especially those with administrative assignments (ministers, directors, and the like), demands that they lead dual lives. Like Lenin's *seredniak* ("middle peasants"), they must have two souls. Even though their function is in principle that of overlordship, the supervisors cannot help becoming submerged in their fief. The nexus is truly dialectical. Successful execution of the party trust is often the condition of political survival. However, the cooperation and loyalty of subordinate personnel cannot be elicited by pressures and sermons alone. High performance depends on good will, and support on mutual give-and-take, and consequently a degree of organizational "patriotism" is indispensable for success. Hence, the understandable proclivity of party nominees to enter into unholy alliances with their underlings. And, for this reason, a *politburo* or central committee member acting as a lobbyist for the bureaucracy under his control frequently does it out of selfish motives, apart from any sympathy he may harbor. The lower his political rank, or to put it differently, the smaller the organizational segment supervised, the stronger this tendency to cross identification. Only an absolute despot, like Stalin in his later years, can remain aloof from all such associations.

Thus, on top of factional alignments (which however well concealed have always been as much a fact of communist politics as of Western democracies), there exist within the high party echelons various "organizational" divisions: central planners versus ministers, bureaucrats versus managers, heavy industry men versus light industry men, and so forth. These divisions lend themselves to uneasy coalitions, generally transient by nature and sensitive to the slightest shift in personal involvement. Yet their ability to materialize rapidly in response to a conducive political situation has been amply demonstrated in Poland in 1956, in the Soviet Union in 1957, and more recently in Czechoslovakia.

Lest this amateurish foray into political sociology be taken for an espousal of the "interest group" (or "pluralistic") model of communist politics,[50] I must qualify my remarks. In accordance with my penchant for "kremlinology," the ramifications of the foregoing are so limited as to border on triviality. Plainly, my point is that the party, including its highest echelon, is *intrinsically* embroiled in conflicts that occur within the economic organization. Consequently, when faced with the complexities and uncertainties of reorganization, the political leaders of the Soviet Union and other East European countries, as an *iudex in causa sua,* can hardly afford to act with Olympian impartiality. For some of them reorganization entails survival, advancement, or demise. Therefore, far from being a matter of detached analysis and social engineering alone, the disputability of reorganization invariably serves as political tinder. Of this there is incontrovertible evidence in times of crisis, and especially during the succession scramble that follows Number One's death or removal from power.

I need not elaborate on this. Suffice it to stress the close coincidence of intensified organizational debates (and of reorganization itself!) with the infighting that took place among the successors of Lenin, Stalin, Khrushchev, and Bierut. If, as one may suspect, Gomulka is at present finally on his way out in Poland, the reopening of a fierce organizational controversy can also be expected there before long. I even venture to predict such an eventuality. Should this scenario be endorsed by history, it will also substantiate the main gist of my speculations, that *reorganization is a somewhat erratic by-product of power struggle, rather than its cause.* All three factions engaged in the Polish power struggle—the remnants of the "Pulawy group," Gomulka's center, and Moczar's "partisans" —are known for their *immobilisme* in matters of economic organization. And yet, Poland will probably attain the long-awaited radical reform in the course of their conflict. This paradoxical effect will be due to the "partisans' " relentless attacks against the remaining bastions of "Pulawian" strength in the central economic bureaucracy, as well as to the concessions that all the contestants are likely to make—in an attempt to gain popular support—to the reform-mongering *intelligentsia.* An additional contributory factor may be provided by the general disorientation and chaos which usually accompany political upheaval.

The toppling of Novotny in Czechoslovakia has given the semblance of an opposite chain of causation. Here, according to most reports, the reform of economic organization was directly and explicitly at stake: Novotny was openly against the reform, whereas the incoming new guard (Dubcek and others) went on the record as its supporters. But again, one must not take things at face value. Behind Novotny's fall lies a drama of bizarre intrigues, conspiracy, and betrayal in the best Kremlin tradition. It is known, for instance, that the crucial (tied) vote of the party presidium, which sealed Novotny's fate, was decided by the sudden volte-face of "the ideological dictator, Hendrych . . . a reactionary . . . (who) also had a long-standing grudge against his boss."[51] Then there was also the mysterious role of the army brass (Sejna, Janko). Most important of all, however, the chief impetus to the anti-Novotny movement appears to have originated in Slovak nationalism, which has no logical connection with a "marketization" reform that is bound to favor the more-developed regions of Bohemia and Moravia. Finally, Dubcek's new team includes some worn-out political figures. Svoboda's presidency is mainly an honorific post, a gesture to placate the Russians. But the appointment of the bureaucrat Cernik (by no means an economic reformer) as premier signifies the probability of a real compromise.

Much study in depth will be necessary to unravel the whole story of Prague's "revolution within the revolution," and we may have to wait until the party's secret archives are opened before any conclusive answers can be reached. But as yet I see no compelling argument to revise my view that communist economic reorganization is intimately bound up with the vagaries of *realpolitik*.

Nevertheless, to maintain that policy problems, such as reorganization, *cannot be* at the bottom of intraparty divisions and power struggle would be doctrinaire. Under certain conditions they could conceivably become decisive, but historically they have not been so in any major instance. The Procrustean quality of the issue-centered approach to communist politics is best illustrated by the cynical shifts in Stalin's early political alignments and by his subsequent quasi-Trotskyite domestic policies. Gomulka's ascendancy to power, backed inchoately by "liberals" and "conservatives" alike, provides another illustration. Issues, apart from survival issues, shed little light on the nature of the compromise reached by the strife-torn Polish directorate in the fall of 1956. Finally, the spectacle of the "Pulawians"—who were notorious for their vociferously and staunchly Stalinist past—turning "ultraliberal" en masse is another case in point. In each of these instances the logic of power is transparent, whereas the relationship to issues, including those of economic organization, escapes systematic categorization.

Similarly, a consistent "interest group" approach is inadequate. No communist leadership has permitted the representatives of diverse interests the degree of aggregation, integration, and autonomy that are necessary to a genuinely pluralistic society. Groups and factions no doubt exist, but they operate primarily on sufferance or by default of the official guardians of party unit, without solid institutional foundations, and contrary to the still sacrosanct ideological orthodoxy. Furthermore, they are more akin to coteries and cliques than to the more stable entities of modern politics that are rooted in the socioeconomic structure. By contrast, communist groups are heterogeneous clusters of men thrown together through momentary expediency and/or biographical accident. Such groups lack permanency and are often politically incongruous, volatile in their avowed programmatic commitments, and generally unpredictable. Beria's reportedly "liberal" leanings were certainly contrary to be vested interests of the security apparatus that was his power base. The previously mentioned "Pulawians" in Poland have shown a remarkable ability to sever their commitments to Stalinism, "command economy," and Moscow. Only personal ties based on a common experience (Jewish background, wartime sojourn in the Soviet Union) have kept together this now decimated but once powerful force of the Polish party.

"The social structure and the State are continually evolving out of the life-process of definite individuals, but of individuals . . . as they really are; i.e. as they are effective . . . and are active under definite material limits, pre-suppositions and conditions independent of their will"

—wrote young Marx.[52] Under the historical conditions of the Soviet Union and East Europe, where political—and not so long ago, physical—survival at the top have depended chiefly on one's skill at cynical maneuvering, all politics degenerated to personal *realpolitik.*

The characteristic fusion of political and economic power under communist regimes has amplified the usual economic repercussions of politics to a point where the issue of reorganization becomes inseparable from the *kto kogo* ("who whom") of party purges. This has added elements of fortuitousness to intractability to social engineering. Communist economic reorganizations can, on occasion, spur efficiency or otherwise promote purely economic causes. This is *always* their avowed objective. Still it would be inappropriate to judge the "rationality" of organizational change by economic criteria alone. Mannheim's methodological directive that "no assessment of efficiency is possible without first asking 'Efficiency for what?' "[53] must be kept in mind by anyone dealing with the problem. If one were to consider *Gosplan's* downgrading in 1949 on strictly economic grounds, the measure would appear misguided. If anything, the Soviet economy such as it was required more, not less, centralized coordination at the time of postwar reconstruction. However, if Stalin had resolved—out of sheer paranoia or for other reasons—to demolish Voznesensky and his associates politically, the resultant weakening of the planning apparatus may seem a purposeful enough step.

The political background of Gomulka's cold shouldering of Polish economic reformers is even more revealing. The 1956–57 crisis was caused by a confluence of economic and political factors. Among them, no doubt, was the malfunctioning of the "command economy," but inefficiency and waste, although clearly discernible to all, were merely an additional irritant to the situation. They were ridiculed and scorned and, I think, secretly a bit cherished as a proof of the incompetence of an unpopular regime. Yet other issues were certainly of major importance. Not the least of these fell into the political sphere epitomized by the strong feelings of Polish nationalism and the deep resentment of crude Soviet domination. As to the economic grounds for discontent, they were to be found in the grand strategy of forced-draft industrialization or, more generally, in the whole economic policy pursued by the party. The achievements of the Six-Year Plan were almost unnoticed, and the sacrifices it imposed on society came to be universally resented. The official cant contributed to this in no small measure; for instance, the regime had never admitted Soviet exploitation (in the form of underpriced "reparation deliveries" of coal) or the extent of military burdens required by the Warsaw Pact. Another taboo issue was that of the extensive economic privileges enjoyed by the elite, but everyone in Poland knew of the "shops behind yellow curtains" where desirable goods were sold at reduced prices to a select group, while workers' wives stood in queues for life's bare necessities and often went home empty-handed.

The opportunity for venting grievances was seized in 1956, when the party was paralyzed by factional strife. I have already mentioned the ensuing flood of criticism, yet it is worth stressing that neither this criticism nor the demands for change were limited to the technicalities that preoccupy economists. What was at stake during those memorable months went far beyond pricing formulas, methods of allocation, managerial decentralization, and such. The public cares little for all this. As still defined in Eastern Europe today, "socialism" itself was at stake: the legitimacy of one-party rule. Also Polish relations with the Soviet Union were in jeopardy. Gomulka was only able to prevent violence in the streets because of his newly acquired image of the national hero defying Soviet tanks. Later, by pointing to Budapest and by appealing to the instinct for national survival, he succeeded in eliciting popular support in the 1957 elections. But the new leader was aware that these were incomplete victories. The party was still divided and incapable of controlling the situation. Its *apparat* was disoriented, the secret police demoralized, and the general administration in a state of semichaos. The economic bureaucracy and the "command system" were much needed to restore the center's authority over this post-October flux. To overhaul them there and then would have appreciably complicated an already difficult task. Therefore, basic reforms were postponed indefinitely. But naturally, as stabilization progressed, resistance to change was nourished by other influences too, and the central bureaucracy, once it had recovered from the shock, found its main ally in the fundamental inertia of the system.

One frequently comes across the view that Gomulka made a serious political mistake in shelving a radical economic reform after October 1956. I think this common belief is based on a misunderstanding. Gomulka, now as then, has two overriding aims: first, to preserve the one-party dictatorship and, second, to steer Poland safely between the Scylla and Charybdis of local geopolitics. Both goals were probably better served in 1956–57 by the chosen course of action than they would have been by the kind of reform that was hoped for by the bolder economists. I have already mentioned the domestic rationale for preserving the existing economic order. As to external maneuvering, a show of conservatism did much to assuage Soviet anxieties. Perhaps it was also helpful in obtaining from the Russians economic concessions consisting of renunciation of "unequal trade" and cancellation of old Polish debts which were both of considerable political value as well. Finally, the public's dissatisfaction with the state of the economy was much diminished by Gomulka's acquiescence in decollectivization, his new farm program, and his promise of a consumer-oriented policy that could be carried out *within* the framework of central planning. To underwrite the risks of "marketization" in view of all this might have seemed not only bad politics but also poor economics, regardless of the intrinsic merits of such an overhaul. But again, to delay basic reforms for more than a decade, as Gomulka has done, may still turn out to be politically disastrous, even if it is not so economically. When, under "partisan" pressure, Gomulka rids the Warsaw party and state apparatus of the last "Zionist" associated with the cause of economic reform, Moczar may yet try to overthrow him under the banner of reform. Such is the dialectic of communist *realpolitik*.

Toward a Theory of Reorganizations?

What then is the paradigm of organizational change in communist economies? Has the historical record borne out the previously outlined hypotheses? And, above all, to what degree has Marxian optimism—the faith in the rationality of the postcapitalist order—withstood the test of practice? These questions defy clear-cut analysis. In gathering up the threads of speculation and fact, I draw some tentative conclusions.

Perhaps the most important is the recognition of a commonplace: the *economic* organization of the Soviet Union and Eastern Europe has been an integral part of their *political* structure. Two corollaries follow from this.

To begin with, since the populace of the countries involved has been notoriously resentful of or, at best, apathetically resigned to communist minority rule, such economic props to social discipline as bureaucratic hierarchy, administrative central planning, reliance on "command," restrictions on managers and unions, and so forth, have been *politically* functional. Economically they may have been detrimental; still, given the fact that neither repression nor indoctrination is by itself capable of safeguarding the powers usurped by the Communists, the economic strait jacket has performed a political function which, in the absence of more spontaneous social mechanisms for cohesion and equilibrium, should not be underrated. Whether these dictatorial regimes could effectively preserve their position outside the context of Soviet-like economic organization, for example, under some form of "market socialism," is as yet uncertain. Both the Soviet NEP and the Yugoslav experiment[54] cast some doubt on this. And, curiously enough, the Chinese political turmoil, erupting after a *sui generis* economic decentralization, also gives grounds for skepticism.

The second corollary grows out of the internal structure of communist regimes. The interlocking of the party *apparat* with the machinery of economic administration has the effect of suppressing organizational controversy and conflict in times of enforced party "unity," as under Stalin's ossified dictatorship and that of his East European satraps. But under "collective leadership," with its periodic power struggles, just the opposite tendency manifests itself strongly. Political rivalries and feuds, interwoven with intraorganizational conflict, undermine institutional stability. Economic controversies flare up, escalated and even exploited by clashing interests. The issues may, of course, be germane enough, but the push and pull of cliques is likely to detract from the merits of their resolution. As in the anecdotal case of Cleopatra's nose, the personal prejudice and expediency of a handful of well-placed men can influence a nation's pattern of economic organization. This is typified by the complete latitude in shaping the Polish "command economy" enjoyed by the triumvirate Minc-Szyr-Jedrychowski between 1949 and 1956. The allocational priorities were subject to scrutiny by the whole *politburo* (and, on strategic issues, by Moscow), but in such lesser matters as partitioning the economy, designing the framework of planning, and so forth, the trio's authority was virtually unlimited. This manner of creating institutions does not necessarily prevent their viability and, indeed, opportuneness. Nonetheless, save on Hegelian assumptions (that existence is rational, and rationality exists), it would be impossible to vindicate the scientific basis and eudaemonic purpose of social engineering undertaken in such a situation.

Nor are there any firm grounds on which to base a theory of socialist "stages." Whether implied by technological or policy determinism, a *Stufenlehre* ignores the historic uniqueness of and the voluntarism in the emergence of Soviet-type economic organization. Admittedly, the prototype of the "command economy" has been used rather successfully to launch a semiagrarian society into an industrial takeoff. But to argue, as have Deutscher, Nove, and others,[55] that it was a "necessary" or "inevitable" stage in Soviet development is either a tautology ("what is, must be") or metaphysics (to be put in the same category with Hegel's theurgy of rationality). In more down-to-earth terms, the alleged correspondence between the Soviet model of organization and its technological-productive bases has never been ascertained. No doubt many options must have existed in matters of organizational detail. The zigzagging course of Soviet reforms is evidence of this. Furthermore, the possibility that a drastically different mode of organization, for example, a guided market economy, would have worked as well cannot be excluded either.

Power politics was invariably involved in the choices. But ideology —in the Marxian sense of false consciousness—played a part, too. Especially weighty was the impact of Marx's obsessive mistrust of the "elemental chaos" of the market and, by association, of all economic decentralization. The labor theory of value has also had definite organizational repercussions insofar as the physical rationing of producer goods is a logical consequence of pricing that is divorced from scarcity. In general, the Soviet dislike of "bourgeois" theory and practice—an attitude that owes as much to Slavophiles and *narodniki* as to *Das Kapital*—has left a pernicious imprint.

On this, let me quote the sympathetic criticism by Oscar Lange. Having noted the shocking "extent of sacrifices in the standard of living and in political freedom which the Soviet government imposed upon its people," Lange continues: "It may be argued, of course, that with a choice of different techniques of economic policy, the same objectives might have been achieved at a much lower economic cost and also at a lower cost in human values. Very probably this is true. Most of the techniques of economic administration were discovered by the Soviet government through a process of trial and error. Techniques of economic administration well familiar to the 'bourgeois' economists . . . were rejected contemptuously by the Soviet administrators . . . [because of] ideological suspicions."[56] The cited passage (from a eulogy of Russia's war effort) rightly emphasizes the accidental and arbitrary factors in Soviet economic design. The feats of industrialization notwithstanding, the peculiar economic institutions of Russian communism were the creation of a misinformed fiat.

Leaving the Russian conundrum aside, no one could seriously maintain that technological and/or economic considerations have necessitated the adoption of uniform Soviet-like patterns of organization elsewhere in Eastern Europe. Although this is still glossed over in official mythology— and surprisingly also by some unorthodox writers[57]—the sovietization of the "people's democracies" was but a concomitant of international *realpolitik* in the postwar period of Soviet expansion. The notoriety of methods employed by Stalin in his promotional campaign precludes any speculation on this subject. Here too, and clearly so, historical accident rather than structural requirements dictated the shape of economic organization. The fact that the uniform Soviet-like pattern was forced upon countries of such structural diversity and disparate economic-technological levels merely brings out the arbitrary and voluntaristic nature of the initial organizational "stage" of East European socialism.

Regardless of its origins, once a functioning economic organization gives rise to its own "necessities" and "inevitabilities." Wiles's *Political Economy of Communism* revolves around the idea that "there is such a thing as the logic of institutions."[58] What I am proposing here is that institutions have dynamics of their own as well. Heuristically, this would be a kind of *organizational determinism*—an extension of Carl Landauer's suggestion to which I referred earlier.

The economics of this problem has been incisively analyzed by Ward.[59] Among his conclusions, one is of particular interest here: "The

Soviet system is relatively stable with respect to organizational change, except for a tendency toward a cyclical organizational response to information flows about performance. For example, secondary control organizations tend to proliferate in the leadership's effort to improve information about performance. A point is reached, however, beyond which additional organizations reduce the leadership's knowledge of performance, thus creating pressure for return to a simpler set of organizations."[60]

I take the "relative stability" of which Ward speaks to refer to the resistance to such drastic changes that would amount to self-liquidation of the "command economy." In lesser (but not necessarily negligible) matters, there have obviously been recurrent pressures for reorganization, that is, a tendency toward institutional *instability*. Ward's "cyclical organizational response" falls under the rubric of changes resulting from the already discussed interplay of economics, intraorganizational conflict, and politics.

The "response," that is, the reorganization, has been limited by considerations of economic uncertainty and political expediency. Outside of Yugoslavia, communist social engineering has shown a characteristic bias toward the conservation, replication, and proliferation of bureaucratic hierarchies and administrative measures. This is due to the influence of existing institutions on institutional change, or what I have rather loosely described as "organizational determinism." Poland may serve as *pars pro toto* to illustrate the problem.

The chronic malfunctioning of the Polish economy had already prompted various remedial measures in the early 1950s. However, with the basic features of Soviet-type organization considered sacrosanct, the reforms could only deal with the symptoms of the malaise rather than with its etiology. Over the years, the economic agencies of the government have undergone an almost continuous reorganization. New ministries and central administrations were created, sometimes only to be abolished after a short period. Existing agencies were divided or merged. The scope of activities of the various parts of the bureaucratic machine was constantly being defined and redefined. There was also much traffic in top personnel—usually a game of musical chairs played by a select group of political appointees. In an economy that must have an "office" for everything, this kind of permanent reorganization might have seemed an appropriate response to its difficulties. But, in practice, it did not work. Sometimes the changes involved little more than giving new names to old institutions, as, for example, the transformation of the State Commission for Economic Planning (PKPG) into the Commission for Planning (KP) at the Council of Ministers in 1956. Usually they were more substantive, though, as I mentioned before, the solution of one problem often meant the creation of two new ones. As a rule, the reshuffling of the bureaucratic apparatus merely attested to the universality of Parkinson's law. In any case, the frequency and erratic nature of organizational change were sufficient proof of its futility.

Most of the reforms in planning, management, and finance have been equally ineffective. Procedural changes, timetable rearrangements, aggregation and disaggregation of targets, and similar measures of which there were so many during the 1950s had only a marginal impact on the style and content of planning. Indeed, the observer must often have felt like a visitor to a wonderland; the more things changed, the more they seemed the same. Perhaps this should not have struck anyone as surprising. After all, the "command economy" was a reality, a working system, and not without its own logical coherence. As such it was bound to exhibit a considerable resilience. Its objectives were centrally defined by a direct specification of gross outputs *and* final demands. The various material (and similar) balances served as a consistency check. The data on technology were constantly verified through the peculiar information-generating process of administrative "bargaining" in which the center pressed for more output and less input, and the lower echelons for the opposite. Whether this type of allocation was "not inherently wasteful or theoretically unsound," as suggested in an early article by Montias,[61] is debatable. As the means for steering the economy toward its set goals it did the job, but it required a preponderance of physical targets, innumerable material balances, and frequent administrative intervention. Serious difficulties arose when, for some reason, the planners lacked (or gave up) direct control over any part of the input-output mechanism. In a quasi-natural economy of primal programming there was little room for decentralized decision making and initiative which were expected to fill the void. The economic directors (Minc, Szyr, Jedrychowski, and the lesser figures) may have tried to delegate some of their responsibilities. They had certainly shown genuine enthusiasm for firms' "counterplans" and for other forms of grass-root participation encouraged by the slogans of "democratic centralism" in planning. But without more fundamental changes in the "command economy," these attempts to lighten the burden of minutiae in central planning and to release managerial initiative were doomed, as clearly illustrated by the failure of the reforms that were introduced between 1955 and 1958. It was easy enough to delete from the plan a few details, such as the ridiculous "target" for the procreation of wild rabbits (this really happened!). But more significant reductions of central controls and physical allocation procedures were hampered from the start by the defective price structure. The doctrinaire attitude toward pricing has been a major obstacle to a constructive reform of Polish planning. In this respect at least, Marxian economics, with its insistence on the labor theory of value that was translated into "average cost plus" pricing of producer goods, *did* exercise an undeniable influence on practical affairs. Essentially, it acted as a stabilizer of the "command" system, thus fortifying the vested interest of the bureaucracy.

Another tool deployed to rid the economy of its ills was the campaigns. Periodically, to the accompaniment of loud propaganda, Polish managers and workers were reminded of the importance of such things as "cost reduction," "economizing on raw materials," "higher productivity," "high quality of products," and most of all "the fulfillment and overfulfillment of production targets." Much of this had no more than a nuisance value. Other campaigns, waged on special occasions, such as "the intensification of the class struggle against the *kulaks*" and "the battle for improvement in the discipline of labor" during the early 1950s, conveyed important information about the regime's intentions. But no amount of what the Poles have cynically come to call *dretwa gadka* ("numb speech") could improve organizational performance. Actually, contrary to the regime's expectations, things seemed rather to be getting worse. Nevertheless, the combination of allied political and bureaucratic interests with organizational inertia has forestalled radical changes to date.

Even the 1965 reform has barely touched the edifice of the "command economy." Not only is the reform half-hearted in its intention but its implementation has consisted of long drawn out partial moves that reinforce the self-protective "servomechanism" of administrative central planning. With material balances, etc., still at the core of the allocation processes, the bureaucratic propensity to counter any undesirable by-product of partial decentralization by imposing new (or reimposing old) direct controls must take the upper hand. This may be termed the Law of Self-preservation of Bureaucratic Organization, another variation on the familiar Parkinson theme. It would seem that a "minimum critical effort" is necessary to dispose of the economic legacies of Stalinism. Neither technological change nor multiplication of policy objectives is by itself sufficient warranty that the critical level of effort will be forthcoming. And, unless one is prepared to generalize from the very recent and still inconclusive evidence of the latter-day reform movement, rather than from fifty years of experience, there is no indication that communist leaders can undertake it as a project in scientific social engineering.

The Prospects for the Future:
A Conclusion

The 1960s have marked the end of organizational uniformity in the communist world. Eastern Europe and the Soviet Union are in flux. Their leaders profess an interest in a self-regulatory market mechanism, although in this respect the official proposals, let alone the actual reforms, do not parallel the radical solutions adopted by Tito's Yugoslavia. It would be premature to predict the outcome of these trends.[62] But, in my view, technological and/or economic reasons alone do not adequately explain the incipient movement toward "marketization" of East European socialism.

The defects of Soviet-type planning and management are as grave as ever, but the inefficiency and wastefulness must at present be *less* rather than more burdensome than in the past when output hovered closer to the subsistence level. As to the alleged imperatives of the "square law" and the multiplication of policy goals, they complicate the process of administrative planning and management, but not beyond the hope of handling the added difficulties with a *moderate* application of computers and mathematical programming techniques.[63] And consumer-oriented policies could also be implemented directly by the center, if intelligent use were made of market surveys and demand studies.

The within-the-system reforms required for the streamlining of the "command economy" would probably be inferior to a *smoothly working* market. They would admittedly be costly, although in the short run perhaps less so than total reorganization. Yet these are hardly decisive considerations. The communist leaders have never striven for (or, for that matter, comprehended) economic optimality, and I doubt whether they do now. The reasons for a cataclysmic overhaul of the entire economic organization have always been political.

The conversion of the relatively backward Yugoslavia into a quasi-syndicalist version of market socialism came following Tito's expulsion from the Cominform and was as much an act of political defiance vis-à-vis Moscow as an economic experiment. Today, too, "marketization" schemes are a symptom of the decomposition of communist polities as much as an attempt at economic rationalization.

Communist economies are doing badly, but not disastrously so. Despite the temporary setback during the early 1960s, their traditional organization is still a vehicle of creditable growth (averaging 3 percent to 5 percent a year according to conservative estimates). The "routinization of economic growth," emphasized by Grossman, is now, as before, the fundamental "organizational innovation" of Soviet-style socialism.[64] Moreover, there is also a visible improvement in the consumer market, both in quantity and in quality of supplies. Even central planning and management show some signs of progress (although politically paralyzed Poland is a notorious exception). Foreign trade is expanding too, and if unsatisfactorily it is clearly because of the lack of exportable surpluses (due to the lopsided development of the area rather than to current failings of economic organization). Why then the sudden fascination with dramatic economic reform? And why, in particular, the inroads made by the proponents of the market?

It has been pointed out that "the growth and modernization of any economy that is already organized on the command principle renders the maintenance of balance progressively more difficult, and therefore militates for strengthening of this principle, particularly in the form of further centralization."[65] Although I see no insurmountable technical or economic obstacles to such a solution, I feel that politics will bar the road to further centralization.

The long-range aftereffects of the de-Stalinization campaign have wrought irreparable damage to the protective strata of the "command economy." Ideology is in decline everywhere in Eastern Europe. And so is political terror. Even in countries like Poland, which have witnessed a resurgence of cruder ideological pressures and police activity, the re-Stalinization is shallow: rulers as well as ruled know this. Indeed its symptoms seem well nigh grotesque, thus attesting to the wisdom of Marx's observation that in repeating itself the tragedy of history becomes a farce.

Nowhere in Eastern Europe, with the apparent exceptions of Albania and Rumania, have the party directors succeeded in reestablishing the internal cohesion upset by the developments that were triggered by Khrushchev's secret speech at the Twentieth Congress of the CPSU. The "pecking order" in the assorted *politburos* and presidia is nowadays unstable and uncertain. The new communist *realpolitik* is that of checks and balances among "collective leaders." The organizational complement of this delicate political equilibrium is a progressive fragmentation of authority (including economc decision making), fostered as a safeguard against a takeover à la Stalin, Bierut, or Rakosi. In this new environment ministries can challenge the planning commissions, central boards and trusts can defy ministries, and so on down the hierarchical line. Even though the old system shows resistance to change and, in many instances, defeats partial reform measures,[66] it is visibly weakening. The opening of new informal channels of communication and the changes in the content of messages are gradually eroding central planning from within.

The manifest disunity and the resultant weakening of the communist leadership opens the gates to social pressures incompatible with the strict regimen of Soviet-type economic organization. Not only is the public's yearning for liberalization and "marketization" exploited by groups and factions (for example, the new Czech leadership) against political rivals. Once in full swing, popular sentiment is hard to contain and the Communists may find themseves in the situation of the sorcerer's apprentice. In this respect, the "societal hypothesis" has some relevance in explaining the turn away from the "command economy." But, at the risk of boring the reader, I repeat that the ultimate cause of changes lies in the *realpolitik* within the small circle of leaders, and not in the larger social forces that entered the poitical scene in the post-Stalin succession crisis. On this I am in full agreement with the conclusions reached by Rostow according to whom "without change or conflict at the top . . . we can expect no dramatic overt reflection of these [social] forces, all of which have arisen from the dynamics of . . . evolution but lie outside the capabilities of the regime wholly to control."[67]

On the international level, too, the evolving bloc *realpolitik* works against further centralization. The centuries-old East European nationalism is once again on the rise, and the Soviets seem to have lost their ability to bring the satellites in line. As in the case of Tito's Yugoslavia or, for that matter, of China, a radical departure from the Soviet organizational model is a symbol and not only a result of regained national independence. (This also makes it an effective way to bid for popular support within the East European countries.) Rumania, combining Latin unpredictability with the windfalls from her oil trade, may for the moment be the excepton. On the whole, however, the boldness of the sundry reform programs could well serve as an index of East European emancipation from Soviet rule.

One widely held view connects the East European interest in "marketism" with the necessities of foreign trade. This may be important, especially in the smaller and more developed countries, like Czechoslovakia and Hungary. Yet it must not be forgotten that the present sense of need for multilateral and flexible international commerce cannot be separated from the virtual breakdown of COMECON. Growing "polycentrism" renders supranational coordination of planning under Soviet dictates unworkable, and the market, international and domestic, is seen as the only feasible substitute. This, too, is a by-product of the bloc's new *realpolitik*. Were the Kremlin still in full command of Eastern Europe, the COMECON-directed "cooperation and specialization" would have remained an additional stabilizer of the established economic organization.

In short, the *élan vital* of the "command economy" has been spent everywhere in Eastern Europe, not excluding the Soviet Union and Rumania. Therefore, however serviceable, the existing organizational structure will eventually be replaced.

One could think of many theoretically feasible modes of organization with which to replace the Stalinesque edifice. Still, the gaze of communist reformers seems to be fixed on the once-maligned market mechanism whose economic advantages and administrative simplicity have now been rediscovered by the East Europeans.[68] It should be stressed, however, that the theoretical recognition of the benevolence of the "invisible hand" is only one of the stimuli to reform. Centrifugal forces of a purely political nature are even more important. In fact, it is precisely because of the political crisis that the market has been rediscovered at all. Before 1956 both the theoretical literature of the Lange-Lerner variety and the manifest viability of market economies (including Yugoslavia) went totally unnoticed by the present advocates of "marketism."[69] Today, by contrast, the attraction of self-steering demand and supply is overriding many a serious warning voiced by the theoretical opponents of "marketization."[70]

Market socialism of one kind or another seems to be slowly gaining ground, despite local setbacks caused by remaining ideological idiosyncrasies, organizational inertia, and vested bureaucratic interests. Its progress marks the disintegration of the traditional communist polity and, by feedback, accelerates the centrifugal tendencies within the East European countries and in the bloc as a whole. Unless, through an unforeseeable turn of history, the *ancien régime* is reconstituted, the future organization of the communist economies may yet come dangerously close to that of contemporary capitalism. Thus, ironically, half a century of social engineering will have brought the postcapitalist society back to its point of departure.

Postscript

This essay was written in 1966 and revised in April 1968. The subsequent developments in Eastern Europe require a postscript. First, I may have underestimated the importance of issues (political liberalization and economic reform) in the overthrow of Novotny and the rise of the Dubcek leadership. Indeed, for the first time in history, we witnessed a situation approaching a self-liquidation of a communist regime. Second, I have overemphasized the change in the *realpolitik* of the communist world: the Soviet Union is willing and able to intervene *manu militari* in other communist countries. But, if anything, these events reconfirm my views. I believe that the gist of the argument of this essay still stands.

Footnotes

[1] J. Stalin, *Problems of Leninism* (Moscow: Foreign Languages Publishing House, 1954), p. 802.

[2] K. Marx and F. Engels, *Selected Correspondence 1846–1895* (New York: International Publishers, 1942), pp. 475–77.

[3] C. Landauer, *European Socialism. A History of Ideas and Movements from the Industrial Revolution to Hitler's Seizure of Power* (Berkeley: University of California Press, 1959), p. 145.

[4] See, for instance, Bergson's statement on Soviet reforms in A. Balinsky

et al., Planning and the Market in the USSR: The 1960's (New Brunswick: Rutgers University Press, 1967). Similar views have now become a part of public thinking on communist economies in general, see "New Economic Strategies in Eastern Europe" in the First National City Bank, N.Y., *Monthly Economic Letter* (October, 1965).

[5] Z. Frank and J. Waelbroeck, "Soviet Economic Policy Since 1953: A Study of Its Structure and Changes," *Soviet Studies*, XVII, No. I (1965), 31.

[6] R. Campbell, "On the Theory of Economic Administration," *Industrialization in Two Systems. Essays in Honor of Alexander Gerschenkron*, ed. H. Rosoksky (New York: John Wiley & Sons, Inc., 1966).

[7] Z. Frank and J. Waelbroeck, *op. cit.*, p. 29.

[8] R. Campbell, *op. cit.*, pp. 192–93.

[9] This corresponds to the "goal model" in A. Etzioni, "Two Approaches to Organizational Analysis: A Critique and a Suggestion," *Administrative Science Quarterly*, V, No. 2 (1960), 258–60.

[10] P. J. D. Wiles, *The Political Economy of Communism* (Cambridge: Harvard University Press, 1964), p. 50.

[11] A. Nove, *The Soviet Economy. An Introduction*, rev. ed. (New York: Frederick A. Praeger, Inc., 1966), pp. 66–67.

[12] E. Crankshaw, *Khrushchev's Russia* (Baltimore: Penguin Books, Inc., 1959), esp. Chap. 3.

[13] See R. Conquest, *Power and Policy in the USSR: The Study of Soviet Dynastics* (London: Macmillan & Co. Ltd., 1961) for a cogent statement of the "kremlinological" position.

[14] D. Bell, *The End of Ideology. On the Exhaustion of Political Ideas in the Fifties* (New York: Collier Books, 1961), Chap. 14. Contains a useful survey of theories dealing with Soviet reality.

[15] See his *Revolution Betrayed* (New York: Pioneer Publishers, 1957).

[16] N. Wiener, *The Human Use of Human Beings. Cybernetics and Society*, 2nd ed., rev. (Garden City: Doubleday & Company, Inc., 1954), p. 21.

[17] J. W. Forrester, "The Changing Face of Industry—The Role of Industrial Dynamics," *Report to Management*, No. 11 (Graduate School of Business Administration, University of Southern California, 1964).

[18] R. Campbell, *op. cit.*, p. 203.

[19] T. G. March and H. A. Simon, *Organizations* (New York: John Wiley & Sons, Inc., 1958), p. 1.

[20] Campbell, *op. cit.*, p. 188. Note, however, that I distinguish sharply between the "technological" and "organizational" constraints on the "system of production possibilities."

[21] L. Hurwicz, "Conditions for Economic Efficiency of Centralized and Decentralized Structures," *Value and Plan*, ed. G. Grossman (Berkeley: University of California Press, 1960), p. 168.

[22] P. Selznick, "Foundations of the Theory of Organization," *American Sociological Review*, XIII, No. 1 (1948), 25.

[23] Re difficulties of such a definition see J. Berliner's discussion of the quoted Hurwicz article in *Value and Plan*, pp. 176–81. See also O. Wakar *et al.*, *Zarys teorii gospodarki socjalistycznej* (Warszawa: P. W. N., 1964), p. 163, which points out that "decentralization, as a rule, means something different to every user of the term" in the current East European discussion.

[24] For an interesting example, see S. and B. Rome, "Programming the Bureaucratic Computer," *Spectrum*, I, No. 12 (1964).

[25] See H. Guetzkow and H. A. Simon, "The Impact of Certain Communication Nets Upon Organization and Performance in Task-Oriented Groups," *Management Science*, I, Nos. 3–4 (1955).

[26] J. A. Schumpeter, *The Theory of Economic Development. An Inquiry into Profits, Capital, Credit, Interest and the Business Cycle* (New York: Oxford University Press, Inc., 1961), p. 66.

[27] For instance, the bureaucratic elite committed to administrative planning may have to be pensioned off to clear the way for a successful "marketization" of the Soviet-bloc economies. A lump sum payment of their pensions would represent the negative salvage value of the administrative organization. This is not an entirely unrealistic example: the attempt to streamline Polish administrative structure in 1957 provided for severance compensation for the laid-off personnel.

[28] L. Coch and J. R. P. French, "Overcoming Resistance to Change," *Human Relations*, I, No. 4 (1948), gives some insight into this phenomenon. The implications of this microstudy (of one company undergoing a specific change) are quite general.

[29] This is at the heart of "the so-called human relations school, now receiving wide currency in managerial applications" in the U. S. [See A. H. Rubenstein and C. H. Haberstroh, eds., *Some Theories of Organization* (Homewood, Ill.: Dorsey Press, 1960), pp. 169ff.] During the last few years Soviet-bloc countries have exhibited a growing interest in similar problems, for instance see the Polish works on industrial sociology by A. Sarapata, K. Doktor, *Elementy socjologii przemyslu* (Warszawa: P. W. N., 1962) and A. Matejko, *Socjologia zakladu pracy* (Warszawa: P. W. N., 1961), also a volume written by economist A. Wakar *et al.*, *op. cit.*, pp. 179ff.

[30] J. A. Schumpeter, *Capitalism, Socialism and Democracy*, 3d ed. (New York: Harper & Row, Publishers, 1962), Chaps. 11–14.

[31] See, e.g., E. H. Bowman and R. B. Fatter, *Analysis for Production Management*, rev. ed. (Homewood, Ill.: Richard D. Irwin, Inc., 1961), Chap. 12.

[32] Much of Karl R. Popper's critique of such experiments is relevant to the problem discussed here; see his *Poverty of Historicism* (New York: Harper & Row, Publishers, 1964), esp. pp. 64ff.

[33] *Op. cit.*, p. 1663.

[34] See J. G. March and H. A. Simon, *op. cit.*, pp. 140ff.

[35] A. Nove, "The Problem of 'Success Indicators' in Soviet Industry," *Economica*, XXV, No. 97 (1958).

[36] See, e.g., J. Berliner, *Factory and Manager in the USSR* (Cambridge:

Harvard University Press, 1957); D. Granick, *Management of the Industrial Firm in the USSR* (New York: Columbia University Press, 1954); and J. Kornai, *Overcentralization of Economic Administration* (London: Oxford University Press, 1959).

[37] A chronicle of the manifold and perplexing reorganizations of Soviet industry can be found in A. V. Venediktov, *Organizatsiia gosudarstviennoi promyshlennosti v SSSR*, I and II (Leningrad: 1957 and 1961).

[38] See G. Grossman, "Economic Reforms: A Balance Sheet," *Problems of Communism*, XV, No. 6 (1966); and K. Bush, "The Reforms: A Balance Sheet," *Problems of Communism*, XVI, No. 4 (1967).

[39] E. Zaleski, *Planning Reforms in the Soviet Union, 1962–1966, An Analysis of Recent Trends in Economic Organization and Management* (Chapel Hill: University of North Carolina Press, 1967), pp. 190–91.

[40] *6 lat temu... (Kulisy Polskiego Pazdziernika)* (Paris: Instytut Literacki, 1962), p. 41.

[41] See J. M. Montias, *Central Planning in Poland* (New Haven: Yale University Press, 1962), esp. Chap. 10; and my "Economic Reform in Poland: The Cautious Avantgarde," *The Quarterly Review of Economics & Business*, VII, No. 3 (1967).

[42] F. H. Knight, *Economic Organization* (New York: Harper & Row, Publishers, 1965), p. 3.

[43] *Op. cit.*, p. 1661.

[44] See A. Etzioni, *op. cit.*, pp. 272ff.

[45] P. M. Blau, *Exchange and Power in Social Life* (New York: John Wiley & Sons, Inc., 1964), pp. 336ff. offers an illuminating discussion of organizational dynamics in these terms.

[46] R. Conquest, *op. cit.*, p. 6.

[47] W. Jedlicki, *Klub Krzywego Kola* (Paris: Instytut Literacki, 1963), esp. Chap. 1. For another example, see a brilliant fictionalized account of Warsaw's political maneuvers in the "underground" novel by T. Stalinski, *Widziane z góry* (Paris: Instytut Literacki, 1967).

[48] East European countries (e.g., Czechoslovakia, Poland, East Germany), unlike the Soviet Union, have *formally* multiparty constitutions. In fact, however, the Communists have ruled without challenge since 1948.

[49] I am borrowing this term from K. Mannheim; see his *Diagnosis of Our Time* (New York: Oxford University Press, Inc., 1944), p. 166.

[50] For a circumspect statement see, e.g., two articles by H. G. Skilling, "Interest Groups and Communist Politics," *World Politics*, XVIII, No. 3 (1966), and "The Party, Opposition and Interest Groups: Fifty Years of Continuity and Change," *International Journal*, XXII, No. 4 (1967).

[51] H. Schwartz, "Prague's Revolution Within the Revolution," *New York Times Magazine*, March 31, 1968, p. 80.

[52] K. Marx and F. Engels, *German Ideology* (New York: International Publishers, 1939), p. 13.

[53] K. Mannheim, *op. cit.*, p. 167.

[54] B. N. Ward, "Political Power and Economic Change in Yugoslavia," *American Economic Review*, LVIII, No. 2 (1968), 576–78.

[55] Cf. I. Deutscher, *Stalin. A Political Biography*, 2d ed. (New York: Oxford University Press, Inc., 1967), *passim;* A. Nove, "Was Stalin Really Necessary?", *Encounter*, April, 1962, and his rejoinders in *Encounter*, November, 1962.

[56] O. Lange, "The Working Principles of the Soviet Economy," *U.S.S.R. Economy and the War*, ed. R. J. Kerner (New York: Russian Economic Institute, 1943), pp. 25–26.

[57] See, e.g., O. Kyn, "The Market Mechanism in Socialist Economy," *Soviet Affairs*, ed. M. Kaser (London: Oxford University Press, 1966), No. 4, p. 64.

[58] P. J. D. Wiles, *op. cit.*, p. 1.

[59] B. N. Ward, *The Socialist Economy. A Study of Organizational Alternatives* (New York: Random House, Inc., 1967), *passim*, esp. pp. 174ff.

[60] *Ibid.*, p. 263.

[61] J. M. Montias, "Planning with Material Balances," *American Economic Review*, XLIX, No. 5 (1959), 974.

[62] See the conclusions of R. Campbell, G. J. Staller, A. Bergson, and J. M. Montias in their discussion, "Economic Reform in Eastern Europe and in the U. S. S. R.," *American Economic Review*, LVIII, No. 2 (1968), 547–85.

[63] Cf. H. Apel, *Weben und Wunder der Zonenwirtschaft* (Köln: Verlag Wissenschaft und Politik, 1966), p. 133.

[64] G. Grossman, "Soviet Growth: Routine, Inertia, and Pressure," *American Economic Review*, L, No. 2 (1960), 62–63.

[65] G. Grossman, "Notes for a Theory of the Command Economy," *Soviet Studies*, XV, No. 2 (1963), 122.

[66] This is especially clear to an observer of the Soviet reforms: cf. A. V. Bachurin, "Aktualnyie problemy khoziaistvennoi reformy," *Teoriai praktika khoziaistvennoi reformy*, ed. L. H. Gatowski (Moskva: Ekonomika, 1967), esp. pp. 67–68.

[67] W. W. Rostow, *The Dynamics of Soviet Society* (New York: The New American Library, 1954), p. 295.

[68] Cf. O. Sik, "Socialist Market Relations and Planning," *Socialism, Capitalism and Economic Growth. Essays Presented to Maurice Dobb*, ed. C. H. Feinstein (Cambridge: Cambridge University Press, 1967).

[69] Cf. W. Brus, M. Phorille, *Zarys ekonomii politycznej socjalizmu*, I (Warszawa: P.Z.W.S., 1951).

[70] Cf. A. Zauberman, "Recent Developments in Soviet Planning Techniques," *Economia Internazionale*, XX, No. 2 (1967), 21–22.

> Because Socialism concentrates economic power, and because this concentration necessarily gives an extraordinary degree of power to some individuals, regardless of how much one might decentralize the socialist economic system, democracy is more necessary to socialism than to any other type of economic system.
>
> Carl Landauer, *Planwirtschaft und Verkehrswirtschaft* (Munich-Leipzig: Duncker and Humblot, 1931), pp. 145–46.

Gregory Grossman
University of California
Berkeley

The Solidary Society:
A Philosophical Issue
in Communist Economic Reforms[1]

In the above-cited book, nearly four decades ago, Carl Landauer argued —with his wonted clarity of vision and sharpness of thought—that an acceptable socialist order must rest on three premises: a market for both consumer goods and producer goods, profit sharing for employees in the nationalized establishments, and a democratic polity. The first he deemed necessary to render central planning manageable and the economic process efficient. The second, profit sharing, he considered indispensable to ensure the employees' interest in the fortunes of their firms, a precondition of meaningful industrial democracy. And political democracy he regarded absolutely necessary, as our quotation attests, to prevent the socialist economy from becoming an instrument of oppression of the many in the hands of a few, an eventuality that to Landauer (and his fellow social democrats) would have meant the very negation of socialism.

The book was hardly off the press when developments in the then only "socialist" state, Stalin's USSR, proved painfully and tragically to millions of its subjects—and some years later to millions more in Eastern Europe—the reality of Landauer's fears and the wisdom of his humanitarian vision. What at the beginning of the thirties (if not earlier) he affirmed as the necessary foundations of the socialist economy—planning-*cum*-market, worker participation in both the decisions and the fruits of management, political democracy—and what was completely suppressed by Stalinism became the great issues in the "socialist" part of Europe in the sixties and will probably be for some time to come. The reformist movement, which today exists in virtually every country of Stalin's erstwhile empire, though under very unequal degrees of sufferance, is essentially a movement to bring into being Landauer's three premises of a socialist order.

To be sure, Landauer was not writing about Russia or Rumania; in the aforementioned book and in his subsequent programmatic works on socialism and planning he was writing about Germany and other highly developed countries. He was concerned with an efficient and just industrial society, not with the rapid transformation of an agrarian country into an industrial power. Clearly, a program applicable in the one case need not be applicable in the other. But the humanitarian vision and the basic democratic values need not—indeed the past four decades tell us that they *must* not—be faulted by this difference, lest the authoritarian means become the philosophical end and the organizational tool the all-pervading political reality.

The abyss that has separated the social democrats from the Stalinists since the twenties has primarily been a philosophical one. Similarly, what the reform movement in Eastern Europe today is questioning is basically the Stalinist philosophical conception of society. For Stalinism, including some of its present-day milder successor versions, rests on a very definite view of the nature of society and of the social order under what it calls socialism. This view underpins the economic order as much as any other aspect of reality; that is, it underlies the economic system (the "command economy") with its high degree of (at least formal) centralization, the extreme measure of mobilization of economic resources, and the rejection of the market mechanism in the allocation of economic goods. This view is that of what might be called a *solidary society*. To its discussion we now turn.

The orthodox "Stalinist" Soviet ideology sees the whole Soviet society as essentially a solidary unit motivated by a common set of values and striving toward a single general goal, the construction of communism. It includes a single set of intermediate objectives devoid of inner conflicts and cross-purposes and led by a single political party that is itself centrally controlled and directed. The whole Soviet people is visualized marching shoulder-to-shoulder behind its leaders along the high road to communism. The aims of all are the aims of each; in their goals, society, state, Party, and individual are as one. There is no room for particular purposes that diverge from those of the society. Pluralism is equated with disarray—as under "bourgeois democracy"; the market mechanism is equated with chaos—as under capitalism. The social principle of organization is epitomized by the Leninist phrase "democratic centralism," which means government by the leaders *with* the people (that is, with the people's enthusiastic collaboration), not *by* the people.

Such, at last, has been the classic Soviet conception, the ideology of Lenin and Stalin. Presently we shall see that this vision of a perfectly solidary society never corresponded to reality, but for the moment let us concentrate on the orthodox communist conception of a solidary society —or the "solidary conception" for short.

The roots of the solidary conception are several:

1. Its ideological roots lie, first, in Marxist historical determinism, which assures the leaders of the rightness of their goals and justifies their demand that the rest of society obey and conform.
2. It rests on the Marxist tenet that where there are no classes there is no "antagonistic" social conflict. In the Soviet Union (and in other communist countries) the propertied classes have been eliminated or suppressed. All important productive assets have been socialized. The two remaining classes, workers and peasants, are not property-owning and therefore cannot be in mutual "antagonistic" conflict.
3. The solidary conception of society is, in a sense, only the other side of the ruling party's authoritarianism and totalitarianism. It seems to be the nature of an authoritarian regime in power—and not only a communist one—to insist that all of society be monolithically behind it. Every member and group within society must share the official ideology and goals; anything different is heresy to the faith and treason to the cause. And the more existing social values are to be transformed from above, the greater the insistence on ideology solidary.
4. The solidary conception also derives from the chronic situation of national emergency that has characterized communist regimes. No matter that the emergency may be at times imagined (not to say contrived)

rather than real, that it is a by-product of the regime's own internal and external conduct, and that the sense of emergency, ironically, often derives from the regime's awareness of a *lack* of solidarity between itself and all or parts of society. The national emergency provides justification for insisting on the solidarity of the whole society and for threatening those who would not fall in line.

5. We should not overlook the fact that the Soviet Union's historical heritage was not nonconducive to authoritarianism and the notion of social solidarity. For centuries prior to the Bolshevik Revolution, Russia had been governed by autocratic tsars with the help of a centralized state, a bureaucracy, an official church, and a ruling ideology. The tsarist conception of Russian society was also a solidary one. The state tended to identify itself with society. The formation of autonomous social groups was either forbidden or discouraged during much of the tsarist era, while the tsar posed as the protector of all classes. Conflict between groups and classes expressed itself in large part in vying for the autocrat's favor. Both landlords and serfs (the latter existed until 1861) and both employers and workers saw the tsar as the final arbiter in their mutual relations. In economic matters, notably, ultimate authority resided with the tsars, whose explicit or tacit assent, and often whose active initiative, provided the ultimate legitimation of economic activity.[2] In her two great spurts of modernization ("Westernization") before the Soviet era—in the first quarter of the eighteenth century under Peter the Great, and from about 1885 to World War I—Russia depended on the state's active leadership, initiative, and direct economic activity. To some extent the same was true of China's early industrialization before the communist era[3] and, in varying degrees, of the experiences of several of the East European countries that were to fall into the communist orbit after World War II.[4]

But to return to the Soviet situation, the formation of organized groups, and especially political interest groups other than those under the Party's control, is absolutely proscribed. (From here on we shall use the word "groups" to refer only to those groups[5] that are *not* under the regime's effective control.) Such groups as antedated the October Revolution or Stalin's consolidation of power in the late twenties were either abolished or brought under the regime's effective control, as, for example, the trade unions, which, though communist led, enjoyed some autonomy in the twenties, or—to take a quite different example—the Orthodox Church.[6] The only significant *institution*—not a group in the present meaning—that remained largely independent of the regime was the family; in fact, after attempting to weaken the family immediately after the Revolution, from the mid-thirties on official policy sought to strengthen it to promote social stability.[7]

Not only is the organization of autonomous groups proscribed but the very existence of particular or group interests has been steadfastly denied by ideology and propaganda until recently. Apart from the pitiful survivals of the erstwhile propertied classes, there can be (it was asserted) no individuals or groups in the Soviet Union whose true interests do not completely coincide with those of society as a whole, that is, of the state and the Party. Those who think differently have to be convinced and educated to see the true light. And if they attempt to organize themselves into groups of like-minded individuals, they are engaged in treasonable activity against the working class and thus invite severe repression and punishment. In the Stalinist system there is no room for even the most innocuous organized expression of group interest apart from the regime.

Specifically, there is no room for any economic particularism. No such things as *legitimate* economic interests or separate regions, industries, producer groups, and so forth, distinct from the economic interests of society as a whole are recognized; and, of course, no corresponding organizations are permitted. Equally inadmissible are any vertically segmented particular interests, such as those of the workers, the managers, or the planning bureaucracy, that do not coincide with those of society. In short, whatever particular or group interests exist are by definition (in the official view) in full harmony with the interests of society and with each other. It follows that any conflict of group interests with Soviet society is ruled out.

The Economy in a Solidary Society

The economic institutions fashioned by Stalin have generally been consistent with the solidary conception.[8] All economic decisions of significance have been centralized, the most important being reserved for the dictator himself. Nearly all means of production have been nationalized. Nearly all investment—the crucial activity in a country bent on maximum growth—has been socialized. Formal, quantitative national goals have been set up for almost every facet of activity for five-year and one-year terms. These national goals have been broken down into goals for every administrative unit, down to the individual firm, and have been imposed by directives. Prices, too, have been largely centrally set. The firm's autonomy has been minimized, although it could not be completely suppressed because even Stalin and his super-planners would not profess to foresee and control every detail. To the extent that the firms had autonomy they have been guided by the *khozraschet* principle, that is, to economize and to maximize net profit; but, as already indicated, obedience to the explicit directives comes first. Money has been deprived of much of its "moneyness"; its use by individual firms has been severely circumscribed to constrain their freedom of action. As noted, the market mechanism was all but dead within the socialist sector. The possibility of the mushrooming of divergent interests and purpose, brought about by the exercise of money power in a market contest, has thus seemingly been blocked.

The state has acted as though the whole economy were indeed "one big office and one big factory." New firms have been granted capital by the state without provision for repayment or interest charges; the same has been done when the capital of preexisting firms has been augmented. Capital assets have been transferred among firms with no monetary compensation, as a truck might be transferred between units in an army. Firms have had to set aside depreciation reserves—generally quite inadequate in amount—but these went into the state's general funds and lost all identification with the enterprise that generated them. Correspondingly, funds for the replacement of capital assets have had to be obtained from the central authorities. Except for relatively small amounts provided by law, firms have had no legal right to retain profits generated by them, whereas losses were naturally covered by the state. Nearly all materials, fuel, supplies, and types of equipment of any importance have been rationed to the firms by central authorities. Enterprises producing such commodities have been able to dispose of them only in compliance with explicit allocation orders. Surplus amounts of either inventories or money can be seized by higher authorities almost at will.

As noted, the firm is charged by directive ("plan") with a certain production program, expressed in physical terms (or quasi-physical terms, such as values at fixed prices). This fact tends to substantiate the impression of unity of purposes and aims between the individual firm and the state. For if the state wants more of commodity X it orders the appropriate ministries to produce more of X, and the ministries in turn increase the firms' production targets for X (or have additional plants built). Of course, many other steps may have to be taken concurrently to make the production of more of X possible. At times even prices might be manipulated to enhance the firms' incentive to produce more of X. But basically, if society wants more of X, the firms are told to produce more of X; thus, social and particular (firms') objectives coincide in form. Similarly, if the planners want industry to consume less of Y, they order all concerned to consume less of Y by perhaps substituting Z. There is hardly any need to use indirect policy instruments —no manipulating of taxes, subsidies, interest rates, credit terms, tariffs, prices, and the like. Compare this with the military: if the high command of an army wants to bring fire on a certain target it orders one of its units to do so. The unit's objective and the army's are identical in form.

Competition—real, not "socialist," competition[9]—among firms has been rejected. Competition leads to conflict among the competitors, which cannot be allowed. It leads to industrial secrets and therefore retards the diffusion of innovations (but more on this presently). Worst of all, it fosters a spirit of antagonism, of one against all; it splinters society, distracts it from its goals. Competition is responsible for many of the ills of capitalism and there is no need to reproduce them in the socialist society. The socialist economy is a solidary one, one for all and all for one, all sharing equally in technical and economic knowledge, and all united in the fulfillment of the state's goals.

Perhaps one of the most forceful expressions of the solidary conception as applied to the economy is in the realm of interfirm legal relations.[10] To be sure, firms are required to enter into contracts with each other. At first glance this may seem superfluous, as each firm's production program was minutely prescribed from above, whereas interfirm commodity flows (as just mentioned) were subject to detailed allocation orders. Yet the Soviet system of contracts is not devoid of logic. The interfirm contracts attempt to bring about a meeting of minds on secondary details and, more important, a definition of mutual obligations and mutual responsibility in many particulars of commodity flow that even the production targets and allocation orders could not specify. The contracts are thus in execution of what is known in Soviet legal terminology as the "planning acts" of the sovereign authority, but they are also a logical complement to the *khozraschet* system of management insofar as a minimal amount of decentralized decision making is inevitable.

Since the contracting parties usually have no choice *whether* to enter into contracts with each other, being in effect ordered to do so, often they cannot agree on the terms of the contract. Such cases ("precontract disputes") are submitted to adjudication, in the process of which the intent of the higher authorities as expressed in relevant legislation and planning acts is of paramount consideration.

Similarly, the issuance of a new planning act that is in conflict with a given contract invalidates the contract, or at least a portion thereof. Furthermore, and perhaps most revealing of the solidary conception underlying interfirm relations, breach of contract is not adjudicated on the strength of the contractual provisions alone but with reference to the intent of the planning authorities. Thus, the party that broke a contract is not held liable if its nonperformance, in the eyes of the appropriate arbitration tribunal, was in conformity with the national purposes as manifested in the acts of the planning authorities. This, of course, has made interfirm relations uncertain and must have placed considerable strain on management. But the point is not to ensure the certainty of contractual relations; rather, it is to enforce obedience to and full conformity with the will and intent of the central authority within a solidary body economic.

Another important manifestation of the solidary conception is the system of so-called collective agreements (contracts) that traditionally exist in every communist country except Yugoslavia. These agreements are not the result of a resolution of the opposing interests of management and labor; rather, they are solemn declarations of how the two will join forces to attain the tasks imposed on both from above.[11]

It is equally consistent with the solidary conception—and with the aim of rapid industrialization—that the director of the Soviet enterprise, though deprived of authority by his superiors in everything pertaining to the external relations of the enterprise, enjoy very broad powers within the enterprise and especially in regard to *his* subordinates. Although elaborate legislation exists governing employer-employee relations, some aspects (such as the maximum wage bill and the structure of the labor force by broad categories) are written into the firm's plan. Wage rates are centrally set. The trade union often (especially in later years) takes up the individual worker's grievances against management and has to concur in cases of dismissal. But basically the director is boss in his own firm. His powers are especially great in rewarding individuals for good and loyal performance with money or with important material benefits (housing, vacations).[12] The principle of "one-man management" (*edinonachalie*) is a cardinal one in the Soviet philosophy of organization, as it is in nearly all solidary organizations, such as the military, most authoritarian political parties, and so forth.

We mention this principle also because it is one of the more vulnerable points in the solidary conception. The one-sided dominance of the director—and to some extent management and planners in general, and behind them Party and state—over the work force is in stark contrast to the ideals of socialism, industrial democracy, worker control, absence of alienation, and so forth, that are at the philosophical roots of all Marxism, including that of the Soviet variety. Some of the worst cant in Soviet propaganda relates to this point ("Soviet workers do not strike because they would only be striking against themselves!"). And it is here, as we shall see, that some of the critique is focused and some of the major issues of the future communist society are maturing.

Socially and politically, the individual is an integral part of the solidary conception. Every citizen of the Soviet Union is expected to share the common ideology, to practice the "moral code of the builders of socialism (later, of communism)," to be ever alert and vigilant, and to march toward the common goal shoulder-to-shoulder with his fellow citizens. But economically, a major exception to this conception is made in regard to the individual. It is recognized that before the arrival of "full communism" Soviet man still requires material remuneration and incentives to do what he was expected to do for the social good anyway (". . . to each according to his labor," said Marx). That is, man's acquisitive instincts are openly catered to—at any rate, this side of the private ownership of means of production. Whatever society's goals, the individual's economic objective is to earn money, and as long as he does so legally he has the regime's full blessing. The result has been very considerable inequality of earnings. The purpose has been, of course, as under capitalism, to make the individual work better and harder for the social good. But the by-products have often been for the social ill, at least as seen through official eyes. First, acquisitiveness easily led people into illegal activities, especially in a society where so much is illegal. Second, and perhaps more important, it seriously undermined the supposed solidarity of Soviet society. In trying to maximize his earnings, and often in trying only to obtain enough food, the individual found himself in conflict with his neighbors, his employer, and the "establishment" as a whole. And management often found itself in conflict with the state's (and society's) interests, as will presently be described. There is a good deal of truth in the Maoist and Guevarist criticisms that by stressing material incentives the Soviet regime has consciously fostered a money-grubbing climate that has undermined and corrupted the noble cause of communism.[13]

The Non-Solidary Reality

But if particular interests and conflict within the body economic have, until recently, lacked legitimacy in the official ideology, their existence in the Soviet-type economy has been obvious. In fact, it has been so obvious as to constitute a major continuous theme in the Soviet press and a chronic problem to the authorities. In this way they have long ago received *de facto* official recognition.

In its quest to earn personal rewards and to avoid penalties, Soviet-style management worked out a characteristic pattern of conduct that is documented *ad nauseam* in the literature of the communist countries and has by now been carefully studied by Western observers. To be sure, Soviet management did much to maximize output and thereby met the demands of the state. It built production facilities, modernized equipment, borrowed and developed technology, trained labor, accomplished all the other things expected of it and thereby contributed to the impressive record of communist industrialization. But it also tended to neglect quality, paid insufficient attention to costs, ignored customer interests in terms of specifications and delivery dates, all too often produced unusable and unsalable articles in mass quantities, and frequently resisted innovation. It submitted false reports to planners, did its best to bargain out easy targets, concealed resources, hoarded materials, diverted goods into unauthorized channels, and engaged in a multitude of illegal or questionable activities, both to glorify production and to line its own pockets.

The lack of competition among producers—all being state owned —eliminated the tendency to keep secret economic and technological information. Thus there was little if any of the conflict known in market economies. But this advantage—long claimed for socialism in comparison with capitalism—tended to be seriously offset by a lack of incentive to innovate.[14] The net gain in terms of technological progress has hardly been positive.

In behaving in these ways Soviet management acted rationally in the sense of pursuing its self-interest under the circumstances, as it was urged to do by the officially designed system of bonuses and rewards. The result, however, was to belie the solidary conception and to create a multitude of conflicts of interest, especially between firms and their superior entities, on the one hand, and the state (as well as society), on the other. The firm's interest was to fulfill the plan with the least trouble and to earn good bonuses for management, which constantly clashed with the state's interest not only to squeeze the most production from the available resources but also to have the plans faithfully fulfilled and quality specifications observed and in being accurately informed of what was going on. What was required by the state was not necessarily most advantageous for the firm. Instead of all pulling together cheerfully for the common good, each firm in some measure pulled in its own direction.

Interest groupings were not supposed to arise; however, firms in the same region or ministerial organization sometimes shared certain interests (although they could more often be rivals for resources and favors), higher authorities eventually shared and protected the interests of their subordinates, various governmental bureaus and Party organizations also eventually shared such regional or industrial interests. The result was "localism" and "departmentalism"—the practice of preferring one's own region or ministry in the distribution of economic goods— twin tendencies to frustrate the planners' wishes which the regime had been continuously but unsuccessfully fighting from the outset. Localism and departmentalism were not supposed to exist under the solidary conception of society. Hence, they were decried as vicious excrescences rather than as normal by-products of group self-interest. Laws were passed, but the circumstances that spawned them remained intact and the tendencies persisted.

For a long time the blame for the firms' acting at cross-purposes with the desires of the state tended to be placed on the incompetence or insufficient social consciousness of the chief actors, that is, the managers and the planners. The system itself was not questioned, at least not openly. Managers were blamed for incompetence and negligence, for placing their own interests above those of the state, for flouting "plan discipline" and "financial discipline," and even for consciously "wrecking" (though this has seldom been mentioned since World War II). Planners were also blamed for incompetence, insufficient mastery of technical subjects, "bureaucratism," buck-passing, and the like. However, under the system even supermen could not have achieved reasonably good harmony between the actions of the firms and the desires of the state, owing to the inadequacy of the information with which the system operated. Not that there was too little information; rather there was much too much in sheer volume. But the main directives to the firms were in physical terms—production targets and input-utilization standards—and these were too crude to control a complex economy successfully. Any attempt to introduce greater detail into the physical directives added to the strain of an already overburdened system of communication and centralized decision making. (In recent years, approximately 20,000 commodities were individually "planned" and physically allocated at the national level alone in the USSR. It must also be remembered that the communication and data-processing technology continues to be quite primitive.) On the other hand, unburdening the planning apparatus by aggregating the physical categories only gave more scope of action to the managers with no assurance that they would exercise it in the state's (or society's) interests, given the existing structure of prices and incentives. And finally, the plans and the directives were not drawn up by supermen; often they were internally and mutually inconsistent, tardy, and technically weak.

An interesting case is what the economist calls "external diseconomies," the social costs that are an unintended but tangible by-product of economic activity. Let us consider those external diseconomies that consist of a deterioration of the ecology: air and water pollution, deforestation, soil erosion, increased flood hazard, predatory exploitation of mineral resources. It has been a long-standing thesis of various anticapitalist doctrines, including those of the Communists, that these enormous depredations are the inevitable result of the chaos, planlessness, and selfishness of capitalist production. They would have no place under socialism. As it happened, however, Soviet industrialization was accompanied as much by this type of major social cost as was American early industrialization, and apparently for essentially the same reasons. The chief causes of external diseconomies are (1) an excessively foreshortened time horizon, and (2) the exclusion of these social costs in the decision maker's private costs. As for the first cause, Soviet leaders and planners operated under a sense of urgency that, if anything, was even more pressing than that of the private entrepreneur. Sometimes the urgency was not even the state's but the individual politician's. For instance, when Khrushchev put 100 million acres of arid soil under the plow in his virgin lands campaign of the middle fifties, he wanted immediate results in the form of grain in order to discomfit his opposition in the Kremlin (which he did in June 1957, after the first good harvest). That the same soil would a few years later begin to turn into a dust bowl was probably of minor importance to him. As for the second cause, the social costs were often ignored in the calculations of the planners, engineers, and managers, who were under enormous pressure to show results in terms of output. Indeed, not only social costs but also accounted-for costs tended to be ignored under these circumstances! And even if not ignored, in many instances these costs could not have been formally taken into account because the used-up resources—land, minerals, timber—did not carry any prices under Soviet practice (following the Marxist tenet that only man-made goods have "value"). Thus, no account was taken of the large amounts of fertile land flooded by the huge Volga dams—this at a time when every effort was being made to raise agriculture production. (The same dams, incidentally, ruined the rich Caspian fishing grounds by blocking access to spawning sites.)

To sum up, by about the middle fifties the situation in the Soviet-type countries was as follows. The ruling ideology insisted on the solidary nature of the socialist society. It identified the goals of the society, the Party, the state, and the individual with one another. The individual, therefore, was exhorted to act continuously in the state's interests, and should he be uncertain at any point what these interests in the specific contests were, the Party would give him the necessary guidance. In theory, the individual's material rewards were coordinated with the state's interests and spurred him in the right direction. No separate group interests were recognized, and no organized action to protect and advance such interests was tolerated. In reality, however, the structure of material incentives was poorly coordinated with the state's interests and impelled individuals to work as cross-purposes with the interests of the state (and society). The prevailing physical planning was too crude to control this divergence of interests, and Party and police intervention were incapable of preventing it. The structure of material rewards also gave rise to particular interests and to the grouping of such interests in the form of "localism" and "departmentalism." One result of this situation was the hyperbureaucratization of society as an enormous apparatus was built up to plan, manage, and inspect the "command economy." But the bureaucracy itself was fragmented—and the Party—identifying themselves with certain economic ("business") interests, at least for specific purposes.

These defects of the Soviet-type system have of course been well known for decades both to foreign critics and to domestic observers (although the latter were forced to keep largely silent until the late fifties). But the first successful attack on these features of the Soviet system and on the closely related solidary conception of society occurred in Yugoslavia soon after the Tito-Stalin break. Although the break came into the open in June 1948, it took several years for its philosophic and institutional aftereffects to become apparent.

Before the Tito-Stalin break, the Yugoslav communist regime was foremost in Eastern Europe in the faithful copying of Soviet institutions and doctrines for domestic use. Though held back at the time, a certain disillusionment with the Soviet-type system began to set in among Yugoslav leaders even before the break with Moscow. The break removed all external constraints to reexamining both the doctrines and the ideology under which the country had been operating for several years, although the country's difficult economic position and, for a while, its virtual political isolation were conducive to fundamental questioning and rethinking.

With time, the Yugoslavs developed a distinctive, though far from monolithic, political philosophy which proceeded from Marxist premises and represented both a critique of the Stalinist socioeconomic model and a set of positive prescriptions.[15] The critique of Stalinism was threefold: (1) The Soviet-type economic system inevitably creates an enormous bureaucracy that extends into all walks of life, which oppresses the individual, deprives him of dignity and of creative capacity, and generates a new kind of class society based on control if not ownership of property. (2) The Soviet-type economic system is wasteful and inefficient (in ways that have already been summarized in this essay). (3) Since the individual producer (worker) does not have any significant say about his work but is instead subject to the strict authority of management and the state bureaucracy, he is as much "alienated" under the Soviet system as he would be, according to the classical Marxian analysis, under capitalism. Hence, the humanist and industrial-democratic promise that socialism held out in the traditional Marxist view is not being realized in the Soviet system. For these reasons, the Yugoslavs have tended to characterize the Soviet system as "state capitalism"—perhaps one of the most unkind epithets that they, as fellow Marxists, could bestow on the USSR.[16]

Their own distinctive economic system attempts to avoid these defects. It has been much experimented with in detail since it made its appearance in the early fifties, but the essential features have been quite stable. They may be briefly summarized as follows:

1. The economy is planned, but the plans indicate only general lines of development and the allocation of the national product among broad categories. They avoid the detail that characterizes Soviet plans, and, most importantly, they do not prescribe specific targets for enterprises. Yugoslav plans have been compared with French "indicative" plans, a similarity that has been growing in recent years because of the evolution of planning in both countries.

2. Since no directives are issued to individual enterprises, the chief function of resource allocation and coordination—in the short run, but in good measure also in regard to investment—is entrusted to the market mechanism. The Yugoslav market mechanism has functioned very much like any modern mechanism—except for capital and labor, where the Yugoslav institutions are more distinctive—allowing for the prevalence of price control in most of the period in question. The individual firms are in competition with each other, although the small size of the economy and its insulation from the rest of the world owing to exchange control have often tended to make the number of competing firms in an industry rather small. Monopoly is therefore a problem in the Yugoslav economy, but the reasons for this are not entirely systematic.

3. There is some private activity. Most agricultural production is carried on by private peasant farms; there is also much small-scale private enterprise outside of agriculture, the legal limit being a maximum of five employees on private account.

4. Local government, which enjoys a good deal of autonomy from the center, exercises some important economic functions, especially the initiation of new enterprises and the provision of local services (including housing).

5. Perhaps the most distinctive feature of the Yugoslav system is the so-called "workers' self-management," whereby a firm's policy is made by elected bodies (workers' councils, management boards) from among the firm's workers (employees), whereas the hired manager is primarily responsible to these elected bodies and through them to the workers at large. The workers in a Yugoslav enterprise thus also partake of some of the rights and functions of corporation stockholders in capitalist countries. The corollary of this arrangement, insofar as incentives are concerned, is that a large part of the firm's net income is either distributed to the personnel or retained for investment. Thus the Yugoslav firm can be thought of as a profit maximizer or, more accurately, as a profit-per-worker maximizer.[17]

We need not digress here to examine how well the system works or how close Yugoslav reality approaches its model; there are many problems and many deviations from the ideal in any economy. At any rate, it seems to work with an efficiency that compares wtih that in Soviet-type countries, has manifested one of the highest growth rates in the world over the past one and one-half decades, is less plagued with excessive bureaucracy (though far from free of it) than its neighbors to the east, and has managed to give the worker a greater sense of meaningful participation in the economic (and governmental) process.

What is important for our purpose is that Yugoslavia has moved some distance in officially rejecting the notion of a solidary society. To be sure, basic commitment to Marxism and socialism is still required by the regime, and calls for ideologically determined social solidarity continue to be made by voices in authority. But this has not prevented the emergence of a considerable variety of opinion and of factional political struggle within the single-party regime. Organized economic interest is explicitly recognized and to some extent even encouraged, conflict among such interests is regarded as normal, and its resolution in the market—and to a growing extent, in the political arena—is taken for granted.[18]

Thus, each enterprise represents an economic interest grouping that is in conflict with its clients, suppliers, competitors, and so forth. (No doubt, there are also group conflicts within enterprises which are resolved through intrafirm politics and bargaining.) The firm's goal is admittedly selfish: to make profit, not to fulfill a national plan or to meet specific output targets. Firms combine into trade associations. There are also chambers of commerce. The 1963 constitution went even further; it established multicameral legislatures on the federal and republic levels, each containing an economic chamber elected by producers, which passes on all economic legislation. (Yugoslavia does not have a true parliamentary government but is beginning to move in that direction.

These organizations presumably defend and promote the interests of producers, but, in theory at least, their ultimate constituents are the "self-managing" workers. Moreover, there are trade unions. At first glance it seems that there is no room for them in an ostensibly worker-run economy, yet their existence is recognition of the fact that there is a multiplicity of interests within a "self-managing" working class as well. Strikes have been permitted in recent years—also a seeming incongruity in worker-run enterprises, but only at first view. Yugoslav trade unions have been playing an active role on the national level promoting consumer and worker-*qua*-worker interests.

Something that might be identifiable as "business" interest seems to be emerging. It brings together the point of view of management, its concern with production and profits, its opposition to bureaucratic controls (and possibly to interference by the Party, though we do not know much about this point), its desire to be unmolested by excessive control on the part of self-managing workers or trade unions. Firms in given industries, comprising both managerial personnel and rank-and-file

198

workers, share certain common interests which seem to be to some extent institutionalized in the trade associations. Producers in a certain republic or district or locality ("commune") also may have interests in common, which tend to receive institutionalized expression because of the relative autonomy of local government and local Party organizations. Regional expression of interest is of course greatly heightened in Yugoslavia because of the vast historical and economic contrasts within the country. Though the regional interests may be potentially disintegrative on a national scale, they tend to accentuate the differentiation of distinct economic interests by providing them at times with territorial political power bases.

On a more abstract level, Yugoslav political philosophy invokes the notion of *contradiction* to explain these phenomena and to give them a constructive significance. "Contradiction" is a standard Marxist term which can perhaps be often rendered into more familiar English by the word "conflict." "Antagonistic" contradictions are those that beset a class society; they are irreconcilable class conflicts. Orthodox *Soviet* ideology maintains that after the proletarian revolution some contradictions in society would still continue to exist, even into the stage of socialism, but they would no longer be antagonistic; rather, they would be reconcilable, "nonantagonistic" contradictions. But not much was made of this notion in Stalin's day. Since the middle fifties a rather large amount of literature on "contradictions" and on the closely related theme of "interests in society" has emerged in the USSR. Most of this has appeared in philosophical journals and much of it has a rather arid effect upon the Western reader. Yet even this literature has begun to question the categorical Stalinist assertion of the fundamental identity of all interests in the Soviet society, although (to our knowledge) on the purely philosophical plane it has not evolved nearly as far as has its Yugoslav counterpart.[19]

By contrast, Yugoslav theory sees contradictions as "the energizing force behind socialist transformation and progress."[20] Both Soviet and Yugoslav philosophy see antagonistic contradictions disappearing but nonantagonistic ones persisting as the socialist society develops. But in the Yugoslav view, the nonantagonistic contradictions stemming from specific interests (personal, group, regional) and clashing among themselves and with the general social interest perform a positive role in propelling the society forward.[21]

The Yugoslav paradigm seems to carry an important lesson for our inquiry. The explicit recognition of particular interest groups and conflict among them, and between them and the state (and society), coupled with the establishment of appropriate institutions for the routine resolution of such conflicts (especially the market mechanism) brings about a better harmonization of "business behavior" with the interests of the state (or society) than does the Stalinist denial of internal conflict and insistence on a solidary conception of society. Moreover, although it need not entail less conflict as such (if conflict could be somehow measured on the social scale), the Yugoslav economic system gives less appearance of conflict on the *microeconomic level*, insofar as the conflict is resolved more or less impersonally in the marketplace rather than in personal confrontation within a bureaucratic setting. A failure to recognize the constructive role of conflict in society in itself seems to magnify conflict.[22]

In East European countries other than Yugoslavia, open criticism of the Stalinist economic system (as against criticism of specific defects) had to await the partial lifting of political controls that came with "de-Stalinization" in the USSR and its satellites, that is, after the Twentieth Congress of the Soviet Communist Party in February 1956. But it came quickly. Within only four months, at the Second Congress of the Polish Economists in June 1956, far-reaching criticism of the Soviet-type economic system was already freely and widely voiced, and proposals for different institutional arrangements were put forward.[23] The Polish Revolution of October 1956 gave further impetus to this process, the critical and reformist literature grew rapidly, and for a while it looked as though Poland might indeed adopt a more liberal socialist economy. As it happened, the new Polish communist regime proved itself to be fearful of major moves and nearly all the bold proposals and semiofficial schemes were abandoned (with one significant exception, the de-collectivization of Polish agriculture).

Although the abortive course of Polish economic reformism, once by far the most vibrant in the Soviet bloc, dealt a setback to the cause of economic reform in Eastern Europe, by no means did it stop this movement in the early stages. On the contrary, since 1956, economic debate unfolded remarkably in both the Soviet Union and the rest of Eastern Europe and by the early sixties reached a volume, an intensity, and (though varying from country to country) a relative degree of freedom of expression that few competent observers would have been willing to predict only a few years earlier.

There is no space here for even the briefest summary of this fascinating development.[24] It is sufficient to point out that the tone of this literature—whether stemming from academic economists or managers or administrators—has been overwhelmingly critical of the old Stalinist economic model and economic doctrine, and the predominant view on the positive side has been in favor of decentralization of the economic structure. Few have been willing in recent years to defend the Stalinist system outright, and the debate in large measure has amounted to disagreement on the desirable degree of decentralization and closely related matters (such as price formation). Though not frequently mentioned in the literature, the Yugoslav example has undoubtedly been very much in the background of these debates.

The proponents of reform in Eastern Europe have overwhelmingly been pressing for a substantial, and sometimes radical, decentralization of the system. At the heart of such positive proposals has been the greater autonomy of the individual firm, especially in day-to-day decisions if not with regard to long-term investment, and, in the more far-reaching proposals, the establishment of a market mechanism to coordinate the decisions and activities of the individual enterprises. If the firm is to act autonomously it must be given an appropriate objective. This aim is profit, which in the thinking of East European economic reformism has a threefold salutary function: it epitomizes and measures the firm's own contribution to the national economy, it directs resources to relatively higher priority uses, and at the same time it creates a financial fund from which rewards for such socially beneficial activities can be paid to the firm's management and staff. That this threefold functional role of profits is closely analogous to the role of profits in the "Western" theory of competitive capitalism is clear to anyone familiar with Western economies; the similarity has been the source of some embarrassment to Eastern reformists. Of course, the functional role of profit is predicated entirely on the prices from which it derives. And so the principles and methods of price formation and whether it should be administrative or automatically performed in the market have been a major focus of the debates.

But it would not be correct to suggest that the Soviet and East economic debates of the last decade have been limited to issues of institutional reform alone. They have also deeply involved the most fundamental propositions of economic doctrine and the meaning of Marxist economics. Although all of the options that are expressed, at least openly, are nominally within the Marxist fold and profess a basic allegiance to socialism, this has not prevented them from being of the greatest diversity. In addition, it is clear, or may be inferred, from much of the reformist literature that the authors have much more in mind than a mere improvement in the efficiency of the "economic mechanism."[25] By calling for the decentralization of economic decision making they are simultaneously calling for some decentralization of power in society, a partial democractization, and a greater opportunity for the expression of consumer interests. They are really often indirectly calling for a different, more democratic, more pluralistic, more consumer-oriented society. Surely economic decentralization in itself would not guarantee the attainment of such overall sociopolitical ends. But neither can the sociopolitical sphere be insulated from fundamental changes in the economy, as the Yugoslav experience shows,[26] and as the Czechoslovak episode of 1968–69 strongly suggests.

At the heart of the reformist ideas in the USSR and Eastern Europe is the notion that the social purposes are not threatened by the presence and exercise of particular interests; on the contrary, particular interests can and should be harnessed for society's benefit. Thus, the firm is to be granted autonomy to allow it to pursue its own interests unabashedly, that is, to earn profit for distribution to its own personnel or for other internal purposes. This does not mean that social aims are dismissed. Rather, they are to be met indirectly by following the producers' own and direct interests, as in a "capitalist" market economy. Again, this implies that the firm obtains the right signals, works with the right costs and prices, and is impelled by the right incentives. But this problem is pushed onto the planners, who now have to guarantee socially meaningful prices either by directly setting them at appropriate levels or by fashioning such institutions (especially within the framework of market relations) as will accomplish the same in the marketplace.

Indeed, today some of the most enthusiastic proponents of (socialist) profit making and of the (socialist) market are in the Soviet Union and Eastern Europe. For instance, the authors of an unsigned introductory section to a summary of the views of a large number of Soviet economists and mathematicians, who gathered, in a rather stormy meeting, to discuss economic reforms in March 1964, take a proprofit position:

> At present, more and more economists lean towards the view that one should accept as the [microeconomic] optimality criterion the ratio of profit to the sum of fixed and circulating capital . . . Some [Soviet] economists say that the use of profit as the optimality criterion amounts to the injection of bourgeois conceptions [into the socialist economy]. Our objective [it is said by these critics] is the satisfaction of needs, and the profit criterion allegedly contradicts this aim. It is true that with irrational management of the economy it may happen that the production of goods which poorly meet [consumers'] needs will yield more profit than the output of more urgently needed and higher quality goods. But the perfection of our economic system, which the economists must work out, will preclude such occurrences. The magnitude of profit will reflect the degree of satisfaction of needs. Under such conditions profit will serve as the synthetic indicator of the ineluctable law of socialist management: the achievement of the highest results with the least outlay. After all, profit is nothing but the difference between results and outlays.[27]

A Czechoslovak economist, writing in 1965 under the challenging title, "Creative Development in Marxist Economic Thinking," in the official journal of the Soviet bloc, argued that the idea that the market mechanism is "alien to socialism, a mere survival of capitalism, is indicative of a superficial understanding of Marxist political economy." He pointed out that the market existed before capitalism and should continue under socialism as well; moreover, under socialism it functions better than under capitalism because "the development of socialist commodity-money [i.e., market] relations is not left to the vagaries of chance; on the contrary, they are utilized consciously according to plan to achieve the aims society has set for itself." He then made a categoric statement that would please the most libertarian bourgeois economist: "The market is the final touchstone of the social usefulness of expended labor."[28] And a Hungarian economist writing as the economic reform in his country was being worked out stresses that the desirable economic mechanism should contain "a uniform economic criterion . . . which makes the maintenance of incompatible and incomparable [i.e., noncomparable] plan indices superfluous: this uniform and single criterion is profit."[29]

Nor has it escaped the reformist economists of Eastern Europe that their proposals rest on a rejection of what we have called the solidary conception of society and are instead premised on the recognition of particular interests. Simultaneously, the concept of contradictions as applied to the socialist society is receiving greater attention. It is clear that the explicit rejection of the solidary conception is causing concern in some places. Should even the pretense of solidarity be dropped, would it not be that much harder for the state to advance the process of social integration which is clearly necessary in these societies in transition and flux? Would it not be more difficult to bridle the self-serving impulses of the citizenry and the particularist tendencies of firms, industries, ministries, and regions? We have already seen one answer to this: the refusal to admit the legitimacy of conflicts in itself aggravated conflicts. To quote a passage from a recent article by W. Brus, since the middle fifties the leading proponent in Poland of the use of the market mechanism for *current* resource allocation:

"... the theoretical reservations expressed today about the trends in the economy of the European socialist states are not reduced to criticism of the justice of this or that concrete solution. It is the question whether decentralization as such, introduced simultaneously with increased economic incentives arising from the economic results of the work of a separate team of men, does not constitute a step backward, a breaking up of a unified system of planned economy into separate groups, naturally inclined to oppose each other, to compete, to disregard the general interest. This attitude, however, is marked by no more than apparent logic. Even if we should agree that the future shape of a socialist society has already been correctly determined, [the issue is not] a formal integration, but a real one, where the superiority of social interests will not be imposed but will arise naturally from the belief that the social interest has been correctly defined and from the awareness that personal interests are connected with [such] social interest. Increasing the... independence of enterprises, together with all the ensuing elements of change in the system of economic management, may be considered an advance on the road to socialization, not only because it should create conditions for increased economic results but also because it should bring the mechanism of decision making closer to the common members of society.[30]

The Reforms and the Reaction

By the end of the sixties, the movement for economic reform in Eastern Europe—a vague, heterogeneous, multidirectioned movement, but nonetheless a major reality throughout the whole region—has achieved both much and little. Apparently, the movement for economic reform has met with considerable success: beginning with East Germany in 1964, all countries of the region (except Rumania and Albania, but not excluding the USSR) have put into effect reform measures of a more or less comprehensive character. Typically, these measures have centered on industry but have also taken in other sectors; and, as a minimum, they have revised some of the success indicators for enterprises, raised the importance of profit as both a major target of the firm's activity and as a financial source of various funds under decentralized control, experimented with the formal organizational structure, recalculated wholesale prices, and introduced certain new financial categories at the firm's level, such as the payment of interest on assets. But these formal achievements should not be overrated. With two exceptions, Czechoslovakia and Hungary, the reforms have so far been minor, that is, they have operated within the limits of the basic structure of the command economy rather than affording a substantial scope to the market mechanism. As for the two countries in which major "marketing" reforms have been launched, Czechoslovakia has at this writing (mid-1969) already *experienced* a sharp reversal in this regard in consequence of the rise in power of conservative elements in the wake of the Soviet invasion of August 1968. Only Hungary is proceeding with a major reform, and seemingly a relatively bold one at that, although it is yet too soon to appraise its extent and efficacy.

But a start has been made, although it is a minor one. "Economic reform" is the slogan of the decade, even of relatively conservative spokesmen; at times it acts as a screen behind which to minimize institutional change. And yet, even hypocritical allegiance to economic reform is a tribute that dogma must now pay to economic reality. Perhaps the most eloquent tribute to the viability of reformist ideas in Eastern Europe is the intensification of the campaign against the notion of market socialism that has been going on in the Soviet Union since the spring of 1968.

Given its timing and its language, there can be little doubt that this intensification is a reaction to the "Prague spring" of that year and has maintained its momentum within the USSR because of the Soviet military intervention in Czechoslovakia in August. But it is also quite clear that the campaign is aimed as much against indigenous advocates of market socialism as against parallel views in the other East European countries. In fact, it is interesting to note that the one country that since the beginning of 1967 has been marketizing its economy, Hungary, seems to be never mentioned in these strictures against market socialism.[31]

The chief domestic target of these attacks is a short book, *Plan and Market*, published in 1966 by G. S. Lisichkin, an economic journalist.[32] The book itself is a relatively mild (though well presented) argument for greater attention to the market in resource allocation for current production, that is, for supplementing planning with a market orientation. But it is more explicit and more comprehensible to the general reader than other promarket arguments in recent Soviet literature, and as such it has served as a ready foil for the opposition. Indeed, one gets the impression that much Soviet opinion in favor of marketization is more widespread than what finds its way into print, probably being vented at professional conferences and in unpublished memoranda. Otherwise it would be difficult to understand the vehemence of the reaction.

Perhaps the most definitive attack on market socialism is an editorial in the November 1968 issue of *Planovoe khoziaistvo*, the official organ of the State Planning Commission. Categorizing the notions of market socialism as "petty bourgeois," the editorial argues that the autonomy of enterprises and the installation of a market mechanism would lay the foundation for "anarcho-syndicalism" in the economy and would "counter the interests of socialist construction." It would also retard technical progress. Moreover, the firm's freedom of decision making in a market context is illusory; only under central planning can there be true freedom of choice for the enterprise (although this point is not further elaborated). In addition, only under central planning can each enterprise be certain of the need for an unselfulness of its contribution, and each employee, of his material well-being. (This is apparently an allusion to the fluctuation of rewards when a firm's net income depends on changing market conditions). Thus, the true interests of every state enterprise call for the strengthening and perfection of central planning, rather than for the opposite.

For our purposes, a crucial point is made in the following passage (p. 9):

Given a correct economic policy, in a socialist society there are, and can be, no groups of workers (*kollektivy*) whose material interests lie in contradiction to the objectively necessary planned management of the economy on the part of the state. Hence, the economic activity of the enterprise can be defined only by society's purposes.

This is clearly a reaffirmation of what we have called the solidary conception of society, and it is this philosophical issue that (though not alone) separates the economic neo-Stalinists from the economic reformers.

An interesting distinction along this line has been drawn by the well-known Soviet economist, L. Gatovskii. Writing in April 1969 on the theme "leinin on Democratic Centralism in Economic Management,"[33] Gatovskii stresses the identity of social interests on one side and those of individual enterprises, and of the workers employed in them, on the other. But it is the former that must be determining, as epitomized in the following formula: "that which is in the interest of the whole society should be advantageous for enterprises and their employees."[34] This principle, which he characterizes as Leninist democratic centralism and identifies as the one underlying current Soviet economic reform, is contrasted by him with two others: first, *bureaucratic* centralism, which employs administrative means of economic management and ignores the interests of individual enterprises; and second, which he does not name, but which presumably refers to market socialism, one that rejects all centralism. The latter is epitomized by the formula: "what is advantageous for the enterprise is *ipso facto* advantageous for society." In this case, social interests are not actively determining; instead, they emerge as a result of the interaction of the conflicting interests of thousands of enterprises. No doubt the advocates of market socialism would deny that this kind of socialist laissez faire corresponds to anything that they have in mind; rather, they would insist that often the state can ensure its interests better *through the market*. Nor is it clear how Gatovskii would ensure that society's (that is, the state's) interests "determine" those of individual enterprises without going most of the way toward his opponents' program. Surely, the current Soviet economic reform, which he claims rests on his formula, has already amply shown that it has not done much to make individual enterprises' interests conform to those of the state.[35]

It is interesting to note that Gatovskii insists, again in line with the present official position, that *personal* incentives should be given the greatest scope to further social interests. But as we have already seen, it is precisely the combination of strong personal incentives with imperfect success indicators for enterprises (and larger groupings) that in the economic sphere belied the Stalinist fiction of the solidary society.

Although with the exception of Hungary—and Yugoslavia, of course—there has been as yet, despite all the reforms of the sixties, little systemic change in the economies of Eastern Europe, and although the solidary conception of society still seems to prevail with those who are keeping institutional change to a minimum, nevertheless there are trends in the realm of institutions, as well as in that of ideas, that point in other directions. Take, for instance, the discarding of the old "gross value of output" success indicator for the individual enterprise, which is typical even of the minor reforms, and its replacement by such targets as "gross sales," "profit," and "profitability." Of course, in the Soviet situation this shift in targets has not yet revolutionized the operation of the firms or of the economy as a whole. Yet, in the long run, it may have certain significant psychological effects. "Production" is for the good of the state; it is closely identified with the regime's goals, national plans, historical missions. To pursue production goals is a solidary thing to do, especially in a quasi-militarized economy. But profit and sales are pursued for particular ends (although the state may take its cut of profits). Their social mission is much less obvious, and if perceived at all requires more sophisticated rationalization. Furthermore, the pursuit of profits and sales orients one's mind toward customers, not toward hierarchical superiors (as is the case now). One becomes more conscious of the needs of clients and less aware of the imperatives of the state. The business of running a firm is thus at least in part de-politicized and secularized. As service to the state recedes in day-to-day significance, professional standards, commercial practices, and private or group interests are likely to become more important. And this is also a major reason why the elevation of profit to prime rank as the enterprise's success indicator is opposed by the more conservatively minded economists.[36,37]

Nevertheless, on the philosophical level an important milestone has already been passed in all the countries now embarking on economic reform, however minor. The traditional, orthodox solidary conception of society has been largely discredited and is on the defensive. It is widely recognized as having been detrimental to the solution of economic problems in the real world. Not only is the existence of particular economic interests and aims acknowledged but the central problem of economic reforms is now generally understood to be the establishment of such institutions and procedures as will harmonize particular interests and purposes with social interests and goals. (The latter, of course, continue to be interpreted and defined by the political leadership.) Liberman's formula—"what is advantageous for society should be also advantageous for every enterprise, and what is disadvantageous for society should be extremely (!) disadvantageous for any enterprise"—has become the slogan of the whole economic-reform movement in Eastern Europe. As we have observed, it has even been put forth as a formula characterizing the minimal Soviet reform. The "nonantagonistic contradictions" in a socialist society are now widely seen as an inevitable fact of life to be turned to social benefit through an institutionalized and constructive resolution of conflicts and not to be merely deplored and suppressed.

Footnotes

[1] An earlier version of this paper was presented at the Workshop on Business and the State (September 1966) and the Faculty Seminar on Comparative Study of Communist Societies (September 1967), both in Berkeley. Valuable comments were received, as well as individually from Professors Reinhard Bendix, Joseph S. Berliner, Kenneth T. Jowitt, Nicholas V. Riasanovsky, Howard R. Swearer, and Benjamin Ward—for all of which the author is most grateful, although retaining all responsibility. The copyright to this paper belongs to the organizer of the Workshop on Business and the State, Professor Earl F. Cheit.

[2] A penetrating analysis of the relationship between state, society, and economic interests in Tsarist Russia is in Reinhard Bendix, *Work and Authority in Industry* (New York: John Wiley & Sons, Inc., 1956), Chaps. 1 and 3.

[3] Cf. Albert Feuerwerker, *China's Early Industrialization* (Cambridge: Harvard University Press, 1958), *passim,* and Franz Schurmann, *Ideology and Organization in Communist China* (Berkeley: University of California Press, 1966), pp. 222–23. Schurmann observes: "What distinguished bureaucratic capitalism in [pre-Communist] China from its counterparts in [other] countries was its lack of success in launching basic industrial development." The same cannot be said of pre-Communist Russia; cf. Gerschenkron, *Economic Backwardness in Historical Perspective, passim.*

[4] See, for instance, Nicolas Spulber, *The State and Economic Development in Eastern Europe* (New York: Random House, Inc., 1966), *passim.* For a broader treatment of the historical role of the state in economic development see Gerschenkron, *op. cit., passim.*

[5] Cf.: a group is "any mass of human activity tending in a common direction," Harry Eckstein and David E. Apter, eds., *Comparative Politics: A Reader* (New York: The Free Press, 1963), p. 391. So defined, a group does not have to be formally organized.

[6] In Eastern Europe, a notable example of an institution escaping the state's full control is the Catholic church, especially in Poland.

[7] Cf. H. Kent Geiger, *The Family in Soviet Russia* (Cambridge: Harvard University Press, 1968), esp. Chap. 2.

[8] A survey and analysis of Soviet economic institutions can be found in Alec Nove, *The Soviet Economy: An Introduction,* 3d ed. (New York: Frederick A. Praeger, Inc., 1969).

[9] In "socialist competition" the contestants vie with one another in trying to excel in regime-appointed tasks.

[10] An excellent treatment of this subject is in D. A. Loeber, "Plan and Contract Performance in Soviet Law," *Illinois Law Forum* (Spring, 1964), pp. 128–

79. See also Harold J. Berman, *Justice in Russia*, rev. ed. (New York: Vintage Books, 1963), Chap. 3.

[11] Cf. Bendix, *op. cit.*, pp. 366–67. A fuller treatment of collective contracts will be found in Emily C. Brown, *Soviet Trade Unions and Labor Relations* (Cambridge: Harvard University Press, 1966), pp. 182ff.

[12] On most of these points see Brown, *op. cit.*, *passim*.

[13] On the Chinese position regarding "social mobilization" vs. material incentives see Schurmann, *op. cit.*, pp. 99–103 and 196–202, and Charles Hoffmann, *Work Incentive Practices and Policies in the People's Republic of China, 1953–1965* (Albany: State University of New York Press, 1967). To anticipate our later discussion, a summary of the Chinese criticism of the Yugoslav economic system may be found in R. V. Burks, "Yugoslavia: Has Tito Gone Bourgeois?", *East Europe*, 14:8 (August, 1965), pp. 2ff. Regarding Cuba see Carmelo Mesa-Lago, *The Labor Sector and Socialist Distribution in Cuba* (New York: Frederick A. Praeger, Inc., 1968). It seems that in both countries material incentives have been less avoided than their ideological tenets would make one think.

[14] On the resistance to innovation the interested reader is referred to two articles by the author: "Soviet Growth: Routine, Inertia, and Pressure," *American Economic Review*, L:2 (May, 1960), pp. 62–72; and "Innovation and Information in the Soviet Economy," *American Economic Review*, LVI:2 (May, 1966), pp. 118–30.

[15] The theory of the Yugoslav economy is ably developed by a leading Yugoslav economist, Branko Horvat, in *Towards a Theory of Planned Economy* (Belgrade, 1964). On the Yugoslav firm see, *inter alia*, Benjamin Ward, "The Nationalized Firm in Yugoslavia," *American Economic Review*, LV:2 (May, 1965), pp. 65–74.

[16] Horvat, *op. cit.*, p. 77.

[17] For the pure theory of a Yugoslav-type firm see Benjamin Ward, "The Firm in Illyria," *American Economic Review*, XLVIII:4 (September, 1958), pp. 566–89, and *The Socialist Economy* (New York: Random House, Inc., 1967), Part 3. See also Evsey D. Domar, "The Soviet Collective Farm as a Producer Cooperative," *American Economic Review*, LVI:4(1) (September, 1966), pp. 734–57.

[18] Cf. Jovan Djordjevic, "Interest Groups and the Political System of Yugoslavia," in Henry W. Ehrmann, *Interest Groups on Four Continents* (Pittsburgh: University of Pittsburgh Press, 1958), pp. 197–227. The author, a leading Yugoslav jurist, presented this paper at an international conference as early as 1957.

[19] An interim survey of the Soviet literature since Stalin's death may be found in A. S. Aizikovich, "Vazhnaia sotsiologicheskaia problema" ("An Important Sociological Problem"), *Voprosy filosofii*, 1965:11, pp. 163–69. A Soviet philosopher who affirmed relatively early the positive side of particular interests insofar as they can be harmonized with social goals is G. E. Glezerman; cf. his article in *Kommunist*, 1964:12, which antedates the Soviet economic reform by

over a year. Since the announcement of the reform in September 1965 this has been the official view, it being further claimed that the reform advances this harmonization; cf. *Pravda*, June 25, 1967, p. 3.

[20] M. George Zaninovich, "Yugoslav Variations on Marx," to appear in Wayne S. Vucinich, ed., *Contemporary Yugoslavia: Twenty Years of Socialist Experiment* (Berkeley: University of California Press, 1969).

[21] Cf. Schurmann, *op. cit.*, pp. 53ff. for the place of "contradictions" in Chinese communist thought. It would take us too far afield, however, to pursue this question.

[22] In the words of a Czechoslovak author, writing as the Czechoslovak reform was being introduced: "The so-called contradiction-less unity of strict centralism (i.e., in our terms, a command economy based on the solidary conception) paralyzes the impetus within socialist economics and brings into being a number of contradictions which engender disproportions in the national economy and which, in their entirety, have a retarding effect" (Ladislav Tomesek, "The Relationship between Philosophy and Economics and the New System of Management," *Plánované Hospodárstvi*, 1965:2, here quoted from a translation by Radio Free Europe, *Czechoslovak Press Survey*, No. 1612). For further discussion of "Interest Groups and Communist Politics" see the path-breaking article by H. Gordon Skilling, *World Politics*, XVIII:3 (April, 1966), pp. 435–51.

[23] A good summary account of this event can be found in John M. Montias, *Central Planning in Poland* (New Haven: Yale University Press, 1962), Chap. 9.

[24] A convenient survey may be found in Michael Gamarnikow, *Economic Reforms in Eastern Europe* (Detroit: Wayne State University Press, 1968).

[25] "Economic mechanism" is a phrase recently employed in Hungary in the context of the economic reform. It refers to the totality of institutional arrangements whereby the state's economic goals are realized and serves to underscore the instrumental nature of these institutions and the unassailability of the basic principles and goals of the socialist order.

[26] For an insightful discussion of the connection between economic reformism, Yugoslav style, and broader sociopolitical evolution see R. V. Burks, *loc. cit.*

[27] *Ekonomisty i matematiki za kruglym stolom* (Economists and Mathematicians at a Round Table), Moscow, 1965, pp. 15–16. The authors of the introduction are apparently Iu. Davydov and L. Lopatnikov.

[28] Zdyslav Shults, "Creative Development of Marxist Economic Thinking," *Problems of Peace and Socialism* (June, 1965), pp. 24–26. Cf. O. Kyn, "The Market Mechanism in a Socialist Economy," *St. Antony's Papers*, No. 19 (1965), pp. 61–67.

[29] József Bognár, "Overall Direction and Operation of the Economy," *The New Hungarian Quarterly*, VII:21 (Spring, 1966), p. 13.

[30] W. Brus, "About a Theory of Socialist Enterprise," *Zycie Gospodarcze*

(January 23, 1966), here quoted from a translation by Radio Free Europe, *Polish Press Survey*, No. 1961. In the spring of 1968 Brus was removed from his chair at the University of Warsaw.

[31] Hungary's substantial progress toward market socialism and the apparent absence of open Soviet hostility do suggest that economic reformism was not a major reason for the Soviet military intervention in Czechoslovakia.

[32] G. S. Lisichkin, *Plan i rynok*, Moscow, 1966, p. 95. An interesting feature of this work is the reappraisal of the New Economic Policy of the twenties, a period when market socialism may be said to have existed in the Soviet Union. Lisichkin sees the NEP not merely as a transitional period that prepared the ground for an era of full-scale planning, as has been the standard Soviet view since then, but as an economic system in its own right. There has been a growing interest in the NEP among the economic reformers of other East European countries as well.

[33] *Ekonomicheskaia gazeta*, 1969, No. 16, p. 3.

[34] This formulation was given prominence by Professor E. Liberman in his well-known article, "Plan, Profit, Premia," *Pravda*, September 9, 1962, English text in *Current Digest of the Soviet Press*, XIV:36.

[35] Cf. Getrude E. Schroeder, "Soviet Economic 'Reforms': A Study in Contradictions," *Soviet Studies*, XX:1 (July, 1968), pp. 1–21.

[36] Cf. the warnings by S. G. Strumilin against giving profit too much of a role on the enterprise level in "Pribyl'" ("Profit"), *Komsomol'skaia pravda*, February 16, 1968, p. 3.

[37] Carl Landauer has suggestively inquired into some of the implications of economic rationality for socialist—including Eastern—thought in a recent essay, "Das Eindringen marktwirtschaftlicher Vorstellungen in die sozialistische Ideenwelt" ("The Penetration of Market-Economy Notions into the Socialist Realm of Ideas"), *Hamburger Jahrbuch für Wirtschafts- und Gesellschaftspolitik*, XII, Tübingen, 1967, pp. 142–59.